The Torah Calendar:

The Calendar our Creator Wants us to Keep

Yes and Amen!

By Norman B. Willis

Updated First Edition (v1.6)

This book is published in its first revised edition.
If you have comments, loving suggestions or
questions to help us improve this publication,
please send them to us, to benefit future
readers:

Nazarene Israel
P.O. Box 787
Anderson, CA 96007
USA

Email: servant@nazareneisrael.org.

May the name of YHWH be glorified:

Amein.

Shemote (Exodus) 12:14

14 "Now this day will be a memorial to you, and you shall celebrate it as a feast to YHWH; throughout your generations you are to celebrate it as a permanent ordinance."

Table of Contents:

Author's Notes:

Handwritten annotations:
Law (Torah)
God (Elohim)
THE LORD (YHWH, Yahweh)
Jesus (Yeshua)

Unless otherwise noted I have used the New King James Version (NKJV) as a base text, corrected for the Hebrew names, and a few Hebrew terms. Instead of God I have used the Hebrew term, "Elohim." Instead of the name of THE LORD, I have used the Hebrew name of our Creator, YHWH ("Yahweh"). Instead of Jesus, I have used the Messiah's Hebrew name, Yeshua. Instead of Christ, I have used Messiah. Finally, in place of Law I have typically used the Hebrew term 'Torah.' I have also made an effort to correct any wording that does not reflect the meaning of the source texts.

In works of this sort, we oftentimes deal with errors in translation, and/or scribal errors. When pointing out these errors I have made an effort to display the source material alongside the English text, so that the reader can verify my translations for himself. For the Tanach (the 'Old Testament') I have used the Hebrew Masoretic Text. Unless otherwise noted, Aramaic text comes from the Bibleworks Peshitta with Hebrew Letters (PEH), and Greek text comes from BibleWorks Greek Text (BGT) or BibleWorks New Testament (BNT). Quotations from the Talmud come from the Soncino Classics Collection, and quotations from Maccabees are taken from "The Apocrypha", Destiny Publishers, 1942.

I am occasionally asked why I do not make much more extensive use of footnotes and cross-references in my studies. The answer is that I believe Scripture is the highest and best authority on all matters of doctrine. In

7

my opinion, if one cannot understand a point by reading and studying the Scriptures, whether in translation, or in the original source texts, what point is there in seeking man's opinion? In my experience, seeking man's opinion typically only confuses the situation, and confusion is not of YHWH. What YHWH wants us to do is to seek His face, and to seek His word as the highest and best authority. That is our purpose here. *YES!*

My goal in this study is not to spend a whole lot of time refuting Christian and/or Jewish traditions. Rather, my goal here is simply to show what I believe YHWH's Word actually commands us to do, using only as much commentary as is really necessary to tie the relevant Scripture passages together. I encourage you to be a 'noble Berean', and study out everything I say for yourself, holding fast only to that which is good.

Please do not take my word for anything. Instead, seek out the truth for yourself. However, I pray that this study will aid you in doing just that.

If you find some error, either in the commentary, or in translation, or if you should find a typographical error of some kind, please help by writing to me in love. This will help us to correct the error in future editions, so that others can benefit as well.

May YHWH be with you as you study for Him,

Yes Always

Norman B. Willis
In the Dispersion
2008 CE (@6008 HRT)

Why the Torah Calendar?

9-11-12

The Jews have an ancient meditative saying, that whoever's calendar you keep, that is who you worship. If we will take some time to reflect on this maxim, we may be able to see what the Jews mean.

In Scripture, a servant obeys his master's bidding. By the same token, whoever the servant obeys, that person is His master. But how does this apply to us?

Many believers are unaware that neither the Christian Calendar nor the Orthodox Jewish Rabbinical Calendar is the calendar prescribed by Scripture. But why would this make a difference? Let's illustrate with an extreme example.

A Muslim keeps the Islamic Calendar, and he worships Allah. By the exact same token, a Christian keeps the Roman Gregorian 'Christian' calendar, and in so doing, at least in the language and thought of Scripture, he serves the Roman Papacy. That is because it is the Roman Papacy that tells us to keep that particular calendar, and at least in Scriptural thought, whoevers commandments you keep, that person is your master.

Similarly, a Jew keeps the Orthodox Jewish calendar. However, since the Orthodox calendar is not the one Scripture prescribes, by this same ancient maxim, his elohim ('god') essentially is the Jewish rabbinate, which tells him to keep that particular calendar.

But what if YHWH has a calendar of His own? And what if His calendar is different than all of these other calendars? And what if YHWH told all of Israel to keep His calendar forever, in all of its generations? If we believe that YHWH is our Elohim, and if we claim to obey and serve Him alone, then should we not be keeping His calendar, rather than anyone elses?

Yes, we should

Joshua, the son of Nun, let the children of Israel know that they had to make a choice about who they would serve, and whose commandments they would keep.

> **Yehoshua (Joshua) 24:15**
> **15 And if it seems evil to you to serve YHWH, choose for yourselves this day whom you will serve, whether the elohim which your fathers served that were on the other side of the River, or the elohim of the Amorites, in whose land you dwell. But as for me and my house, we will serve YHWH."**

Whether we are conscious of it or not, each one of us has to choose whom we will serve. Will we keep the Islamic Calendar, and serve Allah? Will we keep the Roman Gregorian 'Christian' Calendar, and thereby serve Pope Gregory, and the Papacy? Will we keep the Orthodox Jewish Rabbinical Calendar, and serve Rabbi Hillel II and the Jewish rabbinate? Or will we choose to serve YHWH our Elohim, and keep only the calendar He commands His people to keep, in His word?

If you choose to serve YHWH, and if you desire to keep the calendar He asks His people Israel to keep in all of their generations, then this study is for you.

Shalom.

About 'Calendrical Drift'

Before we launch into our study about the calendar the Torah tells us to keep, first we should take a look at history, and see how it was that the children of Israel drifted away from the Torah Calendar. Hopefully this will help us to understand how error can creep in, so that we can guard against it happening again.

As we saw in *Nazarene Israel*, the Messiah Yeshua ('Jesus') told us not to think that He was come to destroy the Torah (the Laws of Moses) or the Prophets.

> *Mattai (Matthew) 5:17*
> *17 "Do not think that I came to destroy the Torah or the Prophets. I did not come to destroy but to fulfill.*

We also saw that even after Yeshua's resurrection, the faithful still had to keep the original Torah Calendar, so they would be in the right place at the right time, when YHWH poured out His blessings upon those who were keeping His calendar. For example, the apostles still had to be keeping the Pentecost after Yeshua's resurrection, in order to receive the gift of the Spirit.

> *Ma'asim (Acts) 2:1-2*
> *1 When the Day of Pentecost had fully come, they were all with one accord in one place.*
> *2 And suddenly there came a sound from heaven, as of a rushing mighty wind, and it filled the whole house where they were sitting.*

As we will see later in this chapter, the Apostle Shaul (Paul) tells us that YHWH will fulfill these exact same festival days again, in the future. Just as YHWH poured out blessings on those who were keeping His festival days in the past, He will pour out blessings on those who are keeping His festival days in the future. If we want to be there when those blessings are poured out, then it only stands to reason that we need to be keeping the calendar that He commands. *yep*

As important as it is to keep the Torah Calendar, it can seem somewhat more difficult, and confusing, at least at first. While the Roman 'Christian' calendar date changes at midnight (while one is sleeping), the Torah tells us that the day begins at evening. For example, Genesis 1:31 tells us that "the evening and the morning were the sixth day."

> **B'reisheet (Genesis) 1:31b**
> **31b So the evening and the morning were the sixth day.**

Leviticus 23:32 confirms that the Hebrew day lasts from evening to evening (i.e., from sunset to sunset), rather than from midnight to midnight.

> **Vayiqra (Leviticus) 23:32b**
> **32b "On the ninth of the month at evening, from evening until evening you shall celebrate your sabbath."**

The 'sabbath' discussed in Leviticus 23:32 (above) is the Day of Atonement, but like all Hebrew days, the weekly Sabbath also lasts from evening to evening. Luke 4:16 tells us that Yeshua ('J-sus') kept also this Sabbath, which lasts from sunset to sunset.

12

> *Luqa (Luke) 4:16*
> *16 So He came to Nazareth, where He had been brought up. And as His custom was, He went into the synagogue on the Sabbath day, and stood up to read.*

Even though many Christian churches teach that the day of worship was changed from the evening-to-evening Sabbath to the midnight-to-midnight Sunday at Yeshua' resurrection, we see that the Apostle Shaul (Paul) still continued to go into the synagogues on the Sabbath day long after Yeshua's resurrection.

> *Ma'asim (Acts) 13:14*
> *14 But when they departed from Perga, they came to Antioch in Pisidia, and went into the synagogue on the Sabbath day and sat down.*

Some mainstream churches tell us that since Yeshua fulfilled the Torah perfectly, the days of worship and rest have been changed from the Sabbath and Hebrew festivals to Sunday, Christmas and Easter. However, this doctrine is curious, considering the words *Sunday*, *Christmas* and *Easter* never appear in Scripture.

Is there some good reason to adopt days of worship that never appear in Scripture? And is there some good reason to adopt days of worship that neither the Messiah nor His apostles kept?

Some scholars use Acts 20:7-11 as 'proof' that the disciples gathered together on Sunday; and this might at first seem to make sense.

Ma'asim (Acts) 20:7-11

7 Now on the first day of the week, when the disciples came together to break bread, Shaul, ready to depart the next day, spoke to them and continued his message until midnight.

8 There were many lamps in the upper room where they were gathered together.

9 And in a window sat a certain young man named Eutychus, who was sinking into a deep sleep. He was overcome by sleep; and as Shaul continued speaking, he fell down from the third story and was taken up dead.

10 But Shaul went down, fell on him, and embracing him said, "Do not trouble yourselves, for his life is in him."

11 Now when he had come up, had broken bread and eaten, and talked a long while, even till daybreak, he departed.

Since Judea was under Roman control, it might make sense to think that the disciples were keeping the Roman calendar, in which the day begins at midnight. If this were the case, then it would make sense that the disciples gathered on Sunday morning, listened to Shaul all day Sunday, all Sunday night, and through until the break of dawn Monday morning. However, this would not explain why there were so many lamps in the upper room.

Why would there be so many lamps in the upper room, if the disciples initially met on a Sunday morning? And

14

why would they only eat one meal in a twenty-four hour period? These things do not really make sense.

Religious Jews are a very tradition-oriented people. During the Sabbath they usually worship at the synagogue (or at the Temple), and then after the Sabbath is over they often get together at a friend or a relative's house to break bread and fellowship, so as to extend the day of worship and rest as long as possible. However, this does not reflect a new day of worship on 'Sunday morning', but is simply an extension of the Sabbath. If we look at Acts Chapter 20 in this light we understand that the reason there were so many lamps in the upper room is because they met after sundown.

This same kind of post-Sabbath fellowship meeting is found in the Book of John, where we are told that the first day of the week was "the same day (Sabbath) at evening":

> **Yochanan (John) 20:19**
> **19 Then, the same day at evening, being the first day of the week, when the doors were shut where the disciples were assembled, for fear of the Jews, Yeshua came and stood in the midst, and said to them, "Peace be with you."**

Yeshua was crucified at Passover, in the spring. Israel can already be hot at that time, and if it was hot, then the sensible thing would have been to leave the doors open into the night. However, since there was persecution the disciples closed their doors. Therefore, the only really unusual thing here was that Yeshua showed up. It does not reflect a new day of worship.

But if the disciples were not taught to keep Sunday, Christmas or Easter, then how did these things come about? How did the original Torah Calendar 'drift' to where it is today, with so many Christians keeping days of worship and rest that are nowhere commanded in the word of YHWH?

The earliest known reference to Sunday worship comes from the Christian apologist Justin Martyr, circa 150 CE.

> *And on the day called Sunday, all who live in cities or in the country gather together to one place....*
> *[Justin Martyr, First Apology, Chapter 67 - Weekly Worship of the Christians, circa 150 CE, Biblesoft]*

Scripture numbers the days of the week (first, second, third, fourth, fifth, sixth, and seventh), and then calls the seventh day "the Shabbat" (the abstention/the rest). It never calls any day 'Saturday' or 'Sunday.' In contrast to this, the Ante-Nicene Church Father Justin Martyr tells us that the reason his assembly worshipped on Sunday (on the Roman Calendar) was that it was the day Elohim (G-d) made the world, and that it was the day Yeshua first appeared to His disciples.

> *But Sunday is the day on which we all hold our common assembly, because it is the first day on which God, having wrought a change in the darkness and matter, made the world; and Jesus Christ our Saviour on the same day rose from the dead. For He was crucified on the day before that of Saturn (Saturday); and on the day after*

16

that of Saturn, which is the day of the Sun, having appeared to His apostles and disciples, He taught them these things, which we have submitted to you also for your consideration.
[Justin Martyr, First Apology, Chapter 67 - Weekly Worship of the Christians, circa 150 CE, Biblesoft]

With all due respect, Justin Martyr makes the mistake of thinking that Yeshua ushered in the Roman calendar system. Also notice that while Justin Martyr's reasons for worshipping on Sunday might seem good, we have already seen that neither the Messiah nor His apostles were in the habit of meeting together on Sunday.

However, as we explained in *Nazarene Israel*, YHWH allowed the original Nazarene faith to be eclipsed by Sunday worship for a time, so that belief in Yeshua would be able to spread throughout the world just that much more rapidly. By temporarily debasing the faith, and by tying it to the Roman calendar, YHWH was able to help the faith spread not only throughout the Roman Empire, but also to other lands where sun worship and idol worship was common. Because of the calendar, and because the Romans had a history of bringing foreign idols and gods into their pantheons, Roman Christianity was much easier to spread than the original Nazarene faith. Over time there came to be many more converts to Christianity than there were converts to Nazarene Israel.

Then in the early 300's, Constantine became Emperor of Rome, and issued his famous Edict of Milan, which officially proclaimed a degree of religious tolerance within the Roman Empire. However, the Roman Empire was not without religious frictions. Three

17

The original Nazarene faith.

hundred years after Yeshua, the Church Father Epiphanius asserted that even though the Nazarenes were still keeping the original seventh-day Sabbath, those he termed "true Christians" worshipped only on Sunday, on the Roman calendar.

> *"The Nazarenes do not differ in any essential thing from them (meaning the Pharisees/Orthodox Jews), since they practice the customs and doctrines prescribed by Jewish Law; except that they believe in Christ.*
> *"They believe in the resurrection of the dead, and that the universe was created by God. They preach that God is One, and that Jesus Christ is His Son.*
> *"They are very learned in the Hebrew language. They read the Law (meaning the Law of Moshe).... Therefore they differ...from the true Christians because they fulfill until now (such) Jewish rites as the circumcision, (the) Sabbath, and others."*
> *[The Church Father Epiphanius in his doctrinal book, "Against Heresies," Panarion 29, 7, Page 41, 402]*

Since the Church Father Epiphanius asserted that the Nazarenes were "heretics", we know that the Roman Church was not friendly towards the Nazarenes. Further, although the Roman Empire was officially tolerant to other religions, it was less than a century after Constantine converted to Christianity when the Roman Christians began to stigmatize and then 'officially disallow' the Nazarenes. The Roman Church had formally disallowed the Sabbath approximately fifty years earlier, circa 336 CE, when the Emperor Constantine issued an edict stating that Christians must not "Judaize" by resting on the Sabbath, but that they must rest on "the Lord's Day" (i.e., Sunday).

> *"Christians must not 'Judaize' by resting on the Sabbath; but must work on that day, honoring rather the Lord's Day ('Sun' day) by resting, if possible, as Christians.*
> *However, if any (Nazarene) be found 'Judaizing', let them be shut out from Christ." (Other translations read, "Let them be anathema to Christ.")*
> *[The Church of Imperial Rome; Council of Laodicea under the Emperor Constantine; Canon 29, circa 336 CE]*

Three hundred years after Yeshua both preached and healed on the seventh-day Sabbath, the Sabbath had been officially banned by the Church of Rome.

Following the same general pattern, over time, the Hebrew festival of the Passover also gave way to the pagan festival of Easter (Ishtar). First the timing of the Passover was shifted away from the Hebrew evening-to-evening calendar, to the Roman midnight-to-midnight one. The date was then changed from the 14th of Nisan (Aviv) to a Sunday which fell around that same general timeframe. Then the name of the festival was changed from Passover to Easter, in honor of the Babylonian mother-goddess Ishtar.

A crisis came about in the second century when the bishops of Asia decided to keep the Passover on the Hebrew calendar, as they had been taught by the Apostles Phillip and Yochanan (John). This is recorded in Church history as the famous 'Quartodeciman Controversy' of the second century.

The Church father Eusebius records that the Quarto-deciman Controversy erupted when Bishop Victor of Rome began to insist that all the assemblies must keep the Passover on a Sunday (on the Roman calendar), rather than on the 14th of Nisan (on the Hebrew one).

> *A question of no small importance arose at that time. For the parishes of all Asia, as from an older tradition, held that the fourteenth day of the moon, on which day the Jews were commanded to sacrifice the lamb, should be observed as the feast of the Saviour's passover...But it was not the custom of the churches in the rest of the world...But the bishops of Asia, led by Polycrates, decided to hold to the old custom handed down to them. He himself, in a letter which he addressed to Victor and the Church of Rome, set forth in the following words the tradition which had come down to him. (Eusebius, Church History, Book V, Chapters 23, 25, circa 190-195 CE)*

Eusebius also reproduces the letter that Polycrates, a major figure in Asia, personally wrote to Bishop Victor of Rome, protesting Bishop Victor's decision to change the date of the Passover from the 14th of Nisan (Aviv), to a Sunday. Polycrates points out that the tradition of keeping the Passover on the Hebrew calendar had been given in Asia by the apostles Philip and Yochanan themselves, and that the tradition had been held fast in Asia over generations, by a number of distinguished and devout believers. Polycrates then insisted that all believers should do as the Scriptures said, rather than accept a man-made tradition.

We observe the exact day; neither adding, nor taking away. For in Asia also great lights have fallen asleep, which shall rise again on the day of the Lord's coming, when he shall come with glory from heaven, and shall seek out all the saints. Among these are Philip, one of the twelve apostles, who fell asleep in Hierapolis; and his two aged virgin daughters, and another daughter, who lived in the Holy Spirit and now rests at Ephesus; and, moreover, John, who was both a witness and a teacher, who reclined upon the bosom of the Lord, and, being a priest, wore the sacerdotal plate. He fell asleep at Ephesus. And Polycarp in Smyrna, who was a bishop and martyr; and Thraseas, bishop and martyr from Eumenia, who fell asleep in Smyrna. Why need I mention the bishop and martyr Sagaris who fell asleep in Laodicea, or the blessed Papirius, or Melito, the Eunuch who lived altogether in the Holy Spirit, and who lies in Sardis, awaiting the episcopate from heaven, when he shall rise from the dead? All these observed the fourteenth day of the Passover according to the Gospel, deviating in no respect, but following the rule of faith. And I also, Polycrates, the least of you all, do according to the tradition

of my relatives, some of whom I have closely followed. For seven of my relatives were bishops; and I am the eighth. And my relatives always observed the day when the people put away the leaven. I, therefore, brethren, who have lived sixty-five years in the Lord, and have met with the brethren throughout the world, and have gone through every Holy Scripture, am not affrighted by terrifying words. For those greater than I have said 'We ought to obey God rather than man'.
[Eusebius, Church History, Book V, Chapter 24. Translated by Arthur Cushman McGiffert. Excerpted from Nicene and Post-Nicene Fathers, Series Two, Volume 1.]

Despite the fact that the assemblies of Asia had learned to keep Passover on the Hebrew calendar, the Roman Bishop Victor decided to excommunicate every assembly which did not agree to hold the Passover on a Sunday, on the Roman calendar. While this greatly displeased many of the other bishops (who knew what Polycrates was saying to be true) the power of the Roman bishopric prevailed over Scripture. As sad as it was, unity was preserved in the church, albeit on false pretenses, and on false festival days. The practice of holding the Passover on the 14th of Nisan (on the Hebrew calendar) was ultimately driven underground, and countless seminary students have since been taught that the Quartodeciman Controversy was merely one example of the right of the Church to change the festival days away from the commanded in Scripture.

As we explain in *Nazarene Israel*, power began to be centralized in the Bishopric of Rome immediately after the destruction of Jerusalem, and the apostles' deaths. The Roman Bishop began to decree that pagan symbols and pagan festival days could be 'sanctified', even though this was in direct violation of the Torah, which tells us to avoid all non-commanded religious imagery, and is very clear that we should not worship YHWH after the manner of the other nations of the world.

> *Devarim (Deuteronomy) 12:1-4*
> *1 "These are the statutes and judgments which you shall be careful to observe in the land which YHWH Elohim of your fathers is giving you to possess, all the days that you live on the earth.*
> *2 You shall utterly destroy all the places where the nations which you shall dispossess served their gods, on the high mountains and on the hills and under every green tree.*
> *3 And you shall destroy their altars, break their sacred pillars, and burn their wooden images with fire; you shall cut down the carved images of their gods and destroy their names from that place.*
> *4 You shall not worship YHWH your Elohim with such things."*

Despite YHWH's stern warning, the calendar continued to drift towards the adoption of pagan festival days. Although the exact wording is not preserved, during the Council of Nicea (circa 326 CE), the Roman Church decided that Easter was to be celebrated throughout the world on the Sunday that followed the 14th day of the 'paschal moon.' However, the moon was to be considered 'paschal' only if the 14th day of the moon fell after the Spring Equinox, despite the fact that the Equinox is never mentioned in Scripture. This was clearly an example of YHWH's people choosing to worship Him on days of their own devising.

In the language of Scripture, the proof of belief is obedience. YHWH knows we believe in Him when we do what He commands. However, if we decide to keep days of worship that are determined by observing the sun, the moon, the stars and the host of the heavens, then YHWH considers that we are worshipping (or 'serving') the sun, the moon, the stars and the host of the heavens. YHWH warns us very sternly against this, and tells us that this is the practice that He has given to all the other nations of the world.

> **Devarim (Deuteronomy) 4:19**
> **19 "And take heed, lest you lift your eyes to heaven, and when you see the sun, the moon, and the stars, all the host of heaven, you feel driven to worship them and serve them, which YHWH your Elohim has given to all the peoples under the whole heaven as a heritage."**

It is natural for men to want to observe the movements of the sun, the moon and the stars. The sun brings warmth, and helps our crops to grow. The moon and the stars shine beautifully at night, and help guide the movements of ships. It is so natural to worship and serve the movements of these heavenly bodies that festivals in honor of these things are found in cultures all over the world (i.e., "all the people under the whole heaven"). However, because YHWH did not command us to keep these festival days, He considers them to be idolatrous, and if we insist on observing these festival days even though He told us not to, He considers us to be idolaters.

We need to remember that YHWH is in the heavens, and we are here on earth. YHWH has a different perspective on things than we do. It can sometimes be very difficult for us to understand, or to accept, but the Torah is clear that YHWH does not permit us to establish new festival days of our own; and that if we attempt to do so, there will be extreme consequences.

In Exodus 32, we read about the infamous episode with the Golden Calf.

> *Shemote (Exodus) 32:4-5*
> *4 And he received the gold from their hand, and he fashioned it with an engraving tool, and made a molded calf. Then they said, "This is your god, O Israel, that brought you out of the land of Egypt!"*
> *5 So when Aharon saw it, he built an altar before it. And Aharon made a proclamation and said, "Tomorrow is a feast to YHWH."*

Notice that even though Aharon declared that the festival was in honor of YHWH, YHWH did not feel honored. Rather, He became enraged that His people would keep festival days that He did not command.

Why, then, do so many believers want to keep festivals that are not commanded in Scripture? The only reason the word 'Easter' appears in the King James Version is that is was mistranslated from the Greek word 'Pascha' (πάσχα), meaning Passover. This error has been corrected in almost every other major translation since the King James Version, but the practice of observing Easter remains strong within Christendom.

When we translate Acts 12:4 correctly, we see that the people were still keeping the Passover in the first century.

Acts 12:4	BGT Acts 12:4 ὃν καὶ
4 So when he had arrested him, he put him in prison, and delivered him to four squads of soldiers to keep him, intending to bring him before the people after Passover.	πιάσας ἔθετο εἰς φυλακὴν παραδοὺς τέσσαρσιν τετραδίοις στρατιωτῶν φυλάσσειν αὐτόν, βουλόμενος μετὰ τὸ πάσχα ἀναγαγεῖν αὐτὸν τῷ λαῷ

We know that the Nazarenes were keeping the 'Jewish' observances until the 4th century CE. However, the majority of the Christian Church did not begin to observe Easter until 190-195 CE, when the Passover was driven underground in the days of Polycrates and the Roman Bishop Victor (above).

Further, let us note that the Apostle Shaul does not tell us to keep Easter, but rather to celebrate the Feast of Unleavened Bread (which is a continuation of the Passover).

Qorintim Aleph (1st Corinthians) 5:8
8 Therefore let us keep the feast, not with old leaven, nor with the leaven of

malice and wickedness, but with the unleavened bread of sincerity and truth.

As a second witness to this, Acts 20:6 shows us that the disciples were still keeping the Days of Unleavened Bread many years after Yeshua's resurrection.

> *Ma'asim (Acts) 20:6*
> *6 But we sailed from Philippi after the days of Unleavened Bread....*

We also know that the Apostle Shaul continued to observe the Israelite Festival of the Pentecost on the Hebrew calendar.

> *Qorintim Aleph (1st Corinthians) 16:8*
> *8 But I will remain in Ephesus until Pentecost....*

We know that Shaul kept Pentecost on the Hebrew Calendar (rather than on the Roman Christian one) because he went up to Jerusalem (and not Rome).

> *Ma'asim (Acts) 20:16*
> *16 For Shaul had decided to sail past Ephesus, so that he would not have to spend time in Asia; for he was hurrying to be at Jerusalem, if possible, on the Day of Pentecost.*

In Acts 27:9, the disciples kept the Day of Atonement, even though it was many years after Yeshua had already been resurrected. The Day of Atonement is here called 'the Fast', because it is traditionally observed by fasting.

> *Ma'asim (Acts) 27:9-10*
> *9 Now when much time had been spent, and sailing was now dangerous because the Fast was already over, Shaul advised them,*
> *10 saying, "Men, I perceive that this voyage will end with disaster and much loss, not only of the cargo and ship, but also our lives."*

The reason the voyage was "now dangerous" was that the Day of Atonement takes place in the fall, at the time when the weather changes from summer to winter. Boat travel on the Mediterranean can be stormy in winter, and therefore it is dangerous. However, the point here is that the apostles were still keeping the festival days found in the Torah, and not converted Roman festival days.

YHWH blesses those who keep His festivals.

> *Ma'asim (Acts) 2:1-2*
> *1 When the day of Pentecost had come, they were all together in one place.*
> *2 And suddenly there came from heaven a noise like a violent rushing wind, and it filled the whole house where they were sitting.*

At least some of the blessings associated with keeping His festival days are still to come, in the future. In Colossians 2:16-17, the Apostle Shaul tells us that the Sabbath, the festivals and the New Moon Days are all shadows of things "still to come." That means just as YHWH poured out blessings on those who were keeping His festival days in the past, YHWH will pour out even more blessings on those who are still keeping His festival days in the future. However, Scripture's true meaning is lost in most major versions, including the King James Version. *Wow!*

Note how the King James Version supplies two words in italics (*days* and *is*), which do not exist in the Greek; and how these two words invert the true meaning of the passage.

Colossians 2:16-17, KJV 16 Let no man therefore judge you in meat, or in drink, or in respect of an holy day, or of the new moons, or of the sabbath <u>days</u>: 17 Which are a shadow of things to come; but the body <u>is</u> of Christ.	BGT Colossians 2:16 ¶ Μὴ οὖν τις ὑμᾶς κρινέτω ἐν βρώσει καὶ ἐν πόσει ἢ ἐν μέρει ἑορτῆς ἢ νεομηνίας ἢ σαββάτων· BGT Colossians 2:17 ἅ ἐστιν σκιὰ τῶν μελλόντων, τὸ δὲ σῶμα τοῦ Χριστοῦ.

Because it adds the italicized words (*days*) and (*is*), the KJV leads the reader to conclude that we should not let anyone tell us what to eat, what to drink, or what days of worship to keep. If we accept these added words at their face value, we can easily conclude that it makes no difference at all whether we keep the Sabbath and the festival days, or whether we worship on Sunday, Christmas, the Chinese New Year, Ramadan, or even no festival days at all. Other translations make similar alterations to the text, and these alterations generally help promote the idea that Yeshua actually did come to abolish the Torah and the Prophets, contrary to His own statement at Matthew 5:17-19.

Scripture, however, is very clear that we are not to add anything to His words, or to take anything away (e.g., Deuteronomy 4:2, Proverbs 30:6, etcetera). Therefore, once we realize that the supplied words *days* and *is* do not appear in the source texts, we should take them back out of the English translations.

Here is the exact same passage from the King James, but with the supplied words *"days"* and *"is"* removed:

> **Let no man therefore judge you in meat, or in drink, or in respect of an holy day, or of the new moons, or of the Sabbath; which are a shadow of things to come; but the Body of Christ.**

If we read this passage carefully, we can see that there are three main ideas here (1-2-3):

1. **Let no man therefore judge you in meat, or in drink, or in respect of an holy day, or of the new moons, or of the Sabbath;**
2. **which are a (prophetic) shadow of things (still) to come;**
3. **but the Body of [Messiah].**

To paraphrase, the Apostle Shaul is telling us:

1. **Let no man judge you with regards to the meat you eat, what you drink, or what religious festival days you keep;**
2. **Because these foods, liquids and festival days are all prophetic shadows of things still to come;**
3. **Therefore, let only the Body of Messiah tell you what to eat, what to drink, and what festival days to keep!**

30

If we rearrange the clauses to make the English read better (3-1-2), we can see that what the Apostle Shaul was actually saying was that we should not let anyone but the Body of Messiah judge us in what we eat, what we drink, and what festival days we keep, because these things are all shadows of prophetic blessings still to come.

> *Let no man (but the Body of Messiah) judge you in meat, or in drink, or in respect of an holy day, or of the new moons, or of the Sabbath; for the festivals are shadows of things (still) to come.*
> *[Colossians 2:16-17, reordered]*

Shaul's true meaning is not reflected in the NIV.

> *16 Therefore do not let anyone judge you by what you eat or drink, or with regard to a religious festival, a New Moon celebration or a sabbath day.*
> *17 These are a shadow of the things that were to come; the reality, however, is found in Christ.*
> *[Colossians 2:16-17, NIV]*

The King James, the NIV, and most of the mainstream Christian versions essentially support the old Gnostic hypothesis: that so long as one knows Yeshua is the Messiah, it makes no difference what days of worship one keeps, because the festivals are merely shadows of the things that "were" to come. However, this is far from Shaul's true meaning.

The idea that the foods we eat and the festival days we keep are important prophetic shadows of things still to come did not originate with the Apostle Shaul. The Jews have long held that major prophetic events typically fall on Israel's festival days.

When YHWH poured out the gift of the Spirit on the Pentecost, the faithful still needed to be at the Temple in Jerusalem in order to receive that gift. If Yeshua's resurrection really marked the end of the Torah and the Prophets, as some groups claim, then why did the faithful still need to be in the Temple on the Pentecost? Why was the Spirit not poured out at some other place, and at some other time, such as on Christmas, in Rome?

Some theologians tell us that even though the Apostles continued to keep YHWH's festivals, the reason we now keep Sunday, Christmas and Easter is that Yeshua's resurrection marked the start of a three-to-four-hundred-year period of change, in which the Church would be authorized to make all sorts of sweeping changes to the faith. However, this thesis is very curious, considering these alleged changes were never prophesied anywhere in Scripture, and also considering how many times YHWH sternly warned those who feared Him not to keep any other festival days.

The Torah is a codification of YHWH's Spirit, given as a list of instructions (dos and don'ts). At least according to Jewish tradition, these instructions were first given to Israel at Mount Sinai on the Pentecost, fifty days after the first Passover. Then, thousands of years later, the Spirit itself was poured out on the faithful at Pentecost. The difference was that this time, instead of just giving a codification of the Spirit, YHWH gave the gift of His

Spirit itself. Thus, in actuality there have already been at least two fulfillments of the Feast of the Pentecost, and Colossians 2:16-17 tell us that there are more on the way.

The pattern in Scripture is one of repeated fulfillments of the festivals. The Children of Israel already fulfilled the Feast of Tabernacles when they dwelt in tabernacles (or booths) in the Wilderness in Sinai. The second fulfillment came when Yeshua was born.

Most Christians have been taught that Yeshua was born on December 25th. However, Yeshua could not have been born in winter, because Luke 2:8 shows us that there were shepherds keeping watch over their flocks at that time.

> ***Luqa (Luke) 2:8***
> ***7 And she brought forth her firstborn Son, and wrapped Him in swaddling cloths, and laid Him in a manger, because there was no room for them in the inn.***
> ***8 Now there were in the same country shepherds living out in the fields, keeping watch over their flock by night.***

In Israel, flocks are not typically let out to pasture in the winter. Therefore, this event had to occur some time before winter had set in, and the flocks were penned up. This effectively rules out the month of December.

As we will show in the chapter on Hanukkah, Yeshua was conceived in the middle of winter (probably during Hanukkah time), and was born some nine months later, in the fall, around the time of the Feast of Tabernacles.

From a prophetic standpoint, it makes perfect sense that Yeshua would be born on the first day of the Feast of Tabernacles, because He would be fulfilling the first day of the Feast of Tabernacles. Could this be why Yochanan (John) tells us that the Word became flesh, and dwelt among us?

> **Yochanan (John) 1:14**
> **14 And the Word became flesh and dwelt among us....**

The word 'dwelt' is the Greek word skenoo, Strong's NT4637, meaning, 'to tabernacle.'

> **NT:4637 skenoo (skay-no'-o); from NT:4636; to tent or encamp, i.e. (figuratively) to occupy (as a mansion) or (specifically) to reside (as God did in the Tabernacle of old, a symbol of protection and communion):**

Essentially, then, what Yochanan (John) was saying was:

> **Yochanan (John) 1:14 [interpreted]**
> **14 And the Word became flesh and tabernacled among us....**

In Leviticus 23, YHWH commands that all native-born Israelites who live in the Land of Israel must make a pilgrimage up to Jerusalem three times a year. One of these three annual pilgrimages is the fall Feast of Tabernacles. During this feast, all Israel must dwell in tabernacles (temporary dwellings) for seven days. In Hebrew, these temporary dwellings are called *Sukkot.* In English, they are often called 'booths'.

Vayiqra (Leviticus) 23:42
42 You shall dwell in booths for seven days. All who are native Israelites shall dwell in booths....

The rabbinical ruling in the first century was likely identical to the rabbinical ruling of today, which is that for health and safety's sake, anyone who is sick, old or pregnant does not actually have to stay in a tabernacle, but can rent a room in an inn. However, even though Miriam was pregnant, there was no room at the inn. Therefore Joseph and Miriam had to dwell in a tabernacle (or a booth, or a 'manger'), in keeping with Leviticus 23. While this might have seemed like a turnabout for Joseph and Miriam, all of this came to pass so that Yeshua might be born in a temporary dwelling (a tabernacle) on the first day of the fall Feast of Tabernacles, in prophetic fulfillment of the feast.

But even though Yeshua was the second fulfillment of the Feast of Sukkot (Tabernacles), Zechariah 14 tells us that there will yet be a third fulfillment.

> *Zechariah 14:16-17*
> *16 And it shall come to pass that everyone who is left of all the nations which came against Jerusalem shall go up from year to year to worship the King, YHWH of hosts, and to keep the Feast of Tabernacles.*
> *17 And it shall be that whichever of the families of the earth do not come up to Jerusalem to worship the King, YHWH of hosts, on them there will be no rain.*

There is even a fourth fulfillment prophesied, in the Book of the Revelation:

Gilyana (Revelation) 21:3
3 And I heard a loud voice from the throne, saying, "Behold, the tabernacle of Elohim is among men, and He will dwell among them, and they shall be His people, and Elohim Himself will be among them,
4 and He will wipe away every tear from their eyes; and there will no longer be any death; there will no longer be any mourning, or crying, or pain; the first things have passed away."

This shows us why the Apostle Shaul warned us not to let anyone but the Body of Messiah tell us what days of worship to keep. It is because they are prophetic shadow pictures of wonderful blessings still to come.

The Sabbath (Shabbat)

The Fourth Commandment is the command to keep the Sabbath. The Sabbath was one of the Ten Commands that YHWH inscribed in stone.

> *Shemote (Exodus) 20:8-11*
> *8 "Remember the Sabbath day, to keep it set apart.*
> *9 Six days you shall labor and do all your work,*
> *10 but the seventh day is the Sabbath of YHWH your Elohim. In it you shall do no work: you, nor your son, nor your daughter, nor your male servant, nor your female servant, nor your cattle, nor your stranger who is within your gates.*
> *11 For in six days YHWH made the heavens and the earth, the sea, and all that is in them, and rested the seventh day. Therefore YHWH blessed the Sabbath day and set it apart."*

The Sabbath is the seventh day of the week, and the fact that YHWH inscribed the commandment to rest (i.e., to 'sabbath') in stone should give us some idea of the degree of importance and unchangeability that YHWH assigns to it.

The reason YHWH assigned the Sabbath as the seventh day of the week is that YHWH created the heavens and the earth in six days, and then rested on the seventh day.

B'reisheet (Genesis) 2:2-3
2 And on the seventh day Elohim ended His work which He had done, and He rested on the seventh day from all His work which He had done.
3 Then Elohim blessed the seventh day and set it apart, because in it He rested from all His work which Elohim had created and made.

However, YHWH not only rested on the seventh day, but He also was refreshed.

Shemote (Exodus) 31:12-17
12 And YHWH spoke to Moshe, saying,
13 "Speak also to the children of Israel, saying: 'Surely My Sabbaths you shall keep, for it is a sign between Me and you throughout your generations, that you may know that I am YHWH who sets you apart.
14 You shall keep the Sabbath, therefore, for it is set apart to you. Everyone who profanes it shall surely be put to death; for whoever does any work on it, that person shall be cut off from among his people.
15 Work shall be done for six days, but the seventh is the Sabbath of rest, set apart to YHWH. Whoever does any work on the Sabbath day, he shall surely be put to death.
16 Therefore the children of Israel shall keep the Sabbath, to observe the Sabbath throughout their generations as a perpetual covenant.

17 It is a sign between Me and the children of Israel forever; for in six days YHWH made the heavens and the earth, and on the seventh day He rested and was refreshed.'"

The language here is curious. Since YHWH's power and might is completely without limit, how can YHWH become tired? And if He cannot become tired, then how can YHWH become refreshed?

In modern computer terms, when a computer screen becomes all messed up, perhaps because a computer has been left on too long, and becomes too hot, or because too many computing operations have been performed on it without the computer being able to take a break, the computer screen becomes disorderly. To correct this condition, one presses the 'refresh' button. In exactly the same way, the Sabbath is a kind of a 'refresh' button for mankind, whereby the proper order is restored between Elohim and man, by purposely taking a day to worship, and to rest in Him.

Notice the language here: that the purpose of the Sabbath is to rest in Him. The purpose of the Sabbath is not to rest and relax the flesh by sewing, by hiking, by catching up on one's sleep for the week, or by participating in recreational activities such as boating, fishing or watching television. Rather, the purpose of YHWH's Sabbath is to restore the proper order between YHWH Elohim and man. As we will see, this calls for us to gather together, and serve Him as one united, combined Body of Messiah.

> **Hebrews 10:24-25**
> **24 And let us consider one another in order to stir up love and good works,**

25 not forsaking the assembling of ourselves together, as is the manner of some, but exhorting one another, and so much the more as you see the Day approaching.

YHWH has specific rules for the Sabbath. He tells us that not only are we to do no work, but that we are not to cause anyone else to work on that day: neither our sons, nor our daughters, nor our menservants, nor our maidservants, nor our cattle, nor any stranger who is within our gates.

> *Shemote (Exodus) 20:8-11*
> *8 "Remember the Sabbath day, to keep it set apart.*
> *9 Six days you shall labor and do all your work,*
> *10 but the seventh day is the Sabbath of YHWH your Elohim. In it you shall do no work: you, nor your son, nor your daughter, nor your male servant, nor your female servant, nor your cattle, nor your stranger who is within your gates.*
> *11 For in six days YHWH made the heavens and the earth, the sea, and all that is in them, and rested the seventh day. Therefore YHWH blessed the Sabbath day and set it apart."*

The basic concept is that we are to rest and relax in Him, and to cause anyone and everyone under our power to rest and relax in Him also. In practical terms, this means that we must not hire anyone to do any regular work, or work for pay on the Sabbath.

YHWH both blessed the seventh day, and He set it apart. By way of blessing, He gave His people one day out of their busy weeks that they should have to do no laborious work. This is so true that the children of Israel were not even supposed to cook on the Sabbath.

In the Wilderness of Sinai, the children of Israel were told to gather and prepare twice as much food on the sixth day of the week (sometimes called 'Preparation Day'), so that no gathering or cooking had to be done on the Sabbath.

> *Shemote (Exodus) 16:22-30*
> *22 And so it was, on the sixth day, that they gathered twice as much bread, two omers for each one. And all the rulers of the congregation came and told Moshe.*
> *23 Then he said to them, "This is what YHWH has said: 'Tomorrow is a Sabbath rest, a set-apart Sabbath to YHWH. Bake what you will bake today, and boil what you will boil; and lay up for yourselves all that remains, to be kept until morning.'"*
> *24 So they laid it up till morning, as Moshe commanded; and it did not stink, nor were there any worms in it.*
> *25 Then Moshe said, "Eat that today, for today is a Sabbath to YHWH; today you will not find it in the field.*
> *26 Six days you shall gather it, but on the seventh day, the Sabbath, there will be none."*
> *27 Now it happened that some of the people went out on the seventh day to gather, but they found none.*

28 And YHWH said to Moshe, "How long do you refuse to keep My commandments and My laws?
29 See! For YHWH has given you the Sabbath; therefore He gives you on the sixth day bread for two days. Let every man remain in his place; let no man go out of his place on the seventh day."
30 So the people rested on the seventh day.

The idea is to prepare for the Sabbath all six days of the week, and then to prepare twice as much food on the sixth day, so that one does not have to gather or prepare food on the seventh. With the work of food preparation already done, the Sabbath is just that much more restful.

YHWH tells us He is serious about His people resting from their labors on the seventh day. He even tells us that whosoever does any work on the Sabbath is to be put to death. This is a sign of the covenant between YHWH and us forever, in all of our generations.

Shemote (Exodus) 31:12-17
12 And YHWH spoke to Moshe, saying,
13 "Speak also to the children of Israel, saying: 'Surely My Sabbaths you shall keep, for it is a sign between Me and you throughout your generations, that you may know that I am YHWH who sets you apart.
14 You shall keep the Sabbath, therefore, for it is set apart to you. Everyone who profanes it shall surely be put to death; for whoever does any

work on it, that person shall be cut off from among his people.
15 Work shall be done for six days, but the seventh is the Sabbath of rest, set apart to YHWH. Whoever does any work on the Sabbath day, he shall surely be put to death.
16 Therefore the children of Israel shall keep the Sabbath, to observe the Sabbath throughout their generations as a perpetual covenant.
17 It is a sign between Me and the children of Israel forever; for in six days YHWH made the heavens and the earth, and on the seventh day He rested and was refreshed."'

However, people being what they are, they sometimes put YHWH to the test. So it was that when Israel was in the Wilderness, immediately after YHWH had warned the people that anyone rebelling against His commandments should be put to death, a man chose to profane the Sabbath by gathering sticks. When Moshe asked YHWH what to do, YHWH decreed that the rebellious man was surely to be put to death.

Bemidbar (Numbers) 15:32-36
32 Now while the children of Israel were in the wilderness, they found a man gathering sticks on the Sabbath day.
33 And those who found him gathering sticks brought him to Moshe and Aharon, and to all the congregation.
34 They put him under guard, because it had not been explained what should be done to him.

35 Then YHWH said to Moshe, "The man must surely be put to death; all the congregation shall stone him with stones outside the camp."
36 So, as YHWH commanded Moshe, all the congregation brought him outside the camp and stoned him with stones, and he died.

The reason this man was profaning the Sabbath was that he had chosen to perform routine, laborious work that could have been done either before or after Shabbat. He should have been congregating and worshipping YHWH at that time.

When YHWH appoints a special time to meet with us, we as His bride must make every effort to meet with Him then. If there is any work that can be done before the Sabbath, so that we have more time to spend with Him on that day, then that work should be done apart from the Sabbath day.

Yet even though the man gathering sticks was breaking the Shabbat, Yeshua said that His disciples were not breaking the Shabbat when they plucked heads of grain (and ate them) on the Sabbath.

Matthew 12:1-8
1 At that time Yeshua went through the grainfields on the Sabbath. And His disciples were hungry, and began to pluck heads of grain and to eat.
2 And when the Pharisees saw it, they said to Him, "Look, Your disciples are doing what is not lawful to do on the Sabbath!"

3 But He said to them, "Have you not read what David did when he was hungry, he and those who were with him:

4 how he entered the house of Elohim and ate the showbread which was not lawful for him to eat, nor for those who were with him, but only for the priests?

5 Or have you not read in the Torah that on the Sabbath the priests in the temple profane the Sabbath, and are blameless?

6 Yet I say to you that in this place there is One greater than the temple.

7 But if you had known what this means, 'I desire mercy and not sacrifice,' you would not have condemned the guiltless.

8 For the Son of Man is Master even of the Sabbath."

There are several reasons that Yeshua's disciples were not profaning the Sabbath. Perhaps one of the most obvious is that His disciples were not working for pay. They also were not reaping with a sickle and a basket, either to sell, or to store up for later. Rather, they were spending time with their Husband, and were simply eating what was readily at hand as they walked through the field, much as one might pluck a few pomegranates one came across on the way to the synagogue. Since it was not really 'work' to pluck these grains and eat them, it did not need to be put off until later.

Another thing that is not 'customary work,' and which does not need to be put off until after the Sabbath is healing, and doing good.

Mattai (Matthew) 12:9-12
9 Now when He had departed from there, He went into their synagogue.
10 And behold, there was a man who had a withered hand. And they asked Him, saying, "Is it lawful to heal on the Sabbath?" — that they might accuse Him.
11 Then He said to them, "What man is there among you who has one sheep, and if it falls into a pit on the Sabbath, will not lay hold of it and lift it out?
12 Of how much more value then is a man than a sheep? Therefore it is lawful to do good on the Sabbath."

Sometimes people have questions about hospital staff: since Yeshua said it is OK to heal on the Sabbath, is it OK for believers to work as doctors, nurses, police and fire services, or as other emergency services personnel? Perhaps it will be easier to understand if we use the following analogy:

Scripture likens Israel to a virgin bride, and if Israel is a virgin bride, then one might consider the Sabbath (or any other festival day) as a 'date' between the bride and her future Husband. If the bride only gets to see her Beloved Fiance one day a week, then if she truly cherishes her Fiance, and wants to be with Him, then she will look for ways to make the most of her time with Him. Because of this, she will try to take care of her earthly chores during the rest of the week, so that she can spend as much time as possible with Him on her one special date day.

If someone should come to the bride's door in need of urgent medical care (or even food) on the day she has to spend with her Fiance, her Fiance will probably be quite pleased and happy with her if she stops whatever she is doing, and helps the one in need. However, in contrast, her Fiance will probably not be pleased if she has been lazy during the week, or has overscheduled herself, such that she has left herself all sorts of little chores to do, or is too exhausted to spend quality time with Him.

It is true that not all work can be put off until another time. For one example, dairy animals must be milked seven days a week, and animals such as sheep need a great deal of help during birthing, no matter what day of the week it is. Further, life being what it is, medical emergencies arise seven days a week, and ambulance and medical crews need to be on hand to help save the lives of those who are in need. However, in all of these scenarios, there is work that must be performed at the time the crisis arises, yet there is also other work that can be put off until later. Whatever work can be done either before or after the Sabbath, should be.

What exactly can and cannot be done on the Sabbath is also the question of some debate. Exodus 35 tells us that anyone who works on the Sabbath must be put to death, and then it also gives us a rather curious commandment, not to kindle a fire on the Sabbath day.

> **Shemote (Exodus) 35:1-3**
> **1 Then Moshe gathered all the congregation of the children of Israel together, and said to them, "These are the words which YHWH has commanded you to do:**

2 Work shall be done for six days, but the seventh day shall be a set-apart day for you, a Sabbath of rest to YHWH. Whoever does any work on it shall be put to death.
3 You shall kindle no fire throughout your dwellings on the Sabbath day."

Why would YHWH prohibit us from kindling a fire in our dwellings on Shabbat? In many climates one needs to burn a fire in winter just to keep warm, and the Sabbath would hardly be relaxing or refreshing without heat. However, if we look at this passage in the Hebrew, we may be able to get a better feel for YHWH's intended meaning.

Exodus 35:3 3 "You shall kindle no fire in any of your dwellings on the Sabbath day."	(3) לֹא תְבַעֲרוּ אֵשׁ בְּכֹל מֹשְׁבֹתֵיכֶם I בְּיוֹם הַשַּׁבָּת :

The word 'kindle' here is ta-ba-aru (תְבַעֲרוּ), which is likely the Hebrew source for the English word "to burn." This is also the word used to describe the burning bush in Exodus 3:2. Thus, the commandment not to kindle a fire on Shabbat is probably the commandment not to burn a fire on the Sabbath.

But even if the commandment in Exodus 35:3 is not to burn a fire on the Sabbath, still we are left with the question, why would YHWH command us not to burn a fire for warmth (or for light) on His day of rest and refreshment? Does He desire us to dwell in the dark, and be cold?

Let us consider that the phrase 'your dwellings' is 'moshavotheichem,' (מֹשְׁבֹתֵיכֶם), which means 'your communities.' Since wood had to be gathered by hand, each individual family did not always build their own fires. Rather, in ancient times, families and clans built a community fire. This is where the people of one extended family cooked, and conducted all manner of work requiring fire, such as blacksmithing. Therefore, it seems likely that what YHWH was really prohibiting was the kindling or burning of a work or a cooking fire on Shabbat.

We already saw in the last chapter that there were many lamps in the upper room where the Apostle Shaul was teaching.

> **Ma'asim (Acts) 20:7-8**
> **7 Now on the first day of the week, when the disciples came together to break bread, Shaul, ready to depart the next day, spoke to them and continued his message until midnight.**
> **8 There were many lamps in the upper room where they were gathered together.**

Many scholars dispute the translation "on the first day of the week." The Greek reads, "mia ton Sabbaton" (μιᾷ τῶν σαββάτων), which many scholars maintain is more correctly translated as "on one of the Sabbaths."

Acts 20:7-8	BGT Acts 20:7 Ἐν δὲ τῇ
7 On one of the Sabbaths, when we were gathered together to break bread, Shaul began talking to	μιᾷ τῶν σαββάτων συνηγμένων ἡμῶν κλάσαι ἄρτον, ὁ Παῦλος διελέγετο αὐτοῖς μέλλων

them, intending to leave the next day, and he prolonged his message until midnight.	ἐξιέναι τῇ ἐπαύριον, παρέτεινέν τε τὸν λόγον μέχρι μεσονυκτίου.

If this gathering did take place on one of the Sabbaths, as some scholars contend, it would show us that Shaul believed one could burn non-work-related fires (in this case, lamps) on the Sabbath, for light.

What this shows us is that it is not YHWH's intention that we remain in the cold or the dark on His day of worship and refreshment. That is why, if the penalty for profaning the Sabbath is strict, the rules for keeping the Shabbat must be interpreted with common sense.

It is sometimes suggested that we do not need to assemble on the Sabbath, in that when the children of Israel were in the Wilderness, YHWH told them to remain in their place on the seventh day.

> **Shemote (Exodus) 16:29**
> **29 "See! For YHWH has given you the Sabbath; therefore He gives you on the sixth day bread for two days. Let every man remain in his place; let no man go out of his place on the seventh day."**

However, the context of this commandment to 'remain every man in his place' is not in reference to assembly for worship, but only with regards to gathering and preparing food. Rather than gather and prepare food on the Shabbat, the children of Israel were supposed to prepare a day in advance, so they did not have to cook.

The commandment to assemble for worship on the Shabbat is given in Leviticus 23:3. We will look at the Hebrew here.

Vayiqra (Leviticus) 23:3 3 'Six days shall work be done, but the seventh day is a Sabbath of solemn rest, a set-apart gathering. You shall do no work on it; it is the Sabbath of YHWH in all your dwellings.	(3) שֵׁשֶׁת יָמִים תֵּעָשֶׂה מְלָאכָה וּבַיּוֹם הַשְּׁבִיעִי שַׁבַּת שַׁבָּתוֹן מִקְרָא קֹדֶשׁ כָּל מְלָאכָה לֹא תַעֲשׂוּ I שַׁבָּת הִוא לַיהוָה בְּכֹל וּשְׁבֹתֵיכֶם :

The seventh day is described as a Sabbath of solemn rest, and a set-apart gathering. The Hebrew here is 'miqra qodesh' (מִקְרָא קֹדֶשׁ), which is usually translated as a 'holy convocation' in English. A 'miqra' is a public meeting, and also a prophetic rehearsal.

> *OT:4744 miqra' (mik-raw'); from OT:7121; something called out, i.e. a public meeting (the act, the persons, or the place); also a rehearsal.*

The letter 'mem' (מ) implies a massing, and 'karaw' (קְרָא) means 'called'. Therefore a miqra (מִקְרָא) is a 'called-out massing', or a 'call to a public meeting'. Please notice that this is also a prophetic rehearsal, as we saw in Colossians 2:16-17 (above).

It was Yeshua's custom to fulfill this commandment to go to a public worship and prayer meeting by going to the local synagogue.

Luqa (Luke) 4:16

16 So He came to Nazareth, where He had been brought up. And as His custom was, He went into the synagogue on the Sabbath day, and stood up to read.

As we explain in *Nazarene Israel*, it seems the apostles also intended the returning gentile Ephraimites to fulfill the requirement to gather for prayer by going to the local synagogues on each Sabbath.

Ma'asim (Acts) 15:19-21
19 "Therefore I judge that we should not trouble those from among the gentiles who are turning to Elohim,
20 but that we write to them to abstain from things polluted by idols, from sexual immorality, from things strangled, and from blood.
21 For Moshe has had throughout many generations those who preach him in every city, being read in the synagogues every Sabbath."

As explained in *Nazarene Israel*, Acts Chapter Fifteen tells us that if the returning gentile Ephraimites would begin by abstaining from the four abominations of idolatry, adultery, strangled (i.e., unclean) meats and blood, then they could be allowed to enter into the synagogues on Sabbath, as they would not be defiling the set-apartness of the space. There in the public prayer and worship meetings, they would learn the rest of the Torah over time, as parts of the Torah are read aloud in the synagogues each week.

It is sometimes taught that since Torah scrolls were not readily available in the first century, but since most households can afford a copy of the Scriptures today, that it is not necessary for the people to gather and assemble for public worship on the Shabbat. However, this ignores both Leviticus 23:3, which plainly tells us to assemble on the Shabbat, as well as Hebrews 10:25, which specifically commands us not to forsake the assembling of ourselves, although it is the custom of some.

> **Hebrews 10:24-25**
> **24 And let us consider one another in order to stir up love and good works, 25 not forsaking the assembling of ourselves together, as is the manner of some, but exhorting one another, and so much the more as you see the Day approaching.**

YHWH tells us that the Sabbath is one of His appointed times. In other words, it is one of the times that He has appointed for us to gather together and assemble ourselves, so as to worship Him as one new man.

Leviticus 23:2-5 2 "Speak to the children of Israel, and say to them: 'The feasts of YHWH, which you shall proclaim to be set-apart gatherings, these are My feasts: 3 'Six days shall work be done, but the seventh day is a Sabbath of solemn rest, a set-apart gathering. You shall do no work on it; it is the Sabbath of YHWH	(2) דַּבֵּר אֶל בְּנֵי יִשְׂרָאֵל וְאָמַרְתָּ אֲלֵהֶם מוֹעֲדֵי יְהוָה אֲשֶׁר תִּקְרְאוּ אֹתָם מִקְרָאֵי קֹדֶשׁ ׀ אֵלֶּה הֵם מוֹעֲדָי : (3) שֵׁשֶׁת יָמִים תֵּעָשֶׂה מְלָאכָה וּבַיּוֹם הַשְּׁבִיעִי שַׁבַּת שַׁבָּתוֹן מִקְרָא קֹדֶשׁ כָּל מְלָאכָה לֹא תַעֲשׂוּ ׀

in all your dwellings. 4 'These are the feasts of YHWH, set-apart gatherings which you shall proclaim at their appointed times. 5 On the fourteenth day of the first month at twilight is YHWH's Passover....	שַׁבָּת הוּא לַיהוָה בְּכֹל מוֹשְׁבֹתֵיכֶם : (4) אֵלֶּה מוֹעֲדֵי יְהוָה מִקְרָאֵי קֹדֶשׁ l אֲשֶׁר תִּקְרְאוּ אֹתָם בְּמוֹעֲדָם : (5) בַּחֹדֶשׁ הָרִאשׁוֹן בְּאַרְבָּעָה עָשָׂר לַחֹדֶשׁ בֵּין הָעַרְבָּיִם l פֶּסַח לַיהוָה

It sometimes happens that Ephraimites look for any excuse to forsake the assembling of themselves, even though the Sabbath is the fourth of the commandments that YHWH etched into stone. Let us remember that YHWH is Elohim, and that when He commands His people to assemble, it is best to do as He says.

We may or may not like the others that YHWH has called to be part of His spiritual family here on earth, and if we do not like them, then the tendency can be to want to shun, or avoid them. However, it is important to remember that the apostles bound four beginning fellowship rules for us in Scripture (no idolatry, no adultery, no strangled meat, and no blood), and that so long as our fellow servants are obeying these rules, then we are not at liberty to isolate ourselves, or to set ourselves apart from them.

Service to YHWH is not about being comfortable; nor is it always pleasant. It is, however, almost always edifying, if we hold the right heart attitude towards it.

The New Moon Days

While the Roman Gregorian calendar is based on the movements of the sun, the Torah calendar is based on the movements of the moon, and the agricultural cycles in the Land of Israel.

We will discuss how the agricultural cycles in the Land of Israel relate to the Torah calendar in upcoming chapters, but first we need to discuss the importance of YHWH's New Moon Days, and the commandments He wants us to perform on them.

Whenever a Temple or Tabernacle stands, Israel is to bring a daily sacrifice offering of two lambs, along with their associated meal and drink offerings.

> *Bemidbar (Numbers) 28:2-3*
> *2 "Command the children of Israel, and say to them, 'My offering, My food for My offerings made by fire as a sweet aroma to Me, you shall be careful to offer to Me at their appointed time.'*
> *3 "And you shall say to them, 'This is the offering made by fire which you shall offer to YHWH: two male lambs in their first year without blemish, day by day, as a regular burnt offering.'"*

In addition to the two lambs YHWH commands us to bring as a daily burnt offering, YHWH commands Israel to bring yet two more lambs on the weekly Sabbath (for a total of four, on a regular Sabbath day).

Bemidbar (Numbers) 28:9-10
9 'And on the Sabbath day two lambs in their first year, without blemish, and two-tenths of an ephah of fine flour as a grain offering, mixed with oil, with its drink offering —
10 this is the burnt offering for every Sabbath, besides the regular burnt offering with its drink offering.

The offerings that are to be brought are additive. In addition to the daily and/or the Sabbath offerings, YHWH tells us to bring still more offerings on the first day of the month, which we will see is the day the first crescent sliver of the new moon is sighted.

Bemidbar (Numbers) 28:11-15
11 "'At the beginnings of your months you shall present a burnt offering to YHWH: two young bulls, one ram, and seven lambs in their first year, without blemish;
12 three-tenths of an ephah of fine flour as a grain offering, mixed with oil, for each bull; two-tenths of an ephah of fine flour as a grain offering, mixed with oil, for the one ram;
13 and one-tenth of an ephah of fine flour, mixed with oil, as a grain offering for each lamb, as a burnt offering of sweet aroma, an offering made by fire to YHWH.
14 Their drink offering shall be half a hin of wine for a bull, one-third of a hin for a ram, and one-fourth of a hin for a lamb; this is the burnt offering for

each month throughout the months of
the year.
15 Also one kid of the goats as a sin
offering to YHWH shall be offered,
besides the regular burnt offering and
its drink offering.'"

The reason YHWH requires more offerings on the feast days is that there are more visitors to the Temple during the pilgrimage festivals: hence, there need to be more priests. Since there are more priests present in the Temple on those days, they need more food to sustain them.

It is sometimes thought that the New Moon Day is a commanded Sabbath of rest. However, while there are many reasons to believe this, we should note that the Torah does not command us to cease work on a regular new moon day.

The New Moon Day of the seventh month, however, is different. The New Moon of the Seventh Month is called Yom Teruah (יוֹם תְּרוּעָה). Although technically this phrase translates as the 'Day of Blowing' or the 'Day of Shouting', it is normally called the 'Day of Trumpets.' On this day, all Israel is to cease from its regular work, and assemble in a set-apart gathering.

> *Bemidbar (Numbers) 29:1-6*
> *1 "'And in the seventh month, on the*
> *first day of the month, you shall have a*
> *set-apart gathering. You shall do no*
> *customary work. For you it is a day of*
> *blowing (the trumpets).*
> *2 You shall offer a burnt offering as a*
> *sweet aroma to YHWH: one young*

bull, one ram, and seven lambs in their first year, without blemish.
3 Their grain offering shall be fine flour mixed with oil: three-tenths of an ephah for the bull, two-tenths for the ram,
4 and one-tenth for each of the seven lambs;
5 also one kid of the goats as a sin offering, to make atonement for you;
6 besides the burnt offering with its grain offering for the New Moon, the regular burnt offering with its grain offering, and their drink offerings, according to their ordinance, as a sweet aroma, an offering made by fire to YHWH.'"

Let us note once again that while verse 1 clearly tells us not to work on the new moon of the seventh month (Yom Teruah), there is no such parallel command to cease work on the regular new moon days.

Amos 8 is sometimes used to argue that the regular New Moon Days are also commanded days of rest. However, as we will see, Amos 8 is not speaking about the regular new moon days, but about Yom Teruah.

YHWH often uses plays on words as a kind of a pun. In Amos 8, YHWH makes a play on words between the word 'summer' (keitz, קָיִץ), and 'the end' (ha-ketz הַקֵּץ).

Amos 8:1-6
1 Thus YHWH Elohim showed me: Behold, a basket of summer (קָיִץ) fruit.

2a And He said, "Amos, what do you see?" So I said, "A basket of summer fruit."

2b Then YHWH said to me, "The end (הַקֵּץ) has come upon My people Israel. I will not pass by them anymore.

3 And the songs of the Temple shall be wailing in that day," says YHWH Elohim — "Many dead bodies everywhere, they shall be thrown out in silence."

4 Hear this, you who swallow up the needy, and make the poor of the land fail,

5 Saying: "When will the New Moon (Day) be past, that we may sell grain? And the Sabbath, that we may trade wheat?

Making the ephah small and the shekel large, falsifying the scales by deceit,

6 That we may buy the poor for silver, And the needy for a pair of sandals — Even sell the [chaff of] wheat?"

On first reading, one might easily conclude that YHWH was upset because His people were buying and selling on the regular New Moon Days. However, we need to understand YHWH's play on words here, because the summer (קַיִץ) fruits come at the end (הַקֵּץ) of summer, which is when Yom Teruah is held, in the seventh month. Thus it seems that it was not just any New Moon Day that YHWH was upset about His people breaking, but Yom Teruah. Therefore, in the absence of any stronger evidence that His people were not supposed to buy or sell on the regular new moon days, we cannot say conclusively that the regular new moon days are commanded days of rest from all work.

However, even if we are not required to cease work on the New Moon Days, there is still some question about whether or not we are commanded to assemble. There are four specific passages in Scripture which some see as proof that we are to gather on the regular New Moon Days. Let us take a close look at each them, because the evidence can seem confusing.

The first reference to gathering on the New Moon Day is found in 1ˢᵗ Samuel 20:5, where David tells Jonathan that he should eat at the king's table "tomorrow", because it will be the New Moon Day.

> **Shemuel Aleph (1ˢᵗ Samuel) 20:5**
> **5 And David said to Jonathan, "Indeed tomorrow is the New Moon, and I should not fail to sit with the king to eat."**

It could be that the reference to the New Moon here is a reference to Yom Teruah, as it was in Amos 8. However, it is also possible that it was King Shaul's custom to assemble his court on the New Moon Days. Either way, we cannot prove a Torah requirement to assemble on the New Moon Days, as the Torah does not command us to rest on a regular new moon day.

The second passage that suggests a possibile need to assemble on the regular new moon days is found in Second Kings 4:22-23.

2ⁿᵈ Kings 4:22-23 22 Then she called to her husband, and said, "Please send me one of	(22) וַתִּקְרָא אֶל אִישָׁה וַתֹּאמֶר שִׁלְחָה נָא לִי אֶחָד מִן הַנְּעָרִים וְאַחַת

the young men and one of the donkeys, that I may run to the man of Elohim (Elisha) and come back." 23 So he said, "Why are you going to him today? The day is neither a new moon, nor a Sabbath." And she said, "Shalom (It will be well)."	הָאֲתֹנוֹת ׀ וְאָרוּצָה עַד אִישׁ הָאֱלֹהִים וְאָשׁוּבָה : (23) וַיֹּאמֶר מַדּוּעַ אתי [אַתְּ קרי] הֹלַכְתִּי [הֹלֶכֶת קרי] אֵלָיו הַיּוֹם לֹא חֹדֶשׁ וְלֹא שַׁבָּת ׀ וַתֹּאמֶר שָׁלוֹם

The husband of the woman of Shunem asked her why she wanted to go see Elisha, seeing as it was neither 'a' new moon, nor a Sabbath. Had he referred to 'the' new moon, we might assume he was speaking about Yom Teruah. However, since he remarked only that it was not 'a' new moon, it could be that it was a custom for the people to gather on the new moons. However, we cannot conclude a need to gather on the regular new moon days, since the Torah does not command us to assemble on the New Moon Day.

The third reference to gathering on the New Moon Day is found in the prophecies in Ezekiel. This presents an interesting case, because it does seem to indicate a need to assemble at the eastern gate of the Temple on the Sabbath and the New Moon Days, although the Torah gives us no such requirement at present.

Ezekiel 46:1-3 'Thus says the Master YHWH: "The gateway of the inner court that faces toward the east shall be	(1) כֹּה אָמַר אֲדֹנָי יְהוִה שַׁעַר הֶחָצֵר הַפְּנִימִית הַפֹּנֶה קָדִים יִהְיֶה סָגוּר שֵׁשֶׁת יְמֵי

| shut the six working days; but on the Sabbath it shall be opened, and on the day of the New Moon it shall be opened. 2 The prince shall enter by way of the vestibule of the gateway from the outside, and stand by the gatepost. The priests shall prepare his burnt offering and his peace offerings. He shall worship at the threshold of the gate. Then he shall go out, but the gate shall not be shut until evening. 3 Likewise the people of the land shall worship at the entrance to this gateway on the Sabbaths and the New Moons before YHWH. | הַמַּעֲשֶׂה ׀ וּבְיוֹם הַשַּׁבָּת יִפָּתֵחַ וּבְיוֹם הַחֹדֶשׁ יִפָּתֵחַ : (2) וּבָא הַנָּשִׂיא דֶּרֶךְ אוּלָם הַשַּׁעַר מִחוּץ וְעָמַד עַל מְזוּזַת הַשַּׁעַר וְעָשׂוּ הַכֹּהֲנִים אֶת עֹלָתוֹ וְאֶת שְׁלָמָיו וְהִשְׁתַּחֲוָה עַל מִפְתַּן הַשַּׁעַר וְיָצָא ׀ וְהַשַּׁעַר לֹא יִסָּגֵר עַד הָעָרֶב : (3) וְהִשְׁתַּחֲווּ עַם הָאָרֶץ פֶּתַח הַשַּׁעַר הַהוּא בַּשַּׁבָּתוֹת וּבֶחֳדָשִׁים ׀ לִפְנֵי יְהוָה |

Verse one tells us that the Eastern Gate shall be shut the six working days, but that it shall be opened on the Sabbath, and on the day of the New Moon. Because Ezekiel contrasts the Sabbath and the New Moon with the six "working days", it would seem that the new moon days will be commanded days of rest during the future. This is further reinforced by the fact that we are told that the people of the land will need to assemble before the Eastern Gate on the Sabbaths, and on the New Moons. It would seem that the only way this will be possible is if the people do not have to work on the Sabbath and on the new moon days.

It is not clear why Ezekiel would give us a requirement to assemble on the New Moons in the future when the Torah does not require us to gather on them now. However, Isaiah 66:23 does give us a second witness that in the future, all Israel will be required to gather before Him on the New Moon Days.

Isaiah 66:23 23 And it shall be that from New Moon Day to New Moon Day, and from Sabbath to Sabbath, all flesh shall come to worship before Me," declares YHWH.	‫(23) וְהָיָה מִדֵּי חֹדֶשׁ בְּחָדְשׁוֹ וּמִדֵּי שַׁבָּת בְּשַׁבַּתּוֹ ׀ יָבוֹא כָל בָּשָׂר לְהִשְׁתַּחֲוֺת לְפָנַי אָמַר יְהוָה:‬

In the last chapter we saw that the timing of the Sabbath is determined by a 'count of seven.' However, all of YHWH's other appointed times are based on the new moon days. For one example, the Passover is to be held fourteen days after the new moon of the first month is declared (Exodus 12:6). Yom Kippur, or the Day of Atonement is to be held on the tenth day after Yom Teruah (the New Moon of the Seventh Month) (Leviticus 23:27). Since the timing of these festivals is based on the timing of the new moons, if the new moons are declared on the wrong day, it throws off the timing of all the rest of the festivals as well.

YHWH appoints times when He wants to meet with His prospective bride Israel. Now, if our Fiance has a date with us, but we do not show because for some reason or other we are not paying attention to His calendar, what is He going to think? Do we want to stand the King of the Universe up for a date?

Since the declaration of the New Moon is so essential to knowing when to celebrate YHWH's festivals, we need to know how YHWH wants us to determine the New Moon, so we can meet with Him on the times He appoints. Therefore, let us take some time to learn about the New Moon Days, so we can be certain we are doing things according to YHWH's will.

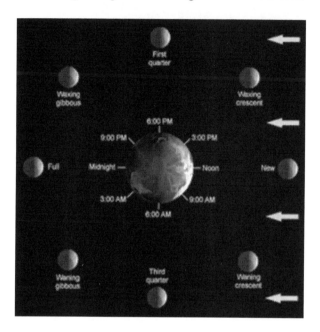

According to modern astronomy, a moon is thought to be 'new' when it sits in line between the sun and the earth (in the 3 o'clock position, above). When the moon is in this kind of linear alignment, the moon is said to be 'in conjunction' relative to the earth.

To look at it another way, when the moon is in conjunction, the moon sits in the same general direction from the earth as the sun does. The reason the moon is not visible is because it is 'conjoined' with the sun (and hence the name, 'lunar conjunction').

A total solar eclipse is a type of lunar conjunction. A total solar eclipse takes place when the moon sits directly in between the sun and the earth, blocking the sun's light. However, the moon does not have to eclipse the sun in order to qualify as a conjunction.

Again, the reason we do not have a total solar eclipses each month is that the orbits of the earth, the sun and the moon are not perfectly flat and parallel. Rather, they sit at angles to each other.

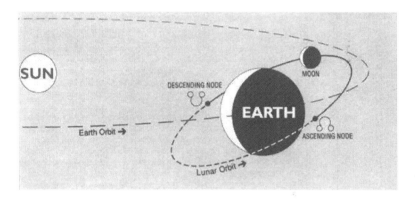

As shown in the diagram on the previous page, the reason the lunar conjunction cannot be seen from the earth is that the sun's light reflects back towards the sun. However, as the moon continues to orbit the earth (counter-clockwise in the earlier illustration), it soon reaches a position (midway between 2 and 3 o'clock in the earlier illustration) where part of the bright side of the moon can now be seen from the earth, at eventide. This thin reflection is called the First Crescent Sliver of the New Moon, and this is the New Moon of Scripture.

In the chart below, the New Moon corresponds to the fourth row down from the top, and the third or the fourth frame from the left. Exactly how bright the moon has to become before it can be seen from the earth has to do with a variety of factors, including clouds, weather, dust in the air, and other factors affecting visibility.

Once the first crescent sliver of the new moon can be seen from the earth, the New Moon Day is declared.

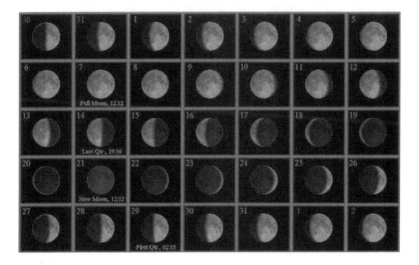

The chart above gives us a typical progression of the phases of the moon over weeks. The first frame (in the upper-left-hand corner) shows the moon in its first quarter, at 50% illumination. Eight days later the moon is full, at 100% illumination. Then, approximately seven days later the moon moves into its last quarter, at slightly more than 50% illumination. Finally, roughly seven more days and the moon again moves into conjunction, and cannot be seen, because all of the sun's light reflects back off of the far side. (This is sometimes called a 'no moon'). Then eight days later it is back in its first quarter again, although in this chart it is at slightly more than 50%.

Notice that there are at least two days in the above chart in which the moon is visibly 'full'. There are also two days in which the moon is in conjunction (i.e., is not visible). This is fairly normal, and it underscores the reason why it is so important to establish the New Moon Day according to the sighting of the first visible crescent sliver.

Because the sun, the moon and the earth do not have perfectly circular orbits, and because their orbits all sit at angles relative to each other, the number of days in which the moon is either in conjunction or is visibly 'full' can fluctuate anywhere in between 1.5 to 3.5 days. Because of this, if we were to hypothetically base the New Moon Day off of the lunar conjunction, either we would have to celebrate the New Moon Day for 1.5 to 3.5 days, or else we would have to choose one of these 1.5 to 3.5 conjunctive days as 'the' New Moon Day. This would be impossible to do, because the Scripture gives us no criteria for how to do that.

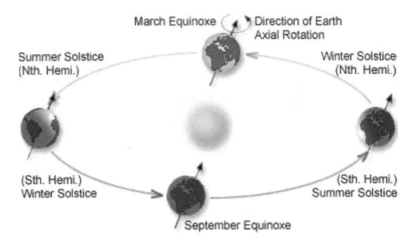

The reason the length of the conjunction fluctuates between 1.5 to 3.5 days is that the earth not only moves in an elliptical orbit, but it also sits at an angle as it orbits the sun (above). All of the heavenly bodies move in imperfect ellipses, and this makes the length of the lunar conjunctions grow longer and shorter over time.

Notice, however, that YHWH does not command us to celebrate the New Moon for 1.5 to 3.5 days, but to celebrate the New Moon Day on one day. Therefore, we need to know how to establish which one day is the New Moon Day.

In First Samuel 20:5, David told Jonathan that the New Moon Day was "tomorrow." This tells us that David did not believe the New Moon Day lasted anywhere from 1.5 to 3.5 days, but that he knew it to be a singular event, taking place on one single day.

> **Shemuel Aleph (1ˢᵗ Samuel) 20:5**
> **5 So David said to Jonathan, "Behold, tomorrow is the New Moon, and I ought to sit down to eat with the king. But let me go, that I may hide myself in the field until the third evening."**

Because YHWH commands us to celebrate the New Moon Day on just one single day, there must be one singular event that marks the start of the New Moon Day. As we will soon see, that singular event is the sighting of the First Crescent Sliver of the New Moon in the Land of Israel, either on the 29ᵗʰ or the 30ᵗʰ day of the month.

The Hebrew month is typically either 29 or 30 days long. But why is this? If the earth were stationary, the moon would make a complete 360 degree orbit about the earth approximately once every 27.5 days (on average). That means if the earth were standing still, it would take the moon 27.5 days, on average, to get back into alignment where the First Crescent Sliver could be seen from the earth. However, since the earth is not stationary (but moves about the sun), it has to travel more than 360 degrees. Therefore it takes the moon two extra days (on average) before it comes back into an alignment from which the First Crescent Sliver can again be seen from the earth.

Because the moon has to travel for approximately two more days before the First Crescent Sliver can be seen from the earth again, it takes approximately 29.5 days (on average) to go from one First Crescent Sliver to the next. In practical terms, what this means is that the Hebrew month is normally either 29 or 30 days long; and that is why, on the evening ending the 29th day of the month, observers in the Land of Israel go outside just before eventide, and look for the first crescent sliver of the new moon up in the sky. If they see the First Crescent Sliver, they go and tell the Priesthood at the Temple Mount.

If the Priesthood does receive at least two verifiable sightings at the end of the 29th day, they declare (or 'sanctify') the New Moon. However, if the Priesthood does not receive at least two verifiable sightings at the end of the 29th day (for any reason), the new month is declared by default at the end of the 30th day. This is because, by definition, a Hebrew month cannot be more than 30 days long; and unless the First Crescent Sliver is physically sighted at the end of the 29th day, the month is assumed to be 30 days long.

The Talmud also bears witness to this. Although the Talmud is not Scripture, the Talmud does give us a historical record of the practices and beliefs the rabbis kept in the Second Temple Period (which was the time period when Yeshua lived and ministered). For example, Talmud Tractate Rosh Hashanah ('Head of the Year') even records the interrogation methods used by the Priesthood, and tells us the questions the priests asked of the witnesses, in order to verify whether or not they had actually seen the First Crescent Sliver.

> *How do they test the witnesses? The pair who arrive first are tested first. The senior of them is brought in and they say to him, "Tell us how you saw the moon, in front of the sun, or behind the sun? To the north of it, or to the south? How big was it, and in which direction was it inclined? And how broad was it?"*
> *If he says "In front of the sun," his evidence is rejected. After that they would bring in the second and test him. If their accounts tallied their evidence was accepted, and other pairs were only questioned briefly, not because they were required at all, but so that they should not be disappointed, [and] so that they should not be dissuaded from coming.*
> *[Mishnah, Rosh Hashanah 23b]*

The reason the priesthood was able to ask the witnesses such specific questions about the moon's appearance is that because the earth sits on its axis at an angle, the moon's summer and winter flight paths are different. Because of this, the horns of the first crescent sliver point in different directions at different times of year. In the summer, the horns point more to the left, whereas in the winter, the horns point more upwards, as the moon lies more 'on its back.'

The moon also appears bigger or smaller in the sky depending upon where the moon is in its orbit. If the moon is closer to the earth, the moon appears larger; and if the moon is farther away, it appears smaller. While it is possible that a malicious witness could keep track of these things well enough to fake his testimony, it is unlikely that such thing would regularly pass the Levitical interrogation.

It is important to note that in the Second Temple Period (i.e., Yeshua's day), the New Moons were not determined by pre-calculation, but by visible sighting. This means that the Rabbinical Jewish Calendar (the so-called Hillel II Calendar) was not in use in Yeshua's time, seeing as it bases the start of its month on complex mathematical predictions, rather than on witnesses to the First Crescent Sliver. It also shows us that calendars such as the Lunar Sabbath and Lunar Conjunction Calendars (which begin the month on the Lunar Conjunction) were not in use in Yeshua's day, because one cannot use witnesses to sight the Lunar Conjunction (because it is invisible).

The general rule is that a month always defaults to a 30 day length unless the First Crescent Sliver of the New Moon has been physically sighted at the end of the 29th day, proving the month was shorter than the 30 day default standard. However, just to be clear, let us note that it is hypothetically possible to have a 28 day long month, or even hypothetically a month that was 27 days long.

It takes the moon an average of 27.5 days to orbit the earth, and then an average of two more days to get back into a position from where it can be seen from earth again. Suppose it is winter, it is cloudy at the time the first crescent sliver is to be sighted. When this happens, the difference between the time the first crescent sliver would have been seen, and the time the New Moon Day was declared by the thirty day default grows by half a day each month. If this happens three months in a row, the expected time until the next first crescent sliver decreases to 28 days. Should this happen five months in a row, the expected time until the next first crescent sliver decreases to only 27 days.

Declared by Default	Actual	Difference	Days to Next Moon
No	29.5	0	29.5
30	29.5	.5	29
30	29.5	1	28.5
30	29.5	1.5	28
30	29.5	2.0	27.5
30	29.5	2.5	27

Thankfully, this kind of thing is very rare, as the Land of Israel is sunny all summer, and is also sunny half the winter. Because Israel is so sunny, the calendar auto-corrects itself before the discrepancy becomes very large, and the New Moon Day is almost always declared in its time.

Some scholars believe that when there are clouds, we should declare the New Moon at the end of the 29th day, if calculations tell us that the First Crescent Sliver of the New Moon would have been visible at the end of the 29th day, had there not been clouds. However, the proponents of this theory also acknowledge that in King David's time, the New Moon Day was determined by the visible sighting of the First Crescent Sliver.

> **Shemuel Aleph (1st Samuel) 20:5**
> **5 So David said to Jonathan, "Behold, tomorrow is the New Moon, and I ought to sit down to eat with the king. But let me go, that I may hide myself in the field until the third evening."**

Since the Hebrews did not use modern astronomical calculations in David's time, the only way David could have said with certainty that the New Moon Day was "tomorrow" was if the first crescent sliver had not been seen at the end of the 29th day, thus assuring that the New Moon Day would be declared at its normal, default 30-day mark.

Finally, to be complete, we should discuss Psalm 81:3. Since scholars disagree over how to interpret this passage, we will use the Hebrew here.

3 Blow in the New Moon Day a shofar, in the keseh on the day of our pilgrimage feast.	(4) תִּקְעוּ בַחֹדֶשׁ שׁוֹפָר ו בַּכֶּסֶה לְיוֹם חַגֵּנוּ

Scholars dispute what the keseh (כֶּסֶה) is. Strong's Concordance defines it this way:

> *OT:3677 kece' (keh'-seh); or keceh (keh'-seh); apparently from OT:3680; properly, fullness or the full moon, i.e. its festival: KJV - (time) appointed.*

When we look up the reference to OT:3680, we get a reference to something 'plump'. This might refer to a full moon, or a moon in its fullness (which is the correct interpretation). However, we also get a reference to something that is clothed, covered, or concealed.

> *OT:3680 kacah (kaw-saw'); a primitive root; properly, to plump, i.e. fill up hollows; by implication, to cover (for clothing or secrecy):*
> *KJV - cladself, close, clothe, conceal, cover (self), (flee to) hide, overwhelm. Compare OT:3780.*

One might infer that the thing which is clothed, covered or concealed is also the new moon, except that a new moon is not 'plump', 'waxed fat,' or 'covered with flesh', as the reference requires.

> *OT:3780 kasah (kaw-saw'); a primitive root; to grow fat (i.e. be covered with flesh):*
> *KJV - be covered. Compare OT:3680.*

It is important that we interpret this correctly, for if the word keseh means 'new moon', then Psalms 81:3 is the command to "blow the shofar on the new moon of our pilgrimage feast (חג)." However, this is impossible, because there are no New Moon Days that are also pilgrimage feasts. This is because while Yom Teruah is an appointed time (מוֹעֵד), it is not a pilgrimage festival (חַג).

We should also recognize the fact that it makes no sense to think that YHWH would use the word 'keseh' (כֶּסֶה) to describe the New Moon, when He just used the word Hodesh (חֹדֶשׁ) to describe it. Therefore, the word keseh (כֶּסֶה) must mean something else.

What the word keseh (כֶּסֶה) refers to is not exactly a full moon, but the moon when it is 'plump', and clothed with light. As we will see in later chapters, this describes the Passover and the Feast of Tabernacles perfectly, as these are pilgrimage festivals, and they begin on or about the full moon, when the moon is generally 'waxed fat,' and 'plump', and is 'clothed with light.' Therefore, Psalms 81:3 is the command to blow the shofar on the Passover, and on the First Day of the Feast of Tabernacles.

3 Blow in the New Moon Day a shofar, in the plump moon, on the day of our pilgrimage feast.	(4) תִּקְעוּ בַחֹדֶשׁ שׁוֹפָר ו בַּכֶּסֶה לְיוֹם חַגֵּנוּ

Aviv Barley and the Head of the Year

Once we know how to determine the New Moon, next we need to know how YHWH wants us to determine the start (or the 'Head') of the Year. In order to do this, let us look at the Exodus, for this is where YHWH tells us when He wants the Head of the Year to be.

In Exodus 9:31-32, YHWH caused a plague of hail to fall on the Land of Egypt. The flax and the barley were damaged ('struck') by the hail, because they were in an advanced stage of development.

Exodus 9:31-32 31 Now the flax and the barley were struck, for the barley was in the head and the flax was in bud. 32 But the wheat and the spelt were not struck, for they are late crops.	(31) וְהַפִּשְׁתָּה וְהַשְּׂעֹרָה נֻכָּתָה ׀ כִּי הַשְּׂעֹרָה אָבִיב וְהַפִּשְׁתָּה גִּבְעֹל : (32) וְהַחִטָּה וְהַכֻּסֶּמֶת לֹא נֻכּוּ ׀ כִּי אֲפִילֹת הֵנָּה

The New King James tells us that the barley was struck because it was in an advanced state of maturity where it was "in the head". The Hebrew word for this is 'Aviv' (אָבִיב).

Soon after the Aviv barley was struck, YHWH told Moshe and Aharon that "this month is the head of months for you; it is the first month of the year to you." This tells us that the first month of the year comes just after the barley in the Land of Israel becomes Aviv.

76

Exodus 12:2 2 "This month is the head of months for you; it is the first month of the year to you."	(2) הַחֹדֶשׁ הַזֶּה לָכֶם רֹאשׁ חֳדָשִׁים l רִאשׁוֹן הוּא לָכֶם לְחָדְשֵׁי הַשָּׁנָה

Like the New Moon Day, the determination of the Head of the Year is critical. The Head of the Year has to be determined correctly, or else all of the other months (and all of the festival days) will be off, and we will not be able to meet with our Fiance when He wants us to be there. Therefore, let us learn more about what 'Aviv' barley really is, so we can be sure we declare the Head of the Year in the right month.

Before cereal grasses bud, the stalk is generally still flexible and soft. Because it is soft, it can take a direct hit from hail without being destroyed. However, just as with human beings, as cereal grasses get older and begin to produce fruit, they become drier, and become more brittle, and thus are more easily damaged.

Although modern agriculture uses different terms, for our purposes, barley and other cereal grasses can be thought to pass through the following stages of growth:

1. Vegetative (growth) stage;
2. Budding and Flowering ('cotton') stage;
3. Seed pod formation stage;
4. Milk stage;
5. Soft Dough ('Aviv') stage;
6. Hard Dough ('Carmel') stage;
7. Ancient ripe.

After flowering, barley forms a seed pod, which soon
fills with a milky fluid. This fluid slowly becomes harder
and more substantive, until finally it becomes more of a
solid than a liquid. Once the contents of the seed pod
have solidified to the point that they resemble bread
dough, the barley has reached the stage where its
development can be thought of as being "in the ear"
(אָבִיב), because the main development of the plant now
takes place in the fruiting ear.

Because aviv barley has a soft dough-like consistency,
it is still not as hard (or as substantial) as it will be when
it is fully ripe. Aviv barley still needs to mature on the
stalk for at least two more weeks before it can be
harvested for long term storage, or used as a Wave
Sheaf Offering. However, even though it is still be too
moist to put into long term storage without drying it first,
Aviv barley is solid enough that one can make a meal
out of it if one first lightly roasts it in fire, a process
known as 'parching.' Parching drives the moisture out
of the immature grain, and makes it hard enough that it
can be cracked, or ground into flour. Parched grains
are mentioned in Leviticus 23:14, Joshua 5:11, 1st
Samuel 17:17, 1st Samuel 25:18, and Leviticus 2:14.
Leviticus 2:14 shows us that parched grains are even
substantial enough to be used as a firstfruits offering.

| Leviticus 2:14 | (14) וְאִם תַּקְרִיב |
| 14 "'Also when you bring an offering of firstfruits to YHWH, you may bring Aviv grain parched in the fire, (or) crushed Carmel shall you offer for your firstfruits offering.'" | מִנְחַת בִּכּוּרִים לַיהוָה ׀ אָבִיב קָלוּי בָּאֵשׁ גֶּרֶשׂ כַּרְמֶל תַּקְרִיב אֵת מִנְחַת בִּכּוּרֶיךָ |

In later chapters we will see why the Aviv must be declared when the first complete shocks of barley in the Land of Israel are Aviv, but first we should make clear that the term 'Aviv' is not correctly considered to be the name of a month, as it is used on the Orthodox Jewish calendar.

The Jews began calling the names by months when they went into the Exile to Babylon. Now, instead of calling the months according to their ordinal numbers, the Jews call the months by names (Nisan, Iyar, Sivan, etceteras). Most of these names have Babylonian pagan origins, and these names are often recorded in Scripture.

> **Hadassah (Esther) 8:9**
> **9 So the king's scribes were called at that time in the third month (that is, the month Sivan)....**

However, the fact that the Jews recorded these names in Scripture does not mean that this is what YHWH wants us to do. The correct practice of calling the days and months by ordinal numbers is demonstrated in Ezekiel 1:1.

> **Yehezqel (Ezekiel) 1:1**
> **1 Now it came to pass in the thirtieth year, in the fourth month, on the fifth day of the month, as I was among the captives by the River Chebar, that the heavens were opened and I saw visions of Elohim.**

The reason this is the correct practice is that this is how YHWH numbers the months: with numbers, not names.

Exodus 12:2 2 "This month is the head of months for you; it is the first month of the year to you."	(2) הַחֹדֶשׁ הַזֶּה לָכֶם רֹאשׁ חֳדָשִׁים רִאשׁוֹן הוּא לָכֶם לְחָדְשֵׁי הַשָּׁנָה

Our Jewish brethren, however, are very fond of their man-made traditions, and it is a rule in Judaism that once any man-made tradition has been established for a certain length of time, it becomes law. In effect, the Jews are saying that so long as a man-made tradition is popular, it does not matter whether or not it accords with YHWH's word. However, this is akin to saying that since the Church has kept Christmas and Easter for thousands of years, they have the right to substitute them in place of YHWH's festivals: but we know that this is not correct. If we reject the Church's claim to the right to change YHWH's word to suit its own tastes, then so too must we reject our Jewish brother's claim to be able to alter YHWH's word.

However, after the Romans destroyed the Temple in 70 CE and then drove the Jews out of Judea, the rabbis were no longer able to observe the ripening of the barley in the Land of Israel. Therefore, they had to develop some other means of determining when the first full shocks of barley would become Aviv in the Land of Israel. They did this by developing the Jewish 'Hillel II' Calendar.

In the fourth century, after a few hundred years of intermediate modification, a man named Hillel II finally developed a mathematical algorithm that approximates the ripening of the barley in the Land of Israel fairly well. It does this by calculating the movements of the sun, the moon and the earth with regards to the Spring Equinox. While this calendar helped to keep the idea of a Torah-based Calendar alive for the two thousand years of the Roman Exile, it also has some serious drawbacks, chief among which is the fact that it does not use the means YHWH uses for establishing the time. While the algorithm was brilliant, and while the Rabbinical 'Hillel II' calendar dates often approximate the Torah Calendar dates very well, they are also often off of YHWH's time by a month or more.

The Hillel II Calendar reinforces the practice our Jewish brothers picked up in Babylon, of calling the months by names (rather than by ordinal numbers). For example, the Hillel II Calendar calls the first month of the year "Nisan." However, in modern Hebrew, the first month of the year is also called "The Month of Aviv," as if Aviv was a name that meant simply, "spring" (which is what the term translates to in Modern Hebrew). However, we know that the term does not translate to "spring", but that it refers to a stage of the ripening of the barley.

Exodus 13:4 4 "On this day in the month of the Aviv, you are about to go forth."	הַיּוֹם אַתֶּם יֹצְאִים ו (4) בְּחֹדֶשׁ הָאָבִיב

Notice that Exodus 13:4 does not say that the Exodus took place in the "the Month called Aviv". Rather, it tells us that the first month of the year is the month that begins in the month of 'the' Aviv (הָאָבִיב). In other words, the Head of the Year is to be declared on the first New Moon Day after the first complete shocks of Aviv barley are seen in the Land of Israel.

Some correctly point out that the Aviv barley mentioned in Exodus 9:31 was not spotted in the Land of Israel, but in the Land of Egypt. While this is true, we should also remember that the children of Israel were simply looking for the Aviv wherever YHWH's Presence dwelt at that time. YHWH chose Jerusalem as the place where He wanted to place His name (1 Kings 14:21, etc.), and that has never changed. Further, Scripture tells us that YHWH's eyes are always upon His land.

> **Devarim (Deuteronomy) 11:12**
> **12 "...a land for which YHWH your Elohim cares; the eyes of YHWH your Elohim are always on it, from the beginning of the year to the very end of the year."**

There are other reasons it is important to base the Head of the Year on the ripening of the Aviv barley in the Land of Israel (and not in any other place). Barley is grown in many regions of the world, and it ripens at all different times. For example, in semi-tropical areas (such as in Arizona and in Texas), barley is considered a winter crop. However, in temperate areas (such as Idaho, Montana and Washington State), barley is grown as a summer crop. Add to this the fact that crops in the Southern Hemisphere usually ripen half a year out from the crops in the Northern Hemisphere, and we can see that barley ripens at all different times throughout the world. If each Israelite were to set the Head of the Year based on the ripening of the barley in his own locality, then Israelites all over the world would be keeping His festivals at all different times. This is contrary to what YHWH wants, which is to meet with His bride, and give her gifts on His festival days, based on Jerusalem time.

Ma'asim (Acts) 2:1-2
1 When the day of Pentecost had come, they were all together in one place.
2 And suddenly there came from heaven a noise like a violent rushing wind, and it filled the whole house where they were sitting.

In the first century, blessings were poured out upon the faithful who had come up to Jerusalem in order to keep the Feast of Pentecost. However, in order to receive that blessing, they had to be there when YHWH said the Pentecost was to be held. Had they been keeping their own calendar, based on the ripening of the barley and the observation of the New Moon in their own localities, they might not have known when to be there in Jerusalem.

Finally, while it is commonly held that a Hebrew year has twelve months, and often has a thirteenth or 'leap' year, the truth is that there is no number of months that a Hebrew year should have. While there are usually twelve months in a year, with a leap month every two or three years, the Hebrew lasts from the first new moon after the Aviv barley is sighted one year, until the first new moon after the Aviv barley is sighted the next. That can be any length of time, depending upon the weather YHWH brings. If YHWH brings a cold winter with little rain and sun, the barley can be very late in maturing, and the year could hypothetically be thirteen or fourteen months long (or hypothetically even longer). Then the next year, if the winter is warm, and wet, and the barley ripens early, the winter could hypothetically be only eleven months. Everything depends upon the weather YHWH sends.

Since the timing of the New Year is known only after the first crescent sliver of the new moon is sighted after the barley in the Land of Israel has become Aviv, it is not very easy to project exact dates for coming years. Further, since the start date of each month fluctuates a day forward or back, it is not really possible to project exact dates past the existing month. The Torah Calendar is not as popular as the Roman 'Christian' Calendar, or the Rabbinical Calendar.

While these things might at first seem like a problem, in reality it is a blessing in disguise for the faithful. The western ideal is to schedule and regiment one's life so as to do more, achieve more, and therefore somehow 'become' more. While high productivity and is often described in positive terms within Scripture, the idea is less to plan and to structure one's time intellectually than it is to listen to what YHWH wants us to be doing, moment by moment. Only when one waits on YHWH from moment to moment can we be in tune with His timing.

> *Tehillim (Psalms) 130:5-6*
> *5 I wait for YHWH, my soul waits,*
> *And in His word I do hope.*
> *6 My soul waits for YHWH*
> *More than those who watch for the morning —*
> *Yea, more than those who watch for the morning.*

YHWH does not want His bride to schedule her life out in the minutest detail literally years in advance. Rather, YHWH wants His bride to show that she understands that her future depends completely on Him.

Ya'akov (James) 4:13-17
13 Come now, you who say, "Today or tomorrow we will go to such and such a city, spend a year there, buy and sell, and make a profit";
14 whereas you do not know what will happen tomorrow. For what is your life? It is even a vapor that appears for a little time and then vanishes away.
15 Instead you ought to say,"If YHWH wills, we shall live and do this or that."
16 But now you boast in your arrogance. All such boasting is evil.
17 Therefore, to him who knows to do good and does not do it, to him it is sin.

While we all have to make plans, the idea that we can plan the future down to the minutest detail literally years in advance is nothing short of blasphemy. Who among us could foresee where he would be today, ten years ago?

Our lives hang by YHWH's will. Really about the best and most efficient thing we as humans can do is to make a list of our projects, tasks and/or goals, and then ask YHWH to order it for us. This allows us to remain productive, and yet remain flexible, so that we can stay focused and on task, and yet follow His leading and guiding in the moment. And most importantly, it honors His role as the Master of our lives.

Are we willing to obey His word, and wait on Him more than those who watch for the morning? Are we willing to acknowledge Him as the Ruler of our lives? If so, then learning not to plan our lives out too far in advance is really a very good thing.

The Passover and Unleavened Bread

The first of Israel's seven annual festivals is a one-day festival, the Passover. It is followed immediately by the second of Israel's festivals, the Feast of Unleavened Bread. Since the Feast of Unleavened Bread begins the very next day, these two festivals are often thought of as one long eight-day festival (and even YHWH refers to them in this regard). These two opening festivals speak of Israel's Redemption from slavery and bondage; and because it will clear up some common theological misconceptions later on, let us review the story here.

Avraham begat Yitzhak (Isaac), and then Yitzhak begat Ya'akov (Jacob, later called Israel). From Israel's loins arose Yosef (Joseph), whom his brothers sold into slavery in Egypt. After serving time in prison, Yosef went on to become second in command of Egypt, to fulfill the word of YHWH that was given to Avraham.

> *B'reisheet (Genesis) 15:12-14*
> *12 Now when the sun was going down, a deep sleep fell upon Abram; and behold, horror and great darkness fell upon him.*
> *13 Then He said to Abram: "Know certainly that your descendants will be strangers in a land that is not theirs, and will serve them, and they will afflict them four hundred years.*
> *14 And also the nation whom they serve I will judge; afterward they shall come out with great possessions."*

Yosef was made second in command of all Egypt because it was clear that he was filled with the Spirit of Elohim, and because he served Pharaoh so well. Pharaoh even invited Yosef to bring his family down to the Land of Goshen (the Nile Delta). However, after all of these honors a new Pharaoh arose, who did not know Yosef. This new Pharaoh placed Israel into slavery, and eventually attempted to exterminate them. Israel wept bitter tears because of the harsh treatment, and the attempts at genocide. Israel's cry reached YHWH's ears, and He put His divine plan into action, to deliver them from bondage.

YHWH sent Moshe (Moses) to tell Pharaoh to let His people go, but Pharaoh hardened his heart, and refused. YHWH therefore brought a series of plagues upon the Egyptians, in order to change Pharaoh's mind. This where we pick up the story.

By Exodus Chapter 10, nine of the ten plagues have already come and gone. Then in verse 28, Pharaoh tells Moshe that he will never see his face again. In the next verse (29) Moshe prophesies that what Pharaoh has said will come true: Pharaoh will never see his face again.

> *Shemote (Exodus) 10:27-29*
> *27 But YHWH hardened Pharaoh's heart, and he would not let them go.*
> *28 Then Pharaoh said to him, "Get away from me! Take heed to yourself and see my face no more! For in the day you see my face you shall die!"*
> *29 So Moshe said, "You have spoken well. I will never see your face again."*

Then in Exodus 11, YHWH tells Moshe that He will bring a tenth and final plague upon Egypt; and that this plague will be so horrific that Pharaoh will drive Israel out of Egypt, just to be rid of them, and the plagues.

Shemote (Exodus) 11:1 1 And YHWH said to Moshe, "I am bringing yet one more plague on Pharaoh and on Egypt. After that he is going to let you go from here. When he lets you go, he shall drive you out from here altogether."	(1) וַיֹּאמֶר יְהֹוָה אֶל מֹשֶׁה עוֹד נֶגַע אֶחָד אָבִיא עַל פַּרְעֹה וְעַל מִצְרַיִם אַחֲרֵי כֵן יְשַׁלַּח אֶתְכֶם מִזֶּה ׀ כְּשַׁלְּחוֹ כָּלָה גָּרֵשׁ יְגָרֵשׁ אֶתְכֶם מִזֶּה ׃

The word 'drive' is "garesh y'garesh", (גָּרֵשׁ יְגָרֵשׁ), which is a doubling of the word "to drive out."

> ***OT:1644 garash (gaw-rash'); a primitive root; to drive out from a possession; especially to expatriate or divorce:***

That YHWH said Pharaoh would 'drive' Israel out of Egypt indicates that the Exodus would not be a slow event, but that it would take place very rapidly.

Then, in the next verse, days before the actual Exodus was to take place, YHWH told Moshe to have the children of Israel plunder Egypt, by asking the Egyptians for objects of silver and gold. The language seems to indicate that the children of Israel asked for these objects right away, since "YHWH gave the people favor in the eyes of the Egyptians" at that time.

88

Shemote (Exodus) 11:2-3
2 "Speak now in the hearing of the people, and let every man ask from his neighbor and every woman from her neighbor, objects of silver and objects of gold."
3 And YHWH gave the people favor in the eyes of the Egyptians. And the man Moshe was very great in the land of Egypt, in the eyes of Pharaoh's servants and in the eyes of the people.

Then, after Israel took the plunder, YHWH commanded each family in Israel to take a lamb on the tenth of the month, in preparation for the first Passover.

Shemote (Exodus) 12:3-14
3 "Speak to all the congregation of Israel, saying: 'On the tenth of this month every man shall take for himself a lamb, according to the house of his father, a lamb for a household.
4 And if the household is too small for the lamb, let him and his neighbor next to his house take it according to the number of the persons; according to each man's need you shall make your count for the lamb.
5 Your lamb shall be without blemish, a male of the first year. You may take it from the sheep or from the goats.'"

This spotless and blemishless lamb, of course, was a prophetic shadow picture of Yeshua. Verse 6 tells us that the children of Israel were to keep these lambs until the fourteenth day of the same month, and then they were then to kill them "between the evenings."

Exodus 12:6	(6) וְהָיָה לָכֶם
6 "'Now you shall keep it until the fourteenth day of the same month. Then the whole assembly of the congregation of Israel shall kill it between the evenings.'"	לְמִשְׁמֶרֶת עַד אַרְבָּעָה עָשָׂר יוֹם לַחֹדֶשׁ הַזֶּה ׀ וְשָׁחֲטוּ אֹתוֹ כֹּל קְהַל עֲדַת יִשְׂרָאֵל בֵּין הָעַרְבָּיִם.

Scholars debate the meaning of the phrase 'between the evenings' (בֵּין הָעַרְבָּיִם). Some believe it means 'at sunset,' but this does not really work. It takes several hours to slaughter and dress out a lamb, and there is not enough time if one begins at sunset.

Many scholars believe there were two evenings in Hebraic thought: one at noon, and the other at dusk. The time in 'between' those two evenings refers to mid-afternoon, when the sun had started to descend, but had not yet set. This harmonizes with Deuteronomy 16:6, which tells us the Passover was to be sacrificed at the time 'when the sun comes' (כְּבוֹא הַשֶּׁמֶשׁ) [back to earth].

Deuteronomy 16:6	(6) כִּי אִם אֶל הַמָּקוֹם
6 "but at the place where YHWH your Elohim chooses to make His name abide, there you shall sacrifice the Passover in the evening,	אֲשֶׁר יִבְחַר יְהוָה אֱלֹהֶיךָ לְשַׁכֵּן שְׁמוֹ שָׁם תִּזְבַּח אֶת הַפֶּסַח בָּעֶרֶב ׀ כְּבוֹא הַשֶּׁמֶשׁ מוֹעֵד

when the sun comes (back to earth), at the time you came out of Egypt."	צֵאתְךָ מִמִּצְרָיִם

The passage continues with the instructions as to how the first Passover was to be eaten.

> **7 "'And they shall take some of the blood and put it on the two doorposts and on the lintel of the houses where they eat it.**
> **8 Then they shall eat the flesh on that night; roasted in fire, with unleavened bread and with bitter herbs they shall eat it.**
> **9 Do not eat it raw, nor boiled at all with water, but roasted in fire — its head with its legs and its entrails.**
> **10 You shall let none of it remain until morning, and what remains of it until morning you shall burn with fire.'"**

Next, verse 11 specifies we are to eat the Passover in haste, with our loins girded, sandals (or shoes) on our feet, and our staff in our hand.

Exodus 12:11 "'And so shall you eat it: loins girded (belt on your waist), your sandals on your feet, and your staff in your hand. And you shall eat it in haste. It is the Passover to YHWH.'"	(11) וְכָכָה תֹּאכְלוּ אֹתוֹ מָתְנֵיכֶם חֲגֻרִים נַעֲלֵיכֶם בְּרַגְלֵיכֶם וּמַקֶּלְכֶם בְּיֶדְכֶם וַאֲכַלְתֶּם אֹתוֹ בְּחִפָּזוֹן פֶּסַח הוּא לַיהֹוָה

The word 'naaleichem' (נַעֲלֵיכֶם) can mean sandals, but it can also mean shoes. A direct translation would be something like, "what you go (i.e., walk) upon."

The phrase 'in haste' is בְּחִפָּזוֹן ('chippazown'), which means, 'in hasty flight.' From Strong's OT:2649:

> *OT:2649 chippazown (khip-paw-zone');*
> *from OT:2648; hasty flight:*

Looking up the reference to Strong's OT:2648, we get:

> *OT:2648 chaphaz (khaw-faz'); a*
> *primitive root; properly, to start up*
> *suddenly, i.e. (by implication) to*
> *hasten away, to fear:*

In other words, the Passover is to be eaten hastily, as if we are ready to flee. This is how our forefathers ate the Passover in Egypt, since they had been told they would be 'driven' out after YHWH had struck all the first born.

> *Shemote (Exodus) 12:12-13*
> *12 "'For I will pass through the land of*
> *Egypt on that night, and will strike all*
> *the firstborn in the land of Egypt, both*
> *man and beast; and against all the*
> *elohim (gods) of Egypt I will execute*
> *judgment: I am YHWH.*
> *13 Now the blood shall be a sign for*
> *you on the houses where you are. And*
> *when I see the blood, I will pass over*
> *you; and the plague shall not be on*
> *you to destroy you when I strike the*
> *land of Egypt.'"*

The blood on the doorposts was to be a sign that the persons within the house were faithful to YHWH, and that they were keeping His commandments. Because they were faithfully keeping His commandments, YHWH would spare them from the destruction that was to come. This was prophetic of how Yeshua Messiah's blood would 'mark the doorposts of our hearts', so that we also might be saved.

While Passover and the Feast of Unleavened Bread are technically two separate festivals, YHWH refers to them as if they are one in the same. For example, verse 14 tells us that "this day" (i.e., the Passover) is a memorial, and a feast by an everlasting ordinance.

> **Shemote (Exodus) 12:14**
> **14 "'So this day shall be to you a memorial; and you shall keep it as a feast to YHWH throughout your generations. You shall keep it as a feast by an everlasting ordinance.'"**

However, still referring to the Passover, YHWH tells us to eat unleavened bread for seven days, and that whosoever eats anything leavened, or whosoever does not remove the leaven from his house shall be cut off from Israel.

> **Shemote (Exodus) 12:15**
> **15 "'Seven days you shall eat unleavened bread. On the first day you shall remove leaven from your houses. For whoever eats leavened bread from the first day until the seventh day, that person shall be cut off from Israel.'"**

The reason YHWH considers Passover and the Feast of Unleavened to be all one festival is that the First Day of Unleavened fades in as the Passover fades out. Next, verses 16 through 18 (below) tell us to assemble on the first and the last days of Unleavened Bread, and not to do any manner of work on those days, except for cooking our food.

> *Shemote (Exodus) 12:16-18*
> *16 "'On the first day there shall be a set-apart gathering, and on the seventh day there shall be a set-apart gathering. No manner of work shall be done on them; but that which everyone must eat — that only may be prepared by you.*
> *17 So you shall observe the Feast of Unleavened Bread, for on this same day I will have brought your armies out of the land of Egypt. Therefore you shall observe this day throughout your generations as an everlasting ordinance.*
> *18 In the first month, on the fourteenth day of the month at evening, you shall eat unleavened bread, until the twenty-first day of the month at evening.'"*

We are commanded to eat unleavened bread from the evening ending the 14th day until the evening ending the 21st day (the start of the 22nd day). We are to have no leaven in our houses at all during that time. Notice that the only way this commandment works is if we hold the Passover on the conjunction of the $14^{th}/15^{th}$.

13	14	15	16	17	18	19	20	21	22
{}	P	1	2	3	4	5	6	7	

> *Shemote (Exodus) 12:19-20*
> *19 "'For seven days no leaven shall be found in your houses, since whoever eats what is leavened, that same person shall be cut off from the congregation of Israel, whether he is a stranger or a native of the land.*
> *20 You shall eat nothing leavened; in all your dwellings you shall eat unleavened bread.'"*

Now let us skip ahead in the narrative, and we will come back to verses 24-25 later. Verses 29-35 show us that the children of Israel did not have time to take an extra day to plunder Egypt, in that they were sent out of Egypt in haste.

> *Shemote (Exodus) 12:33-34*
> *33 And the Egyptians urged the people, that they might send them out of the land in haste. For they said, "We shall all be dead."*
> *34 So the people took their dough before it was leavened, having their kneading bowls bound up in their clothes on their shoulders.*

Sometimes verses 35 and 36 (below) are used to say that the Exodus was actually a slow event (or that the Passover took place on the conjunction of the 13th/14th of Aviv), because the plundering is mentioned in the narrative the morning after the Passover. However, let us notice that the narrative mentions the plundering of Egypt in the past tense ("had asked"), showing that the children of Israel had already plundered the Egyptians before the morning they were driven out.

| Exodus 12:35-36
35 And the children of Israel had done according to the word of Moshe, and they had asked from the Egyptians objects of silver, and objects of gold, and garments.
36 And YHWH gave the people favor in the eyes of the Egyptians, so that they gave them what they asked. And they plundered the Egyptians. | (35) וּבְנֵי יִשְׂרָאֵל עָשׂוּ כִּדְבַר מֹשֶׁה וַיִּשְׁאֲלוּ מִמִּצְרַיִם כְּלֵי כֶסֶף וּכְלֵי זָהָב וּשְׂמָלֹת (36) וַיהוָה נָתַן אֶת חֵן הָעָם בְּעֵינֵי מִצְרַיִם וַיַּשְׁאִלוּם וַיְנַצְּלוּ אֶת מִצְרָיִם |

Verse 39 also confirms that the Exodus was a hasty event, in that the children of Israel had not been able to delay. They were in such a hurry that they did not even have time to prepare food for themselves.

> **Shemote (Exodus) 12:39**
> **39 And they baked unleavened cakes of the dough which they had brought out of Egypt, for it was not leavened, since they were driven out of Egypt, and had not been able to delay, nor had they prepared food for themselves.**

Next, Exodus 12:51 gives yet another witness that the children of Israel did not take an extra day to plunder Egypt, for YHWH says He brought the children of Israel out of Egypt "on that same day" (as the Passover/First Day of Unleavened).

Shemote (Exodus) 12:51
51 And it came to be on that same day that YHWH brought the children of Israel out of the land of Egypt according to their divisions.

Now let us double-back in the narrative and look at verses 24 and 25, because they show us something interesting.

Exodus 12:24-25 24 "And you shall observe this thing as an ordinance for you and your children forever. 25 "When you come into the land which YHWH will give you, as He has promised, you shall observe this service."	(24) וּשְׁמַרְתֶּם אֶת הַדָּבָר הַזֶּה לְחָק לְךָ וּלְבָנֶיךָ עַד עוֹלָם : (25) וְהָיָה כִּי תָבֹאוּ אֶל הָאָרֶץ אֲשֶׁר יִתֵּן יְהֹוָה לָכֶם כַּאֲשֶׁר דִּבֵּר וּשְׁמַרְתֶּם אֶת הָעֲבֹדָה הַזֹּאת

Verse 24 tells us that the Passover is an ordinance for us and our children forever; but verse 25 tells us we will perform a Passover offering when we come into the Land (וְהָיָה כִּי תָבֹאוּ אֶל הָאָרֶץ). While this verse can be understood in several different ways, basically what it says is that we need to offer a Passover sacrifice when we live in the Land of Israel. We should not, however, offer Passover sacrifices in the Dispersion, as we explain in the study, 'About Sacrifices.'

However, the children of Israel kept the Passover while they were still in the Wilderness. In the second year after the Exodus YHWH commanded the children of Israel to keep the Passover in the same fashion as they had done during the Exodus, even including the same rules and regulations.

> *Bemidbar (Numbers) 9:1-3*
> *1 Thus YHWH spoke to Moshe in the wilderness of Sinai, in the first month of the second year after they had come out of the land of Egypt, saying,*
> *2 "Now, let the children of Israel observe the Passover at its appointed time.*
> *3 "On the fourteenth day of this month, at evening, you shall observe it at its appointed time; you shall observe it according to all its statutes and according to all its ordinances."*

Notice, though, that in addition to all of the previous Passover ordinances, YHWH gave us some additional ordinances in verses 6-14. These pertain to those who are unclean because of a dead body, and those who are away on a long journey (who cannot celebrate the Passover in its time).

> *Bemidbar (Numbers) 9:6-14*
> *6 Now there were certain men who were defiled by a human corpse, so that they could not keep the Passover on that day; and they came before Moshe and Aharon that day.*
> *7 And those men said to him, "We became defiled by a human corpse. Why are we kept from presenting the offering of YHWH at its appointed time among the children of Israel?"*

8 And Moshe said to them, "Stand still, that I may hear what YHWH will command concerning you."

9 Then YHWH spoke to Moshe, saying, 10 "Speak to the children of Israel, saying: 'If anyone of you or your posterity is unclean because of a corpse, or is far away on a journey, he may still keep YHWH's Passover. 11 On the fourteenth day of the second month, between the evenings, they may keep it. They shall eat it with unleavened bread and bitter herbs. 12 They shall leave none of it until morning, nor break one of its bones. According to all the ordinances of the Passover they shall keep it. 13 But the man who is clean and is not on a journey, and ceases to keep the Passover, that same person shall be cut off from among his people, because he did not bring the offering of YHWH at its appointed time; that man shall bear his sin. 14 'And if a stranger dwells among you, and would keep YHWH's Passover, he must do so according to the rite of the Passover and according to its ceremony; you shall have one ordinance, both for the stranger and the native of the land.'"

Notice that YHWH added additional rules for those who were unclean for a corpse, and for those who were away on a distant journey. But why would YHWH have more rules for the second Passover, than for the first?

As explained in the Nazarene Israel study, the Torah tells us that in order to participate either in the Sabbath, or in YHWH's Festivals, we must follow special rules for ritual purity (and these rules are different for some of the festivals, than for others). It may be that YHWH decided not to give any these rules to Israel until after they were safely out of Egypt, because He did not want anyone getting confused. Perhaps He wanted all of Israel to apply the blood to their doorposts without fail; and therefore He only gave these rules after the Exodus as kind of a 'next level of learning.' If so, then it shows His love for us, in that He wanted to ensure that all Israel would be able to take part in the Exodus.

The next time Scripture records the children of Israel as offering the Passover is at Joshua 5:10, just after they arrived in the Promised Land.

Joshua 5:10 10 Now the children of Israel camped in Gilgal, and kept the Passover on the fourteenth day of the month at evening on the plains of Jericho.	(10) וַיַּחֲנוּ בְנֵי יִשְׂרָאֵל בַּגִּלְגָּל ׀ וַיַּעֲשׂוּ אֶת הַפֶּסַח בְּאַרְבָּעָה עָשָׂר יוֹם לַחֹדֶשׁ בָּעֶרֶב בְּעַרְבוֹת יְרִיחוֹ

Our forefathers would not have slaughtered the lambs by houses, as they had done in Egypt. Rather, they would have brought the lambs to the Tabernacle, and would have slaughtered them there. This is because YHWH gives us some special instructions for how we are to hold the festivals whenever we live in the Land of Israel.

100

Deuteronomy 12:1 1 "These are the statutes and the judgments which you shall carefully observe in the land which YHWH, the Elohim of your fathers, has given you to possess as long as you live on the soil."	(1) אֵלֶּה הַחֻקִּים וְהַמִּשְׁפָּטִים אֲשֶׁר תִּשְׁמְרוּן לַעֲשׂוֹת בָּאָרֶץ אֲשֶׁר נָתַן יְהוָה אֱלֹהֵי אֲבֹתֶיךָ לְךָ לְרִשְׁתָּהּ ׀ כָּל הַיָּמִים אֲשֶׁר אַתֶּם חַיִּים עַל הָאֲדָמָה

When Israel came into the Land, they were still to hold the Passover in the month of the Aviv; only now, instead of holding the Passover in their homes they were to make a pilgrimage to wherever YHWH would choose to establish His name.

> *Devarim (Deuteronomy) 16:1-2*
> *1 "Observe the month of Aviv and celebrate the Passover to YHWH your Elohim, for in the month of Aviv YHWH your Elohim brought you out of Egypt by night.*
> *2 "You shall sacrifice the Passover to YHWH your Elohim from the flock and the herd, in the place where YHWH chooses to establish His name."*

When the Tabernacle stood, the place YHWH chose to place His name was wherever the Tabernacle was. Later, that place became the Temple in Jerusalem.

> *Melachim Aleph (1st Kings) 14:21*
> *21 Now Rehoboam the son of Solomon reigned in Judah. Rehoboam was forty-one years old when he became*

king, and he reigned seventeen years in Jerusalem, the city which YHWH had chosen from all the tribes of Israel to put His name there.

Yet while it is certainly a blessing to go up to Jerusalem for the festivals, Israel's males are only required to go up to Jerusalem for the festivals when they live in the Land of Israel. We can see confirmation of this in the Apostle Shaul's example. Had it been vital to go up to Jerusalem three times a year no matter where one lived, the Apostle Shaul would certainly have gone; and yet Shaul did not go up to the Temple during the fourteen years he was outside of the Land.

> *Galatim (Galatians) 2:1*
> *2:1 Then after an interval of fourteen years I went up again to Jerusalem with Barnabas, taking Titus along also.*

Until YHWH brings us back to His Land we can keep the Passover either in our homes, or with our local fellowships. However, once we are gathered back into the Land, we will again hold the Passover at the new Temple in Jerusalem, in keeping with Deuteronomy.

> *Devarim (Deuteronomy) 16:5-6*
> *5 "You are not allowed to sacrifice the Passover in any of your towns which YHWH your Elohim is giving you;*
> *6 but at the place where YHWH your Elohim chooses to establish His name, you shall sacrifice the Passover in the evening when the sun comes (back to earth), at the time that you came out of Egypt."*

Ezekiel 40-46 also speaks to this time when all twelve tribes of Israel are brought back to the Land of Israel, and the Temple is rebuilt. Ezekiel 45:21-23 tells us that the Passover will again be offered in the Temple.

> *Yehezqel (Ezekiel) 45:21-23*
> *21 "In the first month, on the fourteenth day of the month, you shall observe the Passover, a feast of seven days; unleavened bread shall be eaten.*
> *22 And on that day the prince (Hebrew: נשׂיא 'Nah-see') shall prepare for himself and for all the people of the land a bull for a sin offering.*
> *23 On the seven days of the feast he shall prepare a burnt offering to YHWH, seven bulls and seven rams without blemish, daily for seven days, and a kid of the goats daily for a sin offering."*

We explore this in more detail in *The Post-Millennial Return* study, but one reason the prince in this passage cannot be Yeshua is that the prince of this passage (above) offers up a sin offering not just for the people, but also for himself. But if Yeshua was the sinless, spotless Passover Lamb, then why would He have to offer a sin sacrifice for Himself? This is inconsistent with the idea that the prince here is Yeshua.

While ideally we would all live in the Land of Israel and make the pilgrimages to Jerusalem three times a year (at the Passover, Pentecost, and the Feast of Sukkot/ Tabernacles), at the time of this writing we are still in the Dispersion and the Temple lies in ruins. How then should we offer the Passover? Should we offer it in our homes, as was done in Egypt, because the Dispersion is a 'type' of Egypt? Proponents of this theory remind us that the Passover service was given as an ordinance forever; therefore they reason we should follow the service that was given in Egypt, whenever we do not reside in the Land of Israel.

>*Shemote (Exodus) 12:24*
>*24 And you shall observe this thing as an ordinance for you and your children forever.*

The majority of scholars, however, believe that:
1. Since YHWH has again chosen Jerusalem, but
2. Since no Temple is presently standing, that
3. We cannot sacrifice a lamb until the Temple is rebuilt. (The present author agrees with this view).

One of the requirements of the Passover is to teach our children about our bitter slavery in Egypt, and how YHWH miraculously delivered us out of it.

>*Shemote (Exodus) 12:25-27*
>*25 "It will come to pass when you come to the land which YHWH will give you, just as He promised, that you shall keep this service.*
>*26 And it shall be, when your children say to you, 'What do you mean by this service?'*
>*27 that you shall say, 'It is the Passover sacrifice of YHWH, who passed over the houses of the children of Israel in Egypt when He struck the Egyptians and delivered our households.'" So the people bowed their heads and worshiped.*

But if one of the purposes of the Passover is to teach our children about the first Passover, how do we do this if we cannot offer a lamb until the Temple is rebuilt? Rabbinic Jews teach their children about the Passover by holding a traditional meal that they call a Passover 'Seder' service. The Jews began eating a seder meal in the Exile to Babylon, and although the Seder plate no longer contains lamb, the seder service remains largely the same as it was in the first century. Further, if we read the account of the Last Supper with the idea that Yeshua was leading a Seder, we can see some striking similarities.

In the Middle East, slaves traditionally stood to wait on their masters as they ate. However, the rabbis taught that since the children of Israel were now free, they no longer had to stand and serve their Egyptian masters. Therefore, the rabbinical tradition became to lean or recline at the Passover table as much as one could, to celebrate their freedom.

> *Mattai (Matthew) 26:20*
> *20 Now when evening came, Yeshua was reclining at the table with the twelve disciples.*

In the Passover Seder service, one also dips food into a bowl (or dish).

> *Mattai (Matthew) 26:23*
> *23 He answered and said, "He who dipped his hand with Me in the dish will betray Me."*

One blesses YHWH, breaks bread, takes four cups of wine (each at specific times), and gives thanks.

105

Mattai (Matthew) 26:26-28
26 And as they were eating, Yeshua took bread, blessed and broke it, and gave it to the disciples and said, "Take, eat; this is My body."
27 Then He took the cup, and gave thanks, and gave it to them, saying, "Drink from it, all of you,
28 For this is My blood of the New (Renewed) Covenant, which is shed for many for the remission of sins."

The Passover Seder service usually concludes with the singing of one or more psalms (or hymns) in praise.

Mattai (Matthew) 26:30
30 And when they had sung a hymn, they went out to the Mount of Olives.

The Peshitta Aramaic tells us that Yeshua and his disciples sang praises (i.e., Psalms).

Mattai 26:30 (Murdock Peshitta)
30 And they sang praises, and went forth to the mount of Olives.

However, even if the Last Supper was held as a seder service, it is important to remember that the Last Supper had to be held the evening before the Passover itself (i.e., on the evening of the $13^{th}/14^{th}$), because Yeshua was offered up as the Passover Lamb, which Torah commands on the afternoon of the 14th of Aviv.

Qorintim Aleph (1st Corinthians) 5:7
For indeed Messiah our Passover was sacrificed for us.

Both the Aramaic and the Greek texts seem to support the idea that the Last Supper took place the evening before the Passover proper, because the words used seem to indicate that the bread used during the Last Supper was leavened (and leavened bread could not have been eaten during the Passover week). For example, in the Peshitta the word bread is לחמא, which is the Aramaic counterpart to the Hebrew word 'lechem' (לחם, leavened bread).

| Matthew 26:26
And as they were eating, Yeshua took bread, and blessed, and brake; and gave to his disciples, and said: "Take, eat; this is my body."
(Murdock Peshitta) | כד ^{PEH} **Matthew 26:26**
דין לעסין שקל ישוע
לחמא וברך וקצא
ויהב לתלמידוהי
ואמר סבו אכולו הנו
פגרי: |

The Greek also seems to support the idea of a raised (or a leavened) loaf, in that the word 'artos' (ἄρτον) is Strong's NT:740, meaning a raised (or leavened) loaf.

NT:740 artos (ar'-tos); from NT:142; bread (as raised) or a loaf.

| Matthew 26:26
26 And as they were eating, Yeshua took bread, blessed and broke it, and gave it to the disciples and said, "Take, eat; this is My body." | ^{BGT} **Matthew 26:26**
Ἐσθιόντων δὲ αὐτῶν λαβὼν ὁ Ἰησοῦς ἄρτον καὶ εὐλογήσας ἔκλασεν καὶ δοὺς τοῖς μαθηταῖς εἶπεν· λάβετε φάγετε, τοῦτό ἐστιν τὸ σῶμά μου. |

However, while this does seem to indicate that the Last Supper was held the night before the Passover, it is not conclusive in and of itself, for even the Torah uses the terms for leavened bread (לֶחֶם) and unleavened bread (מצות) interchangeably in some places. For example, in Exodus 29:23 YHWH commands Moshe to take leavened cakes (לֶחֶם) from a basket of unleavened bread (מַצּוֹת).

| Exodus 29:23 | (23) וְכִכַּר לֶחֶם אַחַת |
| 23 "one loaf of bread, one cake made with oil, and one wafer from the basket of the unleavened bread that is before YHWH...." | וַחַלַּת לֶחֶם שֶׁמֶן אַחַת וְרָקִיק אֶחָד ׀ מִסַּל הַמַּצּוֹת אֲשֶׁר לִפְנֵי יְהֹוָה |

Some suggest that the Last Supper was a traditional Sabbath meal, since traditional Jews often share a loaf of leavened bread called 'challah' at the start of the Sabbath. However, the Last Supper could not have been held on the Sabbath, because Yeshua was in the earth for three full days and three full nights.

> **Mattai (Matthew) 12:40**
> **40 "For as Jonah was three days and three nights in the belly of the great fish, so will the Son of Man be three days and three nights in the heart of the earth."**

Yeshua was risen on the first day of the week, having been raised either on the Sabbath, early on the first day of the week, or on the junction of the two.

> *Mattai (Matthew) 28:1*
> *1 Now after the Sabbath, as the first day of the week began to dawn, Mary Magdalene and the other Mary came to see the tomb.*

The reason the Last Supper was not held on a Sabbath is that if Yeshua was raised either on the Sabbath or the first day of the week, and He had been in the earth for three days and three nights, then the Passover could only have taken place on the fourth day of the week, as per Daniel 9:27.

> *Daniel 9:27*
> *27 Then he shall confirm a covenant with many for one week; but in the middle of the week He shall bring an end to sacrifice and offering.*

One popular argument is that the Last Supper was the Passover meal itself (the evening of the $14^{th}/15^{th}$). The big problem with this argument is that it would require Yeshua to be sacrificed not on the Passover (the 14th of Aviv), but on the afternoon of the First Day of Unleavened Bread (the 15th of Aviv). This would make Yeshua not our Passover Lamb, but our First Day of Unleavened Bread Matza. Nonetheless, this argument is popular in that it seems to find support in the English translations of the Synoptic accounts. For example:

> *Mattithyahu (Matthew) 26:17 NKJV*
> *17 Now on the first day of the Feast of the Unleavened Bread the disciples came to [Yeshua], saying to Him, "Where do You want us to prepare for You to eat the Passover?"*

However, the word that is translated as 'first' is the Greek word 'protos' (πρώτη).

Matthew 26:17 17 Now on the first day of the Feast of the Unleavened Bread the disciples came to Yeshua, saying to Him, "Where do You want us to prepare for You to eat the Passover?"	BGT **Matthew 26:17** Τῇ δὲ πρώτῃ τῶν ἀζύμων προσῆλθον οἱ μαθηταὶ τῷ Ἰησοῦ λέγοντες· ποῦ θέλεις ἑτοιμάσωμέν σοι φαγεῖν τὸ πάσχα; (Mat 26:17 BGT)

This word 'protos' (πρώτη) can mean first, but it can also mean, 'in front of', 'before', or 'prior to.'

> **NT:4253**
> **pro (pro); a primary preposition; "fore", i.e. in front of, prior (figuratively, superior) to:**
>
> **KJV - above, ago, before, or ever. In comparison it retains the same significations.**

What Matthew is really saying, then, is that the Last Supper was held 'before' the Feast of Unleavened Bread.

> *Mattithyahu (Matthew) 26:17*
> *17 Now [before] the first day of the Feast of the Unleavened Bread the disciples came to [Yeshua], saying to Him, "Where do You want us to prepare for You to eat the Passover?"*

Mark uses the same word 'protos' (πρώτη), which should again be translated not 'first', but 'before.'

Marqaus (Mark) 14:12	BGT **Mark 14:12** Καὶ τῇ
12 Now on the first day of Unleavened Bread, when they killed the Passover lamb, His disciples said to Him, "Where do You want us to go and prepare, that You may eat the Passover?"	πρώτῃ ἡμέρᾳ τῶν ἀζύμων, ὅτε τὸ πάσχα ἔθυον, λέγουσιν αὐτῷ οἱ μαθηταὶ αὐτοῦ· ποῦ θέλεις ἀπελθόντες ἑτοιμάσωμεν ἵνα φάγῃς τὸ πάσχα; (Mar 14:12 BGT)

While Matthew uses the word 'protos' (πρώτη), John uses a related word 'pro' (Πρὸ), which is correctly rendered as meaning 'before.'

Yochanan (John) 13:1	BGT **John 13:1** Πρὸ δὲ
1 Now before the Feast of the Passover, when Yeshua knew that His hour had come that He should depart from this world to the Father, having loved His own who were in the world, He loved them to the end.	τῆς ἑορτῆς τοῦ πάσχα εἰδὼς ὁ Ἰησοῦς ὅτι ἦλθεν αὐτοῦ ἡ ὥρα ἵνα μεταβῇ ἐκ τοῦ κόσμου τούτου πρὸς τὸν πατέρα, ἀγαπήσας τοὺς ἰδίους τοὺς ἐν τῷ κόσμῳ εἰς τέλος ἠγάπησεν αὐτούς. (Joh 13:1 BGT)

Luke uses different phraseology altogether:

111

Luqa (Luke) 22:7-8
7 Then came the Day of Unleavened Bread, when the Passover must be killed.
8 And He sent Kepha (Peter) and Yochanan (John), saying, "Go and prepare the Passover for us, that we may eat."

There are several issues here. First, in Exodus 29:23 (above), we saw that YHWH sometimes uses the terms for leavened and unleavened bread interchangeably, leaving it to the reader to figure out the meaning based on context. We also saw in Exodus 12:15-18 (above) that YHWH refers to the Passover and the Feast of Unleavened as one big long festival (since the Feast of Unleavened begins as the Passover ends). Note, then, that since YHWH refers to Passover and the Feast of Unleavened Bread interchangeably, Yeshua and His disciples probably did the same. Further, ancient Hebrews did not always think with the same kinds of 'split-second precision' as modern western cultures do. In a modern western culture, if one says, "Then came the Day of Unleavened Bread", one might think it was the Day of Unleavened Bread itself. However, in an ancient Hebraic culture this can mean, 'the Day of the Passover drew near.'

If we will simply understand that the word 'protos' means 'before', the synoptic accounts automatically reconcile themselves with Yochanan. However, some scholars persist in their attempt to place Yeshua's execution on the First Day of Unleavened Bread, rather than the Passover. One theory called the 'Second Hagigah Hypothesis' even inserts a full day in between the Last Supper in Yochanan 13-17, and Yeshua's arrest in Gethsemane in Yochanan 18. Why?

Some who teach the 'Second Hagigah Hypothesis' suggest that Yeshua's trial took place on the 13th of Aviv, as the 'Preparation Day' of the Passover.

> **Yochanan (John) 19:14**
> **14 Now it was the Preparation Day of the Passover, and about the sixth hour. And he said to the Jews, "Behold your King!"**

However, this is not correct. What Yochanan calls the 'Preparation Day of the Passover' is really the day of the Passover slaughter (i.e., the afternoon of the 14th), as this is sometimes thought of as a day of preparation for the Passover meal, which is eaten on the evening beginning the 14th/15th. Once we understand how Yochanan is applying his terms the apparent conflict dissolves, and we see that Yeshua was put to death on the afternoon of the 14th, perfectly fulfilling the Feast of the Passover. This also makes sense when one considers that the priesthood could have been involved with Yeshua's trial on either the 13th or the early 14th, but would have been busy with Temple matters on the afternoon of the 14th, and would have been unable to participate in any kind of a trial held on the 15th, since it was a high day.

While the Talmud is not Scripture, the Talmud also witnesses to the fact that Yeshua was put to death on the afternoon of the 14th. Yeshua is here called 'Yeshu' (which is a rabbinic slur on His name), and He is accused of using sorcery as the source of His miracles. However, if the entries here are accurate (which is itself another question), it also disproves the so-called 'Second Hagigah' hypothesis, and proves our timeline instead.

113

AND A HERALD PRECEDES HIM etc.
This implies, only immediately before
[the execution], but not previous
thereto.
33 [In contradiction to this] it was
taught: On the eve of the Passover
Yeshu [sic]
34 was hanged. For forty days before
the execution took place, a herald
went forth and cried, 'He is going forth
to be stoned because he has practised
sorcery and enticed Israel to apostasy.
Any one who can say anything in his
favour, let him come forward and
plead on his behalf.' But since nothing
was brought forward in his favour he
was hanged on the eve of the
Passover (i.e., the 14th)!
35 'Ulla retorted: Do you suppose that
he was one for whom a defence could
be made? Was he not a Mesith
[enticer], concerning whom Scripture
says, Neither shalt thou spare, neither
shalt thou conceal him?
36 With Yeshu however it was
different, for he was connected with
the government [or royalty, i.e.,
influential].
[Babylonian Talmud Tractate 43a]

While these comments in Talmud are blasphemous, the fact that Yeshua is recorded in the Talmud gives us yet one more witness to Yeshua's existence; for had Yeshua never existed, the Talmud would not bother to speak of Him.

One question that is frequently asked is whether or not Yeshua instituted a new day of worship at the Last Supper, telling His disciples that whenever they partook of the bread and the wine, they should do it in remembrance of Him.

1st Corinthians 11:23-26	BGT **1 Corinthians 11:23** ¶
23 For I received from the Master that which I also delivered to you: that the Master Yeshua on the same night in which He was betrayed took bread; 24 and when He had given thanks, He broke it and said, "Take, eat; this is My body which is broken for you; do this in remembrance of Me." 25 In the same manner He also took the cup after supper, saying, "This cup is the new covenant in My blood. This do, as often as you drink it, in remembrance of Me." 26 For as often as you eat this bread and drink this cup, you proclaim the Master's death till He comes.	Ἐγὼ γὰρ παρέλαβον ἀπὸ τοῦ κυρίου, ὃ καὶ παρέδωκα ὑμῖν, ὅτι ὁ κύριος Ἰησοῦς ἐν τῇ νυκτὶ ᾗ παρεδίδετο ἔλαβεν ἄρτον BGT **1 Corinthians 11:24** καὶ εὐχαριστήσας ἔκλασεν καὶ εἶπεν· τοῦτό μού ἐστιν τὸ σῶμα τὸ ὑπὲρ ὑμῶν· τοῦτο ποιεῖτε εἰς τὴν ἐμὴν ἀνάμνησιν. BGT **1 Corinthians 11:25** ὡσαύτως καὶ τὸ ποτήριον μετὰ τὸ δειπνῆσαι λέγων· τοῦτο τὸ ποτήριον ἡ καινὴ διαθήκη ἐστὶν ἐν τῷ ἐμῷ αἵματι· τοῦτο ποιεῖτε, ὁσάκις ἐὰν πίνητε, εἰς τὴν ἐμὴν ἀνάμνησιν. BGT **1 Corinthians 11:26** ὁσάκις γὰρ ἐὰν ἐσθίητε τὸν ἄρτον τοῦτον καὶ τὸ ποτήριον πίνητε, τὸν θάνατον τοῦ κυρίου καταγγέλλετε ἄχρι οὗ ἔλθῃ.

Again that this passage tells us to observe the Master's Supper with 'artos' (ἄρτον), meaning 'leavened bread.'

The terms leavened and unleavened bread might be interchangeable here as they were in Exodus 29:23 (above). The Renewed Covenant does seem to use 'artos' as a generic term for bread, as at the supper after Yeshua's disciples met Him on the road from Emmaus (during the Feast of Unleavened Bread).

Luqa (Luke) 24:30 30 Now it came to pass, as He sat at the table with them, that He took bread, blessed and broke it, and gave it to them.	^{BGT} **Luke 24:30** καὶ ἐγένετο ἐν τῷ κατακλιθῆναι αὐτὸν μετ' αὐτῶν λαβὼν τὸν ἄρτον εὐλόγησεν καὶ κλάσας ἐπεδίδου αὐτοῖς, (Luk 24:30 BGT)

However, the Passover and the Master's Supper are two different celebrations; and in First Corinthians 5:8, the Apostle Shaul tells us to keep the Passover with specifically unleavened bread ('azumois', ἀζύμοις).

1st Corinthians 5:7-8 7 Clean out the old leaven so that you may be a new lump, just as you are in fact unleavened. For Messiah our Passover also has been sacrificed. 8 Therefore let us celebrate the feast, not with old leaven, nor with the leaven of malice and wickedness, but with the unleavened bread of sincerity and truth.	^{BGT} **1 Corinthians 5:7** ἐκκαθάρατε τὴν παλαιὰν ζύμην, ἵνα ἦτε νέον φύραμα, καθώς ἐστε ἄζυμοι· καὶ γὰρ τὸ πάσχα ἡμῶν ἐτύθη Χριστός. ^{BGT} **1 Corinthians 5:8** ὥστε ἑορτάζωμεν μὴ ἐν ζύμῃ παλαιᾷ μηδὲ ἐν ζύμῃ κακίας καὶ πονηρίας ἀλλ' ἐν ἀζύμοις εἰλικρινείας καὶ ἀληθείας.

The word 'azumois' (ἀζύμοις) in verses 7 and 8 means specifically "unleavened" (bread). Therefore the command here is to observe the Feast of Unleavened Bread with unleavened bread (ἀζύμοις). In contrast, we are not told to use specifically unleavened bread in First Corinthians 11:23-26 (above). Instead, we are told to keep the Master's Supper with (artos, ἄρτον), which can mean leavened bread.

So what did Yeshua mean by telling His followers to think of Him whenever they broke bread and drank wine? It was probably that Yeshua was telling His disciples to think of Him whenever they took bread and wine in their weekly Sabbath meals, since religious Jews customarily share leavened bread and wine when they get together for fellowship at the start of the Sabbath.

One can argue that Yeshua did institute a new festival day, but these arguments are impossible. Yeshua kept the Torah perfectly, and the Torah forbids us to add to the festivals given in Torah.

> **Devarim (Deuteronomy) 12:32**
> **32 "Whatever I command you, be careful to observe it; you shall not add to it nor take away from it."**

However, this then begs the question, "If the Master's Supper is something we do when we gather together on Sabbath Eve, then how do we hold the Passover?" Rather than relaxing and reclining during a Passover Seder service, the Torah tells us to eat the Passover meal quickly, with our loins girded, with bitter herbs, with sandals (or shoes) on our feet and staves in our hands.

117

Shemote (Exodus) 12:11
"'And so shall you eat it: loins girded (belt on your waist), your sandals on your feet, and your staff in your hand. And you shall eat it in haste. It is the Passover to YHWH.'"

The Torah also tells us to teach our children how YHWH miraculously delivered us from slavery in Egypt.

Shemote (Exodus) 12:26-27
26 And it shall be, when your children say to you, 'What do you mean by this service?'
27 that you shall say,' It is the Passover sacrifice of YHWH, who passed over the houses of the children of Israel in Egypt when He struck the Egyptians and delivered our households.'" So the people bowed their heads and worshiped.

Finally, the Torah tells us that only those who are physically circumcised, and only those who consider themselves to be part of the Nation of Israel, should partake of the Passover. No uncircumcised may eat it.

Shemote (Exodus) 12:43-49
43 And YHWH said to Moshe and Aharon, "This is the ordinance of the Passover: No foreigner shall eat it.
44 But every man's servant who is bought for money, when you have circumcised him, then he may eat it.
45 A sojourner and a hired servant shall not eat it.

46 In one house it shall be eaten; you shall not carry any of the flesh outside the house, nor shall you break one of its bones.

47 All the congregation of Israel shall keep it.

48 And when a stranger dwells with you and wants to keep the Passover to YHWH, let all his males be circumcised, and then let him come near and keep it; and he shall be as a native of the land. For no uncircumcised person shall eat it.

49 One Torah shall be for the native-born and for the stranger who dwells among you."

[For more information as to why the requirement of physical circumcision was not done away with at Yeshua's death, please see the *Nazarene Israel* study.]

While some favor the Passover Seder as a good means of teaching their children about the Passover, it seems wiser to teach one's children to keep the Torah as it is written, eating their meal in haste, as if ready to flee. Then read the story of the Exodus and the accounts of the Last Supper and Yeshua's sacrifice for our sins in the Good News. These are things that honor YHWH, for we are following His commandments, rather than the traditions and teachings of men.

Yochanan (John) 14:15
15 "If you love Me, (then) keep My commandments."

The Wave Sheaf and the Pentecost

If one counts the Passover and Unleavened Bread as one festival, then the second of Israel's festivals is the Pentecost. The word Pentecost means 'count fifty,' but count fifty from what? What is the starting point to this 'count to fifty'? The answer lies in the interplay between Leviticus 23 and Joshua 5.

| Leviticus 23:10-11
10 "Speak to the children of Israel, and say to them: 'When you come into the land which I give to you, and reap its harvest, then you shall bring a sheaf of the first fruits of your harvest to the priest.
11 He shall wave the sheaf before YHWH, to be accepted on your behalf; on the day after the Sabbath the priest shall wave it. | (10) דַּבֵּר אֶל בְּנֵי יִשְׂרָאֵל וְאָמַרְתָּ אֲלֵהֶם כִּי תָבֹאוּ אֶל הָאָרֶץ אֲשֶׁר אֲנִי נֹתֵן לָכֶם וּקְצַרְתֶּם אֶת קְצִירָהּ ׀ וַהֲבֵאתֶם אֶת עֹמֶר רֵאשִׁית קְצִירְכֶם אֶל הַכֹּהֵן : (11) וְהֵנִיף אֶת הָעֹמֶר לִפְנֵי יְהוָה לִרְצֹנְכֶם ׀ מִמָּחֳרַת הַשַּׁבָּת יְנִיפֶנּוּ הַכֹּהֵן : |

Verse 10 tells us that when the children of Israel dwell in the Land of Israel, they are to bring a sheaf of the first fruits of their barley harvest (called an 'Omer', עֹמֶר) to the priesthood. The priesthood then waves this Omer (Wave Sheaf) before YHWH on the day after the weekly Sabbath (מִמָּחֳרַת הַשַּׁבָּת).

120

Next, verse 14 tells us we are not allowed to eat any of the produce of the land until after we have brought this Omer to YHWH.

Leviticus 23:14 14 "'You shall eat neither bread nor parched grain nor fresh grain until the same day that you have brought an offering to your Elohim; it shall be a statute forever throughout your generations in all your dwellings.	(14) וְלֶחֶם וְקָלִי וְכַרְמֶל לֹא תֹאכְלוּ עַד עֶצֶם הַיּוֹם הַזֶּה עַד הֲבִיאֲכֶם אֶת קָרְבַּן אֱלֹהֵיכֶם ׀ חֻקַּת עוֹלָם לְדֹרֹתֵיכֶם בְּכֹל מֹשְׁבֹתֵיכֶם

If we will think about Leviticus 23:14 for a moment, we should be able to see why it is so important to declare the Aviv when the very first complete shocks of barley (either wild or domestic) in the Land of Israel become aviv. Israel has many different microclimates, and barley ripens at different times in each of them. While in the warmer regions barley is considered a spring crop, barley does not ripen at the higher elevations until fall. If the Aviv and the Head of the Year could not be declared until all of the barley in the Land of Israel was Aviv, then the Passover could not be held until fall. Likewise, the Wave Sheaf could also not be offered until the fall. However, this would mean that while the farmers could harvest their crops, they would not be able to eat or sell any part of them until the fall. This would result in severe hardship for the farmers. Because of this it only makes sense to declare the Aviv based on the first of the firstfruits to come ripe.

Next, verses 15 and 16 tell us to count fifty days from the Wave Sheaf offering which was made the day after the weekly Sabbath (מִמָּחֳרַת הַשַּׁבָּת), and then to bring a new grain offering to YHWH. This new grain offering is the Pentecost (also called the Feast of Weeks).

| Leviticus 23:15-16
15 'And you shall count for yourselves from the day after the Sabbath, from the day that you brought the sheaf of the wave offering: seven Sabbaths shall be completed.
16 Count fifty days, to the day after the seventh Sabbath; then you shall offer a new grain offering to YHWH.'" | ‏(15) וּסְפַרְתֶּם לָכֶם מִמָּחֳרַת הַשַּׁבָּת מִיּוֹם הֲבִיאֲכֶם אֶת עֹמֶר הַתְּנוּפָה ׀ שֶׁבַע שַׁבָּתוֹת תְּמִימֹת תִּהְיֶינָה :‏
‏(16) עַד מִמָּחֳרַת הַשַּׁבָּת הַשְּׁבִיעִת תִּסְפְּרוּ חֲמִשִּׁים יוֹם ׀ וְהִקְרַבְתֶּם מִנְחָה חֲדָשָׁה לַיהוָה |

These two verses show us that the Wave Sheaf and the Pentecost always fall on the first day of the week.

1. By definition, the weekly Sabbath (הַשַּׁבָּת) is always the seventh day of the week.
2. By definition, the day after the weekly Sabbath is always the first day of the week.
3. Since the Wave Sheaf is offered the day after the weekly Sabbath (הַשַּׁבָּת), the Wave Sheaf is always offered on the first day of the week.
4. Verse 16 tells us the Pentecost comes fifty days (the day after the seventh weekly Sabbath), after the Wave Sheaf on the first day of the week.
5. Therefore, both the Wave Sheaf and Pentecost always fall on the first day of the week.

On average, Passover falls on the weekly Sabbath only once every seven years. However, when this happens, the First Day of Unleavened Bread also falls on the first day of the week. This happened in Joshua 5:10-12.

Joshua 5:10-12 10 Now the children of Israel camped in Gilgal, and kept the Passover on the fourteenth day of the month at evening on the plains of Jericho. 11 And they ate of the produce of the land on the day after the Passover, unleavened bread and parched grain, on the very same day. 12 Then the manna ceased on the day after they had eaten the produce of the land; and the children of Israel no longer had manna, but they ate the food of the land of Canaan that year.	(10) וַיַּחֲנוּ בְנֵי יִשְׂרָאֵל בַּגִּלְגָּל l וַיַּעֲשׂוּ אֶת הַפֶּסַח בְּאַרְבָּעָה עָשָׂר יוֹם לַחֹדֶשׁ בָּעֶרֶב בְּעַרְבוֹת יְרִיחוֹ : (11) וַיֹּאכְלוּ מֵעֲבוּר הָאָרֶץ מִמָּחֳרַת הַפֶּסַח מַצּוֹת וְקָלוּי l בְּעֶצֶם הַיּוֹם הַזֶּה : (12) וַיִּשְׁבֹּת הַמָּן מִמָּחֳרָת בְּאָכְלָם מֵעֲבוּר הָאָרֶץ וְלֹא הָיָה עוֹד לִבְנֵי יִשְׂרָאֵל מָן l וַיֹּאכְלוּ מִתְּבוּאַת אֶרֶץ כְּנַעַן בַּשָּׁנָה הַהִיא :

Since the children of Israel ate the produce of the land on the day after the Passover, yet since Leviticus 23:14 (above) tells us that they could not eat the produce of the land until after they brought the Wave Sheaf, that means they must have offered the Wave Sheaf on the First Day of Unleavened Bread.

123

						Pass.
Omer	2ULB	3ULB	4ULB	5ULB	6ULB	7ULB
8 Om.	9 Om.	10	11	12	13	14
15	16	17	18	19	20	21
22	23	24	25	26	27	28
29	30	31	32	33	34	35
36	37	38	39	40	41	42
43	44	45	46	47	48	49
Pent.						

Pass. = Passover (Pesach)
Omer = The Wave Sheaf and the start of the 50 Count.
2ULB = Second Day of Unleavened Bread
Om. = Abbreviation for the day of the Omer Count.
Pent. = Pentecost (fiftieth day)

When Passover falls on the afternoon of the weekly Sabbath, as it did in Joshua 5:10-12, the Omer falls on the First Day of Unleavened Bread. When this happens, the first seven days of the Omer coincide with the seven days of Unleavened Bread.

Verse 12 tells us the manna stopped falling the day after they ate the produce of the land, which was also the day after the Wave Sheaf, and the Second Day of Unleavened Bread. It may be that YHWH decided to continue to provide manna until the Second Day of Unleavened Bread, so that no one would feel the need to harvest anything until after the high day was past.

However, since the Passover only falls on the Sabbath once in every seven years (on average), Joshua 5:10-12 is a special case. For this reason we also need to know what to do when the Passover does not fall on the weekly Sabbath. Take for example 2008 CE, when Passover fell on the second day of the week.

	Pass.	1ULB	2ULB	3ULB	4ULB	5ULB
Omer	7ULB	3 Om.	4 Om.	5 Om.	6 Om.	7 Om.
8 Om.	9 Om.	10	11	12	13	14
15	16	17	18	19	20	21
22	23	24	25	26	27	28
29	30	31	32	33	34	35
36	37	38	39	40	41	42
43	44	45	46	47	48	49
Pent.						

Pass = Passover
1ULB = First Day of Unleavened Bread
Omer = Wave Sheaf and beginning of the Omer count
Om.   = Abbreviation for the day of the Omer Count.
Pent = Pentecost (always on the first day of the week)

Because Passover on the Torah Calendar did not fall on the weekly Sabbath in 2008 CE, the First Day of Unleavened Bread did not fall on the first day of the week (when the Omer was to be waved). Therefore, the first seven days of the Omer did not match the seven Days of Unleavened Bread; yet the Wave Sheaf was still offered on the first day of the week.

Some believers take exception to the idea that the Wave Sheaf and Pentecost fall on the first day of the week, perhaps because the Christian Church has long designated the first day of the week as its primary day of rest. Perhaps for this reason and perhaps for others, some believers prefer to use the Rabbinical (Hillel II) Calendar version of the Omer Count, which tells us that the reference in Leviticus 23:15-16 (above) to the day after the weekly Sabbath (מִמָּחֳרַת הַשַּׁבָּת) is actually a reference to the day after the Passover (מִמָּחֳרַת הַפֶּסַח). However, there are many problems with this substitution, some of which are listed below.

125

1. YHWH does not tell us to offer the Omer on the day after the Passover (מִמָּחֳרַת הַפֶּסַח), but the day after the weekly Sabbath (מִמָּחֳרַת הַשַּׁבָּת).

2. If YHWH wanted the Omer offered the day after the Passover no matter when the Passover fell, the instructions for offering the Omer would be included in the instructions for the First Day of Unleavened Bread. However, the instructions for the Wave Sheaf are listed separately.

3. If we substitute the word 'Passover' for the word 'Shabbat' uniformly throughout Leviticus 23:15-16, then we find ourselves instructed to wait seven completed Passovers (i.e., seven complete years) before offering the Pentecost.

    Nonsensical Uniform Substitution:
    15 'And you shall count for yourselves from the day after the Passover, from the day that you brought the sheaf of the wave offering: seven Passovers shall be completed.
    16 Count fifty days, to the day after the seventh Passover; then you shall offer a new grain offering to YHWH.'"

4. Reference verse 16 (above), it is not possible to count fifty days until the seventh Passover.

5. Finally, YHWH gives a set date for every other festival in Scripture (e.g., Passover is on the 14th day of the first month). However, YHWH never gives a set date for the Wave Sheaf, or Pentecost. This is because even though these festivals always fall on the first day of the week, year by year, the calendar dates are different.

When we reach the fiftieth day of the Omer Count (on the first day of the week), Numbers 28:26 tells us to bring an offering of new grain to YHWH. This "Feast of Weeks" (Pentecost) is a rest day, and we are to do no customary work on it.

> **Bemidbar (Numbers) 28:26**
> **26 'Also on the day of the First Fruits, when you bring a new grain offering to YHWH at your Feast of Weeks, you shall have a set-apart gathering. You shall do no customary work.**

Like the Passover, when we live in the Land of Israel, we are to celebrate the Feast of Pentecost in the place YHWH chooses to put His name.

> **Devarim (Deuteronomy) 16:9-12**
> **9 "You shall count seven weeks for yourself; begin to count the seven weeks from the time you begin to put the sickle to the grain.**
> **10 Then you shall keep the Feast of Weeks to YHWH your Elohim with the tribute of a freewill offering from your hand, which you shall give as YHWH your Elohim blesses you.**
> **11 You shall rejoice before YHWH your Elohim, you and your son and your daughter, your male servant and your female servant, the Levite who is within your gates, the stranger and the fatherless and the widow who are among you, at the place where YHWH your Elohim chooses to make His name abide.**

12 And you shall remember that you were a slave in Egypt, and you shall be careful to observe these statutes."

As we saw in the last chapter, that place is Jerusalem (e.g. First Kings 14:21, Second Chronicles 12:13). We also saw that Shaul did not go up to Jerusalem for fourteen years when he was out on his missionary voyages (e.g., Galatians 2:1). This shows us we are not required to make the pilgrimages up to Jerusalem when we do not live in the Land. However, even if we do not live in the Land, it is still good to go up to Jerusalem for the festivals, as the devout also did in the first century.

> *Ma'asim (Acts) 2:1-2*
> *1 When the Day of Pentecost had fully come, they were all with one accord in one place.*
> *2 And suddenly there came a sound from heaven, as of a rushing mighty wind, and it filled the whole house where they were sitting.*

However, this brings up an interesting if difficult point. YHWH fulfills prophecy on His Calendar, not man's. In order to receive the gift of the Spirit when it was poured out in Jerusalem, the faithful had to be in Jerusalem when the Torah said to be there.

We have already seen that Leviticus 23:15-16 (above) tells us to begin the Omer count on the first day of the week that comes after the Passover. We have also seen how Pentecost must also take place on the first day of the week. However, in contrast to this, both Josephus and Philo tell us that in the first century, the Wave Sheaf was offered on the day after the Passover.

Here is Josephus' testimony:

> *The feast of Unleavened Bread succeeds that of Passover and falls on the 15th of the month and continues seven days, wherein they feed on unleavened bread, on every one of which days two bulls are killed and one ram and seven lambs. Now these lambs are entirely burnt beside the kid of the goats which is added to all the rest for sins, for it is intended as a feast for the priest on every one of these days. But on the Second Day of Unleavened Bread, which is the 16th day of the month, they first partake of the fruits of the earth, for before that day (the 16th of Aviv) they do not touch them. And while they suppose it proper to honor God [sic] from which they obtain this plentiful provision in the first place, they offer the first fruits of their barley.*
> *[Antiquities of the Jews, iii, 10:5]*

Here is Philo's testimony, which confirms that in the first century, the rabbinical practice was to bring the Wave Sheaf to the altar the day after the Passover.

> *There is also a festival on the day of the paschal feast, which succeeds the first day, and this is named the sheaf, from what takes place on it; for the sheaf is brought to the altar as a first fruit both of the country which the nation has received for its own, and*

also of the whole land; so as to be an offering both for the nation separately, and also a common one for the whole race of mankind; and so that the people by it worship the living God [sic], both for themselves and for all the rest of mankind, because they have received the fertile earth for their inheritance; for in the country there is no barren soil but even all those parts which appear to be stony and rugged are surrounded with soft veins of great depth, which, by reason of their richness, are very well suited for the production of living things.
[Philo: De Specialibus Legibus 2:162]

Most believers accept that Yeshua was cut off in the middle of the week, based partly on the Renewed Covenant (which we shall examine below), and partly on Daniel 9:26-27, which tells us that in the middle of the week, the Messiah would be cut off, bringing a (temporary) end to the sacrifices.

Daniel 9:26-27	
26 "And after the sixty-two weeks Messiah shall be cut off, but not for Himself; and the people of the prince who is to come shall destroy the city and the sanctuary. The end of it shall be with a flood, and till the end of the war desolations are determined.	(26) וְאַחֲרֵי הַשָּׁבֻעִים שִׁשִּׁים וּשְׁנַיִם יִכָּרֵת מָשִׁיחַ וְאֵין לוֹ ׀ וְהָעִיר וְהַקֹּדֶשׁ יַשְׁחִית עַם נָגִיד הַבָּא וְקִצּוֹ בַשֶּׁטֶף וְעַד קֵץ מִלְחָמָה נֶחֱרֶצֶת שֹׁמֵמוֹת : (27) וְהִגְבִּיר בְּרִית לָרַבִּים שָׁבוּעַ אֶחָד ׀

27 Then he shall confirm a covenant with many for one week; but in the middle of the week He shall bring an end to sacrifice and offering. And on the wing of abominations shall be one who makes desolate, even until the consummation, which is determined, is poured out on the desolate."	וַחֲצִי הַשָּׁבוּעַ יַשְׁבִּית זֶבַח וּמִנְחָה וְעַל כְּנַף שִׁקּוּצִים מְשֹׁמֵם וְעַד כָּלָה וְנֶחֱרָצָה תִּתַּךְ עַל שֹׁמֵם :

Matthew 12:40 tells us that Yeshua would be in the grave for three days and three nights.

> **Mattai (Matthew) 12:40**
> **40 "For as Jonah was three days and three nights in the belly of the great fish, so will the Son of Man be three days and three nights in the heart of the earth."**

We know that Yeshua was resurrected either on the Sabbath, or at the start of the first day of the week (when the Sabbath ends and the first day of the week begins). Either way, He was fully risen on the first day of the week (when the Wave Sheaf is to be offered).

> **Yochanan (John) 20:1**
> **1 Now the first day of the week Mary Magdalene went to the tomb early, while it was still dark, and saw that the stone had been taken away from the tomb.**

131

Seventeen verses later, Yeshua tells Miriam not to cling to Him, as He still had to ascend to His Father. This was in fulfillment of how the Wave Sheaf must be waved before YHWH on the first day of the week.

> **Yochanan (John) 20:17**
> **17 Yeshua said to her, "Do not cling to Me, for I have not yet ascended to My Father; but go to My brethren and say to them, 'I am ascending to My Father and your Father, and to My Elohim and your Elohim.'"**

All of this fits perfectly with the Torah Calendar, which calls for the Messiah to be cut off in the middle of the week, raised three days and three nights later (either on the Sabbath, or at the end of Sabbath, as the first day of the week begins), and then to ascend to His Father on the first day of the week as the prophetic fulfillment of the First Fruits of Barley (the Omer).

1	2	3	4	5	6	7
			Pass.	1ULB	2ULB	**3ULB**
Omer	5ULB	6ULB	7ULB	5 Om	6 Om	7 Om
8 Om	9 Om	10	11	12	13	14
15	16	17	18	19	20	21
22	23	24	25	26	27	28
29	30	31	32	33	34	35
36	37	38	39	40	41	42
43	44	45	46	47	48	49
Pent.						

Pass. =   Passover in the middle of the week
3ULB =   Yeshua raised on the third day (or at end)
Omer =   Yeshua ascends as the Wave Sheaf
Pent. =   Pentecost (always first day of the week)

Yeshua was raised not just 'on the third day', but that He was raised on the third day of Unleavened Bread.

The record fits so perfectly with the Torah Calendar that we could easily move on without further comment, except for the fact that Josephus, Philo, and the Talmud all inform us that during the first century, the rabbis did not follow the Torah Calendar method either for the Wave Sheaf or for the Pentecost. Rather, they used the rabbinical method of determining the Omer count, which has the Wave Sheaf being offered on the day after the Passover, which would put the Pentecost on the fifth day of the week. Here is how these events would have fallen out on the Rabbinical Calendar:

1	2	3	4	5	6	7
			Pass.	**1 Omer**	2ULB	**3ULB**
4ULB	5ULB	6ULB	7ULB	8 Om.	9	10
11	12	13	14	15	16	17
18	19	20	21	22	23	24
25	26	27	28	29	30	31
32	33	34	35	36	37	38
39	40	41	42	43	44	45
46	47	48	49	**R.Pent.**		Sab.
True						

Pass. = Passover
1 Omer = Rabbinic Wave Sheaf offered
3ULB = Yeshua raised on the third day (or at end)
4ULB = Yeshua waived before YHWH
R.Pent.= Rabbinical Pentecost
True = Pentecost on the Torah Calendar

Note how Yeshua's resurrection and ascension equate to nothing prophetic on the Rabbinical Calendar.

Our purpose is not to establish exactly what may have happened back in the first century, but rather to establish what the Torah tells us to do today. However, it appears reasonable that instead of pouring out the Spirit on the Rabbinical/Pharisaical Pentecost, YHWH likely poured it out on the true Pentecost, on the first day of the week. This scenario makes sense when one considers that there would have been only one day in between the rabbinical Pentecost and the coming Sabbath. Rather than head for home right after the rabbinical Pentecost was over (and then have to stop traveling a day later, to rest on Sabbath), it would have made more sense for the pilgrims to tarry in Jerusalem until after the Sabbath, and then go to morning services at the Temple before heading for home, on the first day of the week. This is likely when YHWH poured out His Spirit, and yet this is recorded simply as the day when Pentecost was 'fully' come, perhaps because the disciples did not think of the Rabbinical Pentecost as the true Pentecost. This scenario also makes sense when one considers that the Sadducees were a major sect in first century times, and that Caiaphas the High Priest was also a Sadducee (with a large following).

> **Ma'asim (Acts) 5:17**
> **17 Then the high priest rose up, and all those who were with him (which is the sect of the Sadducees), and they were filled with indignation....**

While Caiaphas had to uphold the Rabbinical Calendar as High Priest, the Sadducees believed that the Wave Sheaf and the Pentecost were only correctly observed on the first day of the week. Therefore it may be that many Sadducees were there in the Temple on that particular first day morning, as it was their Pentecost.

In addition to the many first century Sadducees, there would also have been larger numbers of devout Pharisees dwelling in Jerusalem, having come up from throughout all Judea, and all of the nations of the earth. These would likely also have been in the Temple for the regular morning service on the first day of the week following the Rabbinical/Pharisaical Pentecost.

> *Ma'asim (Acts) 2:5-6*
> *5 And there were dwelling in Jerusalem Jews, devout men, from every nation under heaven.*
> *6 And when this sound occurred, the multitude came together, and were confused, because everyone heard them speak in his own language.*

Again, the purpose of this study is not to exhaustively determine in exact detail what happened in the first century, but only to show what the Torah commands, so that we can keep the Torah Calendar correctly in the present day, no matter how our ancestors (whether Jewish or Ephraimite) may have kept it.

Let us consider some of the many parallels between the Pentecost that took place in the Wilderness of Sinai, and the Pentecost in Acts Chapter 2. According to tradition, fifty days after Israel crossed the Reed (Red) Sea, YHWH gave Israel the Torah. Parallel to that, fifty days after Yeshua's resurrection, YHWH poured out the gift of the Set-apart Spirit.

At the Pentecost in Sinai, the Ten Commandments were written on two tablets of stone. At the Pentecost in Acts Chapter Two, YHWH wrote His Torah on the tablets of our heart, by His Spirit.

When the Ten Commandments were given at Mount Sinai, three thousand men were slain (Exodus 32:28). When the Spirit was poured out in Acts Chapter Two, about three thousand men received salvation.

> *Ma'asim (Acts) 2:41*
> *41 Then those who gladly received his word were immersed; and that day about three thousand souls were added to them.*

While the Passover symbolizes our redemption from physical bondage in Egypt, the Pentecost symbolizes our spiritual redemption and renewal in Yeshua.

There are many verses which tell us that Yeshua was the First Fruits. First Corinthians 15:20 tells us that Yeshua is the First Fruits of all those who have died.

> *Qorintim Aleph (1st Corinthians) 15:20*
> *20 But now Messiah is risen from the dead, and has become the firstfruits of those who have fallen asleep.*

Yeshua was the first born of Miriam (Mary).

> *Mattai (Matthew) 1:24-25*
> *24 Then Joseph, being aroused from sleep, did as the messenger of YHWH commanded him, and took to him his wife,*
> *25 and did not know her till she had brought forth her firstborn Son. And he called His name Yeshua.*

Yeshua is also the first-born of YHWH the Father.

Ivrim (Hebrews) 1:6
6 But when He again brings the firstborn into the world, He says: "Let all the messengers of Elohim worship Him."

Yeshua was also the first one to be raised from the dead.

Gilyana (Revelation) 1:5
5 and from Yeshua Messiah, the faithful witness, the firstborn from the dead, and the ruler over the kings of the earth.

As the first born of the dead, Yeshua is also the first born of many brethren.

Romim (Romans) 8:29
29 For whom He foreknew, He also predestined to be conformed to the image of His Son, that He might be the firstborn among many brethren.

Scripture also tells us that Yeshua is the first fruits of those who will be resurrected unto eternal life.

Qorintim Aleph (1 Cor.) 15:20-23
20 But now Messiah is risen from the dead, and has become the First Fruits of those who have fallen asleep.
21 For since by man came death, by Man also came the resurrection of the dead.
22 For as in Adam all die, even so in Messiah all shall be made alive.

23 But each one in his own order: Messiah the First Fruits, afterward those who are Messiah's at His coming.

Surely Yeshua was the First Fruits of all of these things on His Father's Torah Calendar.

The Fasts of Zechariah Reconsidered

Zechariah 8:18-19 speaks of four man-made traditional fast days which are not commanded in the Torah. Should we keep them?

> *Zekaryah (Zechariah) 8:18-19*
> *18 Then the word of YHWH of hosts came to me, saying,*
> *19 "Thus says YHWH of hosts:*
> *'The fast of the fourth month, the fast of the fifth, the fast of the seventh, and the fast of the tenth shall be joy and gladness and cheerful feasts for the House of Judah. Therefore love truth and peace.'"*

Many people mistakenly believe this passage means that the House of Judah is to keep these man-made traditional fast days with joy and gladness, but this is not YHWH's meaning at all. Rather, YHWH is telling the Jews not to fast, but to be joyful on those days.

How did these fast days get started? When King Nebuchadnezzar of Babylon took the Jews into exile, he burned the House of YHWH with fire, and broke down the walls of Jerusalem all around.

> *Melachim Bet (2ⁿᵈ Kings) 25:8-10*
> *8 And in the fifth month, on the seventh day of the month (which was the nineteenth year of King Nebuchadnezzar king of Babylon), Nebuzaradan the captain of the guard, a servant of the king of Babylon, came to Jerusalem.*

9 He burned the house of YHWH and the king's house; all the houses of Jerusalem, that is, all the houses of the great, he burned with fire.
10 And all the army of the Chaldeans who were with the captain of the guard broke down the walls of Jerusalem all around.

The Jews responded by declaring four traditional fast days: the ninth day of the fourth month, the tenth day of the fifth month, the third day of the seventh month, and the tenth day of the tenth month. Notice that these do not refer to the Day of Atonements, or Yom Kippur, which is the tenth day of the seventh month.

Vayiqra (Leviticus) 23:27-28
27 "Also the tenth day of this seventh month shall be the Day of Atonement. It shall be a set-apart gathering convocation for you; you shall afflict your souls, and offer an offering made by fire to YHWH.
28 And you shall do no work on that same day, for it is the Day of Atonement, to make atonement for you before YHWH your Elohim."

They Orthodox/Pharisees have their reasons for these things, but it is not our purpose to get into them here. Rather, simply let us note that YHWH commands us to be careful not to add to the festivals that He commands us to keep, in His Torah.

Devarim (Deuteronomy) 4:2
2 "You shall not add to the word which I command you, nor take from it, that you may keep the commandments of YHWH your Elohim which I command you."

Let us take a brief review of history, so we can better understand the context of Zechariah 8:18-19.

YHWH told Jeremiah that He would allow the Jews to return to His land after the seventy years of their Exile had been completed.

> *Yirmeyahu (Jeremiah) 29:10*
> *10 "For thus says YHWH: 'After seventy years are completed at Babylon, I will visit you and perform My good word toward you, and cause you to return to this place.'"*

Daniel counted the years, and then prayed that YHWH would remember His people, and have compassion upon them.

> *Daniel 9:1-3*
> *9:1 In the first year of Darius the son of Ahasuerus, of the lineage of the Medes, who was made king over the realm of the Chaldeans —*
> *2 in the first year of his reign I, Daniel, understood by the books the number of the years specified by the word of YHWH through Jeremiah the Prophet, that He would accomplish seventy years in the desolations of Jerusalem.*
> *3 Then I set my face toward YHWH Elohim to make request by prayer and supplications, with fasting, sackcloth, and ashes.*

One man sows, and another man reaps. YHWH then sent word through the Prophet Zechariah, that Judah was to begin returning to His land.

141

Zecharyah (Zechariah) 1:14-16
14 So the messenger (angel) who spoke with me said to me, "Proclaim, saying, 'Thus says YHWH of hosts: "I am zealous for Jerusalem and for Zion with great zeal.
15 I am exceedingly angry with the nations at ease; for I was a little angry, and they helped — but with evil intent."
16 'Therefore thus says YHWH: "I am returning to Jerusalem with mercy. My house shall be built in it," says YHWH of hosts, "and a surveyor's line shall be stretched out over Jerusalem."'

We cover more of the history in the chapter on the Book of Esther, but in the days of Ezra and Nehemiah, the Jews did begin to return to the land, and they also began to build the Second Temple.

Ezra 3:8
8 Now in the second month of the second year of their coming to the house of Elohim at Jerusalem, Zerubbabel the son of Shealtiel, Yeshua the son of Yehotzadak, and the rest of their brethren the priests and the Levites, and all those who had come out of the captivity to Jerusalem, began work and appointed the Levites from twenty years old and above to oversee the work of the house of YHWH.

However, now that the Jews were back in the Land and the Temple was being rebuilt, the Jews wanted to know if they should continue to keep the fast days that they had instituted because of the destruction of the temple. YHWH responded with a series of questions to them, essentially asking them, "When you fasted and mourned these seventy years, did you really fast for Me? (No.) Didn't you really fast for yourselves? (Yes). Because I never told you to fast on those days! Why didn't you just keep the Torah that I gave through Moshe (Moses)?"

> *Zecharyah (Zechariah) 7:1-7*
> *7 Now in the fourth year of King Darius it came to pass that the word of YHWH came to Zechariah, on the fourth day of the ninth month, Chislev,*
> *2 when the people sent Sherezer, with Regem-Melech and his men, to the house of Elohim, to pray before YHWH,*
> *3 and to ask the priests who were in the house of YHWH of hosts, and the prophets, saying, "Should I weep in the fifth month and fast as I have done for so many years?"*
> *4 Then the word of YHWH of hosts came to me, saying,*
> *5 "Say to all the people of the land, and to the priests: 'When you fasted and mourned in the fifth and seventh months during those seventy years, did you really fast for Me — for Me?*
> *6 When you eat and when you drink, do you not eat and drink for yourselves?*
> *7 Should you not have obeyed the words which YHWH proclaimed through the former prophets when Jerusalem and the cities around it were inhabited and prosperous, and the South and the Lowland were inhabited?'"*

In other words, "Why did you make up your own days of fasting? Why did you not just keep My word?"

One might ask why it would be a problem if our Jewish brothers want to make up a few fast days of their own, to honor YHWH above and beyond what YHWH says He wants us to do. The answer is that YHWH does not really consider that to be honoring Him. He gives us another witness, not to add to the commandments that He gives us.

> **Devarim (Deuteronomy) 12:32**
> **32 "Whatever I command you, be careful to observe it; you shall not add to it nor take away from it."**

As we explain in *Tree of Knowledge, Tree of Life*, the grand test is to see if we will do what YHWH asks us to do (which is to keep to the Tree of Life), or if we will 'do our own thing' based upon our own thoughts (which is the Tree of the Knowledge of Good and Evil). When we add an additional festival day, or an additional fast to His calendar that is precisely what YHWH prohibits. King Solomon tells us that those people are liars.

> **Mishle (Proverbs) 30:6**
> **6 Do not add to His words, lest He rebuke you, and you be found a liar.**

And here is why it is especially grievous: In the opening chapter of this book (*Why the Torah Calendar?*) we recounted an old Jewish saying: that whoever's calendar you keep, that is whom you worship. If we are careful to keep YHWH's calendar, and to do only as He commands, then YHWH considers that we are worshipping Him. However, if we keep calendars that have been created by men, then we are worshipping men: and this is to worship an object of the Creation, rather than the Creator.

One's actions show one's loyalty. If we obey YHWH gladly, then our loyalty is with Him. However, if we obey men, then our loyalty is not with YHWH, but with man. In YHWH's sight, this is tantamount to rebellion against His authority.

When I was first called into the Messianic Movement, it seemed to me that the quickest way to recreate the Faith Once Delivered to the Saints was to do as Yeshua and His apostles had done: that is, to start with Second Temple Period Judaism, and reject everything that contradicts with the Torah. However, as YHWH continued to lead and guide me, I began to realize that we cannot always see what conflicts with the Torah; and so I began to realize that a much safer and surer approach is be to begin with the Instructions of Elohim (i.e., YHWH's Torah), and then to add nothing to it, and subtract nothing from it. If I cannot verify a tradition or a teaching by the Words of Elohim (i.e., YHWH's or Yeshua's words), then I cannot consider it to be Torah.

Our Orthodox brethren consider that when YHWH gave the Torah to Moshe, He also gave Moshe the power to modify it, as needed. They further consider that they have inherited this power from Moshe. Therefore they believe that their man-made customs and traditions constitute literal 'Torah Law'; and this is precisely what they call it.

> ### Zecharyah (Zechariah) 8:23
> **23 "Thus says YHWH of hosts: 'In those days ten men from every language of the nations shall grasp the sleeve of a Jewish man, saying, "Let us go with you, for we have heard that Elohim is with you."'"**

145

It is a wonderful thing that YHWH is calling His servant Ephraim out of the nations, to return back home to his inheritance in the Land, the Language and the Law. However, as much as we love our brother Judah, let us be careful not simply to accept his interpretations of 'Torah Law', let we also be found guilty of giving our loyalty not to the Creator, but to the Creation.

May YHWH please deliver all of His people from all unrighteousness, soon and in our day.

In Yeshua's name,

Amein.

The Day of Trumpets (Yom Teruah)

We saw earlier how the Head of the Year should be declared when the first crescent sliver of the new moon is physically sighted from the Land of Israel, after the barley in the Land of Israel has become Aviv.

The declaration of the Head of the Year establishes the timing of all the Spring Festivals, including Passover, the Feast of Unleavened Bread, the Wave Sheaf and even the Pentecost. All of these festival dates can be determined just as soon as the Head of the Year is known. However, until the first crescent sliver of the new moon of the seventh month has been physically sighted the Fall Festival dates cannot be known, because YHWH is ultimately in control of the weather.

The New Moon Day of the seventh month is called 'Yom Teruah' (יוֹם תְּרוּעָה). This is oftentimes translated as the 'Day of Trumpets', although it actually translates more like the 'Day of Blowing,' or the 'Day of Shouting.' Strong's Concordance tells us that the word 'Teruah' (תְּרוּעָה) refers to an acclamation of joy, especially of trumpets, and also as a cry of battle, or an alarm.

> ***OT:8643 teruw`ah (ter-oo-aw'); from OT:7321; clamor, i.e. acclamation of joy or a battle-cry; especially clangor of trumpets, as an alarum [sic]:***

When we look up the reference to OT:7321, we find that the idea is one of 'splitting the ears' with sound, particularly with shouts of joy or alarm.

OT:7321 ruwa` (roo-ah'); a primitive root; to mar (especially by breaking); figuratively, to split the ears (with sound), i.e. shout (for alarm or joy):

In this light, let us consider Numbers 10:8-9, which tells us that whenever Israel went out to battle, the priests would blow the silver trumpets (חֲצֹצְרוֹת), sounding an alarm so that YHWH would remember Israel, and save her from her enemies.

Numbers 10:8-9 8 The sons of Aharon, the priests, shall blow the trumpets; and these shall be to you as an ordinance forever throughout your generations. 9 "When you go to war in your land against the enemy who oppresses you, then you shall sound an alarm with the trumpets, and you will be remembered before YHWH your Elohim, and you will be saved from your enemies.	(8) וּבְנֵי אַהֲרֹן הַכֹּהֲנִים יִתְקְעוּ בַּחֲצֹצְרוֹת וְהָיוּ לָכֶם לְחֻקַּת עוֹלָם לְדֹרֹתֵיכֶם : (9) וְכִי תָבֹאוּ מִלְחָמָה בְּאַרְצְכֶם עַל הַצַּר הַצֹּרֵר אֶתְכֶם וַהֲרֵעֹתֶם בַּחֲצֹצְרוֹת וְנִזְכַּרְתֶּם לִפְנֵי יְהֹוָה אֱלֹהֵיכֶם וְנוֹשַׁעְתֶּם מֵאֹיְבֵיכֶם :

Israel was also commanded to blow the silver trumpets in their appointed feasts, in the beginnings of their months, over the sacrifices of their peace offerings and in their 'day of gladness.' Scholars differ as to whether this 'day of gladness' is a reference to the Sabbath, the Feast of Tabernacles, or some other day.

Numbers 10:10
10 Also in the day of your gladness, and in your appointed feasts, and at the beginning of your months, you shall blow the trumpets over your burnt offerings and over the sacrifices of your peace offerings; and they shall be a memorial for you before your Elohim: I am YHWH your Elohim."

(10) וּבְיוֹם שִׂמְחַתְכֶם וּבְמוֹעֲדֵיכֶם וּבְרָאשֵׁי חָדְשֵׁיכֶם וּתְקַעְתֶּם בַּחֲצֹצְרֹת עַל עֹלֹתֵיכֶם וְעַל זִבְחֵי שַׁלְמֵיכֶם ן וְהָיוּ לָכֶם לְזִכָּרוֹן לִפְנֵי אֱלֹהֵיכֶם אֲנִי יְהוָה אֱלֹהֵיכֶם

But if we are commanded to blow the silver trumpets at the beginning of each of our months, then what makes Yom Teruah any different from any other new moon day? One thing that sets it apart is how Israel is not supposed to work on that day, but is commanded to have a set-apart day of rest.

Numbers 29:1
1 'And in the seventh month, on the first day of the month, you shall have a set-apart gathering. You shall do no customary work. For you it is a day of blowing.

(1) וּבַחֹדֶשׁ הַשְּׁבִיעִי בְּאֶחָד לַחֹדֶשׁ מִקְרָא קֹדֶשׁ יִהְיֶה לָכֶם כָּל מְלֶאכֶת עֲבֹדָה לֹא תַעֲשׂוּ ן יוֹם תְּרוּעָה יִהְיֶה לָכֶם :

In the next five verses, YHWH prescribes the offerings we are to bring Him on this day.

Bemidbar (Numbers) 29:2-6
2 You shall offer a burnt offering as a sweet aroma to YHWH: one young bull, one ram, and seven lambs in their first year, without blemish.
3 Their grain offering shall be fine flour mixed with oil: three-tenths of an ephah for the bull, two-tenths for the ram,
4 and one-tenth for each of the seven lambs;
5 also one kid of the goats as a sin offering, to make atonement for you;
6 besides the burnt offering with its grain offering for the New Moon, the regular burnt offering with its grain offering, and their drink offerings, according to their ordinance, as a sweet aroma, an offering made by fire to YHWH.

Some liken YHWH's offerings to an outdoor barbecue, and a barbecue always smells good to the human nose. However, since YHWH is Spirit, could it be that the reason He says these things are a 'sweet aroma' is that it pleases Him whenever we willingly give up what we want, in order to follow His word?

Leviticus 23 confirms that we are to observe Yom Teruah as a set-apart memorial of blowing, and to bring Him an offering made by fire.

Leviticus 23:23-25 23 Then YHWH spoke to Moshe, saying,	(23) וַיְדַבֵּר יְהוָה אֶל מֹשֶׁה לֵּאמֹר׃

24 "Speak to the children of Israel, saying: 'In the seventh month, on the first day of the month, you shall have a sabbath-rest, a memorial of blowing (the trumpets), a set-apart gathering. 25 You shall do no customary work on it; and you shall offer an offering made by fire to YHWH.'"	(24) דַּבֵּר אֶל בְּנֵי יִשְׂרָאֵל לֵאמֹר ׀ בַּחֹדֶשׁ הַשְּׁבִיעִי בְּאֶחָד לַחֹדֶשׁ יִהְיֶה לָכֶם שַׁבָּתוֹן זִכְרוֹן תְּרוּעָה מִקְרָא קֹדֶשׁ : (25) כָּל מְלֶאכֶת עֲבֹדָה לֹא תַעֲשׂוּ ׀ וְהִקְרַבְתֶּם אִשֶּׁה לַיהוָה

But what is the deeper significance of Yom Teruah? Yom Teruah is sometimes called 'the feast of which no man knows the day or the hour' because, like the Head of the Year, we cannot know in advance the day or the hour it will begin. Rather, we must wait until YHWH shows us the first crescent sliver of His new moon.

As we will see in the chapters that follow, Yeshua was probably conceived during the Festival of Hanukkah, and was likely born on the first day of the fall Feast of Tabernacles. We have already seen that He was put to death in fulfillment of the Passover, and that He also fulfilled the Days of Unleavened Bread, the Omer, and the Pentecost. In like fashion, many scholars believe Yeshua will return in fulfillment of the Day of Trumpets, because just as no man knows the day or the hour of the Day of Trumpets before the first crescent sliver of the new moon is physically seen, Yeshua tells us that no man knows the day or the hour in which He will physically return, either.

Mattai (Matthew) 24:29-32
29 "Immediately after the tribulation of those days the sun will be darkened, and the moon will not give its light; the stars will fall from heaven, and the powers of the heavens will be shaken.
30 Then the sign of the Son of Man will appear in heaven, and then all the tribes of the earth will mourn, and they will see the Son of Man coming on the clouds of heaven with power and great glory.
31 And He will send His angels with a great sound of a trumpet, and they will gather together His elect from the four winds, from one end of heaven to the other.
32 "Now learn this parable from the fig tree: When its branch has already become tender and puts forth leaves, you know that summer is near.

In the Parable of the Fig Tree, Yeshua seems to tell us that we can know the general season of His return in advance, yet we cannot know the exact time. This is in the same way as we can know when the Fall Festival Season approaches, but still we must wait for YHWH to show us the first crescent sliver of the new moon.

Mattai (Matthew) 24:36-44
36 "But of that day and hour no one knows, not even the angels of heaven, but My Father only.
37 But as the days of Noah were, so also will the coming of the Son of Man be.

38 For as in the days before the flood, they were eating and drinking, marrying and giving in marriage, until the day that Noah entered the ark,

39 and did not know until the flood came and took them all away, so also will the coming of the Son of Man be.

40 Then two men will be in the field: one will be taken and the other left.

41 Two women will be grinding at the mill: one will be taken and the other left.

42 Watch therefore, for you do not know what hour your Adon is coming.

43 But know this, that if the master of the house had known what hour the thief would come, he would have watched and not allowed his house to be broken into.

44 Therefore you also be ready, for the Son of Man is coming at an hour you do not expect.

We are to know the general time when the Son of Man will appear, yet we cannot know the exact hour of His appearance until He actually arrives. Therefore, we are to be alert, wait, and watch.

Mattai (Matthew) 25:1-13

1 "Then the kingdom of heaven shall be likened to ten virgins who took their lamps and went out to meet the bridegroom.

2 Now five of them were wise, and five were foolish.

3 Those who were foolish took their lamps and took no oil with them,

4 but the wise took oil in their vessels with their lamps.

5 But while the bridegroom was delayed, they all slumbered and slept.

6 "And at midnight a cry was heard: 'Behold, the bridegroom is coming; go out to meet him!'

7 Then all those virgins arose and trimmed their lamps.

8 And the foolish said to the wise, 'Give us some of your oil, for our lamps are going out.'

9 But the wise answered, saying, 'No, lest there should not be enough for us and you; but go rather to those who sell, and buy for yourselves.'

10 And while they went to buy, the bridegroom came, and those who were ready went in with him to the wedding; and the door was shut.

11 "Afterward the other virgins came also, saying, 'Master! Master! Open to us!'

12 But he answered and said, 'Assuredly, I say to you, I do not know you.'

13 "Watch therefore, for you know neither the day nor the hour in which the Son of Man is coming.

Judaism teaches that the ten days beginning with Yom Teruah and ending with Yom Kippur (the Day of Atonement) are called the 'Ten Days of Awe.' The last service on Yom Kippur is called 'Neilah', which means, literally, 'locked', the concept being that YHWH locks the doors of heaven against us at that time, if we have not already repented and entered into His kingdom.

Qorintim Aleph (1st Cor.) 15:50-52
50 Now this I say, brethren, that flesh and blood cannot inherit the kingdom of Elohim; nor does corruption inherit incorruption.
51 Behold, I tell you a mystery: We shall not all sleep, but we shall all be changed —
52 in a moment, in the twinkling of an eye, at the last trumpet. For the trumpet will sound, and the dead will be raised incorruptible, and we shall be changed.

Many scholars believe that this passage in First Corinthians implies that Yeshua will return on Yom Teruah, since we will be changed at His coming, which will occur at the last trumpet.

Trumpets are also mentioned many other places in Scripture, and trumpets are usually associated with judgment and the final redemption. This is consistent with the theme of the Fall Feasts in general.

While there are many rabbinical traditions associated with Yom Teruah, many of them contradict Scripture. It is not our purpose to detail those rabbinical traditions here, but one of these rabbinical customs has become recorded in Scripture, and therefore we need to discuss it.

Another term for the Head of Months is the Head of the Year, and in Hebrew, the term for the Head of the Year is 'Rosh Hashanah.' As we saw earlier, YHWH tells us that Rosh Hashanah begins on the first day of the first month.

Shemote (Exodus) 12:2
2 "This month is the head of months for you; it is the first month of the year to you."

The rabbis, however, have developed a ruling that Rosh Hashanah should be celebrated not on the first day of the first month, but on the first two days of the seventh month. The development of this tradition is complex, and it is not our purpose to detail it here, but it seems this rabbinical custom may have already been in place by the end of the Babylonian Exile, as evidenced by the fact that Ezra held a set-apart assembly on the first two days of the seventh month.

Nehemiah 8:2-3 shows us how Ezra assembled the people on the first day of the seventh month.

> *Nehemiah 8:2-3*
> *2 So Ezra the priest brought the Torah before the assembly of men and women and all who could hear with understanding on the first day of the seventh month.*
> *3 Then he read from it in the open square that was in front of the Water Gate from morning until midday, before the men and women and those who could understand; and the ears of all the people were attentive to the Book of the Torah.*

Then Nehemiah 8:13 shows us how Ezra led a second day of set-apart assembly on the second day of the seventh month.

Nehemiah 8:13
13 Now on the second day the heads of the fathers' houses of all the people, with the priests and Levites, were gathered to Ezra the scribe, in order to understand the words of the Torah.

The rabbis today celebrate Rosh Hashanah on the first two days of the seventh month, identical with how Ezra the priest did so.

There are many other rabbinical customs surrounding Yom Teruah which we will not attempt to explore here.

The Day of Atonements (Yom Kippur)

The tenth day of the seventh month is called by several names, but it is usually called Yom Kippur, or the Day of Atonement. However, the Torah actually calls it Yom HaKippurim (יוֹם הַכִּפּוּרִים), or 'The Day of the Atonements (plural).'

The Day of the Atonements is the most set-apart day of our year. YHWH tells us not to do any work at all on this day, for YHWH promises to cut off anyone who does not make this a day of complete rest.

Leviticus 23:26-32	
26 And YHWH spoke to Moshe, saying:	(26) וַיְדַבֵּר יְהוָה אֶל מֹשֶׁה לֵּאמֹר :
27 "Also the tenth day of this seventh month shall be the Day of the Atonements. It shall be a set-apart gathering for you; you shall afflict your souls, and offer an offering made by fire to YHWH.	(27) אַךְ בֶּעָשׂוֹר לַחֹדֶשׁ הַשְּׁבִיעִי הַזֶּה יוֹם הַכִּפֻּרִים הוּא מִקְרָא קֹדֶשׁ יִהְיֶה לָכֶם וְעִנִּיתֶם אֶת נַפְשֹׁתֵיכֶם l וְהִקְרַבְתֶּם אִשֶּׁה לַיהוָה :
28 And you shall do no work on that same day, for it is the Day of Atonements, to make atonement for you before YHWH your Elohim.	(28) וְכָל מְלָאכָה לֹא תַעֲשׂוּ בְּעֶצֶם הַיּוֹם הַזֶּה l כִּי יוֹם כִּפֻּרִים הוּא לְכַפֵּר עֲלֵיכֶם לִפְנֵי יְהוָה אֱלֹהֵיכֶם :
29 For any person who is not afflicted in soul on that same day shall be cut off	(29) כִּי כָל הַנֶּפֶשׁ אֲשֶׁר

from his people.
30 And any person who does any work on that same day, that person I will destroy from among his people.
31 You shall do no manner of work; it shall be a statute forever throughout your generations in all your dwellings.
32 It shall be to you a sabbath of solemn rest, and you shall afflict your souls; on the ninth day of the month at evening, from evening to evening, you shall celebrate your sabbath."

לֹא תְעֻנֶּה בְּעֶצֶם הַיּוֹם הַזֶּה | וְנִכְרְתָה מֵעַמֶּיהָ : (30) וְכָל הַנֶּפֶשׁ אֲשֶׁר תַּעֲשֶׂה כָּל מְלָאכָה בְּעֶצֶם הַיּוֹם הַזֶּה | וְהַאֲבַדְתִּי אֶת הַנֶּפֶשׁ הַהִוא מִקֶּרֶב עַמָּהּ : (31) כָּל מְלָאכָה לֹא תַעֲשׂוּ | חֻקַּת עוֹלָם לְדֹרֹתֵיכֶם בְּכֹל מֹשְׁבֹתֵיכֶם : (32) שַׁבַּת שַׁבָּתוֹן הוּא לָכֶם וְעִנִּיתֶם אֶת נַפְשֹׁתֵיכֶם | בְּתִשְׁעָה לַחֹדֶשׁ בָּעֶרֶב מֵעֶרֶב עַד עֶרֶב תִּשְׁבְּתוּ שַׁבַּתְּכֶם :

Yom HaKippurim is called 'the Fast' at Acts 27:9, because it is traditionally observed by abstaining from both food and water for twenty-four hours.

Ma'asim (Acts) 27:9-10
9 Now when much time had been spent, and sailing was now dangerous because the Fast was already over, Shaul advised them,
10 saying, "Men, I perceive that this voyage will end with disaster and much loss, not only of the cargo and ship, but also our lives."

However, while fasting is a good way to afflict one's soul, the commandment is not necessarily to fast, but rather to afflict one's soul from the evening ending the ninth of the month, to the evening ending the tenth.

> *Vayiqra (Leviticus) 23:32*
> *32 It shall be to you a sabbath of solemn rest, and you shall afflict your souls; on the ninth day of the month at evening, from evening to evening, you shall celebrate your sabbath."*

While fasting can lead to desirable spiritual benefits, let us recognize that it is not always medically appropriate for diabetics, intensive care patients and/or nursing mothers to fast. If one's medical condition precludes fasting, then other forms of self-affliction, such as wearing sack cloth next to the skin, still fulfill YHWH's commandment to afflict our souls.

Numbers 29:7-11 gives a second witness that we are to abstain from all forms of work on this day. It also gives us a list of the sacrifices YHWH expects the priesthood to offer on Yom HaKippurim, whenever a Temple or Tabernacle stands.

> *Bemidbar (Numbers) 29:7-11*
> *7 "On the tenth day of this seventh month you shall have a set-apart convocation. You shall afflict your souls; you shall not do any work.*
> *8 You shall present a burnt offering to YHWH as a sweet aroma: one young bull, one ram, and seven lambs in their first year. Be sure they are without blemish.*

9 Their grain offering shall be of fine flour mixed with oil: three-tenths of an ephah for the bull, two-tenths for the one ram,
10 and one-tenth for each of the seven lambs;
11 also one kid of the goats as a sin offering, besides the sin offering for atonement, the regular burnt offering with its grain offering, and their drink offerings."

Hebrews 9:7 tells us these sacrifices were to atone for sins the people committed in ignorance.

Ivrim (Hebrews) 9:7
7 But into the second part the high priest went alone once a year, not without blood, which he offered for himself and for the people's sins committed in ignorance....

However, the High Priest also sent a scapegoat forth into the wilderness.

Vayiqra (Leviticus) 16:1-34
1 Now YHWH spoke to Moshe after the death of the two sons of Aharon, when they offered profane fire before YHWH, and died;
2 And YHWH said to Moshe: "Tell Aharon your brother not to come at just any time into the Set-apart Place inside the veil, before the mercy seat which is on the ark, lest he die; for I will appear in the cloud above the mercy seat.

3 "Thus Aharon shall come into the Set-apart Place: with the blood of a young bull as a sin offering, and of a ram as a burnt offering.

4 He shall put the Set-apart linen tunic and the linen trousers on his body; he shall be girded with a linen sash, and with the linen turban he shall be attired. These are Set-apart garments. Therefore he shall wash his body in water, and put them on.

5 And he shall take from the congregation of the children of Israel two kids of the goats as a sin offering, and one ram as a burnt offering.

6 "Aharon shall offer the bull as a sin offering, which is for himself, and make atonement for himself and for his house.

7 He shall take the two goats and present them before YHWH at the door of the Tabernacle of Meeting.

8 Then Aharon shall cast lots for the two goats: one lot for YHWH and the other lot for the scapegoat.

9 And Aharon shall bring the goat on which YHWH's lot fell, and offer it as a sin offering.

10 But the goat on which the lot fell to be the scapegoat shall be presented alive before YHWH, to make atonement upon it, and to let it go as the scapegoat into the wilderness.

11 "And Aharon shall bring the bull of the sin offering, which is for himself, and make atonement for himself and

for his house, and shall kill the bull as the sin offering which is for himself.

12 Then he shall take a censer full of burning coals of fire from the altar before YHWH, with his hands full of sweet incense beaten fine, and bring it inside the veil.

13 And he shall put the incense on the fire before YHWH, that the cloud of incense may cover the mercy seat that is on the Testimony, lest he die.

14 He shall take some of the blood of the bull and sprinkle it with his finger on the mercy seat on the east side; and before the mercy seat he shall sprinkle some of the blood with his finger seven times.

15 "Then he shall kill the goat of the sin offering, which is for the people, bring its blood inside the veil, do with that blood as he did with the blood of the bull, and sprinkle it on the mercy seat and before the mercy seat.

16 So he shall make atonement for the Set-apart Place, because of the uncleanness of the children of Israel, and because of their transgressions, for all their sins; and so he shall do for the tabernacle of meeting which remains among them in the midst of their uncleanness.

17 There shall be no man in the tabernacle of meeting when he goes in to make atonement in the Set-apart Place, until he comes out, that he may make atonement for himself, for his

household, and for all the assembly of Israel.

18 And he shall go out to the altar that is before YHWH, and make atonement for it, and shall take some of the blood of the bull and some of the blood of the goat, and put it on the horns of the altar all around.

19 Then he shall sprinkle some of the blood on it with his finger seven times, cleanse it, and consecrate it from the uncleanness of the children of Israel.

20 "And when he has made an end of atoning for the Set-apart Place, the Tabernacle of meeting, and the altar, he shall bring the live goat.

21 Aharon shall lay both his hands on the head of the live goat, confess over it all the iniquities of the children of Israel, and all their transgressions, concerning all their sins, putting them on the head of the goat, and shall send it away into the wilderness by the hand of a suitable man.

22 The goat shall bear on itself all their iniquities to an uninhabited land; and he shall release the goat in the wilderness.

23 "Then Aharon shall come into the tabernacle of meeting, shall take off the linen garments which he put on when he went into the Set-apart Place, and shall leave them there.

24 And he shall wash his body with water in a Set-apart place, put on his garments, come out and offer his burnt offering and the burnt offering of

the people, and make atonement for himself and for the people.

25 The fat of the sin offering he shall burn on the altar.

26 And he who released the goat as the scapegoat shall wash his clothes and bathe his body in water, and afterward he may come into the camp.

27 The bull for the sin offering and the goat for the sin offering, whose blood was brought in to make atonement in the Set-apart Place, shall be carried outside the camp. And they shall burn in the fire their skins, their flesh, and their offal.

28 Then he who burns them shall wash his clothes and bathe his body in water, and afterward he may come into the camp.

29 "This shall be a statute forever for you: In the seventh month, on the tenth day of the month, you shall afflict your souls, and do no work at all, whether a native of your own country or a stranger who dwells among you.

30 For on that day the priest shall make atonement for you, to cleanse you, that you may be clean from all your sins before YHWH.

31 It is a sabbath of solemn rest for you, and you shall afflict your souls. It is a statute forever.

32 And the priest, who is anointed and consecrated to minister as priest in his father's place, shall make atonement,

and put on the linen clothes, the Set-apart garments;

33 then he shall make atonement for the Set-apart Sanctuary, and he shall make atonement for the tabernacle of meeting and for the altar, and he shall make atonement for the priests and for all the people of the assembly.

34 This shall be an everlasting statute for you, to make atonement for the children of Israel, for all their sins, once a year." And he did as YHWH commanded Moshe.

While extremely controversial, since the scapegoat was sent forth to bear "all" the sins of the people, some scholars believe the scapegoat even served to atone for sins that had been committed intentionally, provided the sinner had later repented of his sin (as in the case of King David's infamous sin with Bathsheba). The Talmud tells us that the people knew when their sins had been forgiven, for the High Priest tied one piece of scarlet wool on the horns of the scapegoat, and then YHWH would supernaturally cause this piece of scarlet wool to turn white when He had forgiven their sins.

Isaiah 1:18 18 "Come now, and let us reason together," says YHWH. "Though your sins are like scarlet, they shall be as white as snow; Though they are red like crimson, they shall be as wool.	‫(18) לְכוּ נָא וְנִוָּכְחָה‬ ‫יֹאמַר יְהוָה אִם יִהְיוּ‬ ‫חֲטָאֵיכֶם כַּשָּׁנִים כַּשֶּׁלֶג‬ ‫יַלְבִּינוּ אִם יַאְדִּימוּ‬ ‫כַתּוֹלָע כַּצֶּמֶר יִהְיוּ‬

According to the Talmud, a second piece of wool was tied first to the door of the Temple, and then later to a rock, so that those in the Temple would also be able to see when YHWH had forgiven his people.

> *R. Nahman b. Isaac said it was the tongue of scarlet, as it has been taught: Originally they used to fasten the thread of scarlet on the door of the [Temple] court on the outside. 28 If it turned white the people used to rejoice, 29 and if it did not turn white they were sad. They therefore made a rule that it should be fastened to the door of the court on the inside. People, however, still peeped in and saw, and if it turned white they rejoiced and if it did not turn white they were sad. They therefore made a rule that half of it should be fastened to the rock and half between the horns of the goat that was sent [to the wilderness].*
> *[Babylonian Talmud, Rosh Hashanah 31b, Soncino Press]*

The Talmud also tells us that forty years before the destruction of the Temple, the scarlet thread stopped turning white. It now remained red, indicating that YHWH was no longer forgiving His people their sins.

> *For forty years before the destruction of the Temple the thread of scarlet never turned white but it remained red.*
> *[Babylonian Talmud, Rosh Hashanah 31b, Soncino Press]*

Tractate Yoma 39b gives us a second witness that for the last forty years before the destruction of the Temple, the "crimson-coloured strap" no longer turned white.

> **Our Rabbis taught: During the last forty years before the destruction of the Temple the lot [For the Lord] [sic] did not come up in the right hand; nor did the crimson-coloured strap become white; nor did the westernmost light shine; and the doors of the Hekal would open by themselves, until R. Johanan b. Zakkai rebuked them, saying: Hekal, Hekal, why wilt thou be the alarmer thyself?5 [Babylonian Talmud Tractate Yoma 39b, Soncino Press]**

If the Temple was destroyed in 70 CE, forty years prior to that date puts the cessation of this miracle circa 30 CE, which is when many scholars believe Yeshua died for our sins, and was raised again the third day.

The Talmud contains many different sorts of entries, some of which seem factual, and many of which seem controversial. However, if this particular miracle as recorded in Talmud is to be believed, it seems it could only have been a sign from YHWH, showing His people that Yeshua really was their Messiah, and that the blood of mere bulls and goats would no longer be enough to cause Him to forgive His people's sins.

And while Scripture does not specify, there are others who believe that the Day of Atonement is above all a day when we are to make sure we are in right standing before Yahweh our Elohim. It is a day when we are to release others from debts, whether financial, emotional, or spiritual. If our hearts are hard towards anyone for something evil that he has done towards us, it is a day for releasing those old debts, in forgiveness, no matter how fresh the present hurt.

Scripture does not say whether the fast of Isaiah 58 pertains directly to Yom Kippur or not, but many draw parallels to this passage.

> *Yeshayahu (Isaiah) 58:1-12*
> *58 "Cry aloud, spare not;*
> *Lift up your voice like a trumpet;*
> *Tell My people their transgression,*
> *And the house of Jacob their sins.*
> *2 Yet they seek Me daily,*
> *And delight to know My ways,*
> *As a nation that did righteousness,*
> *And did not forsake the ordinance of their Elohim. They ask of Me the ordinances of justice;*
> *They take delight in approaching Elohim.*
> *3 'Why have we fasted,' they say, 'and You have not seen? Why have we afflicted our souls, and You take no notice?'*
> *"In fact, in the day of your fast you find pleasure, And exploit all your laborers.*
> *4 Indeed you fast for strife and debate,*
> *And to strike with the fist of wickedness. You will not fast as you do this day,*
> *To make your voice heard on high.*
> *5 Is it a fast that I have chosen,*
> *A day for a man to afflict his soul?*
> *Is it to bow down his head like a bulrush,*
> *And to spread out sackcloth and ashes?*
> *Would you call this a fast,*
> *And an acceptable day to Yahweh?*

6 "Is this not the fast that I have chosen:
To loose the bonds of wickedness,
To undo the heavy burdens,
To let the oppressed go free,
And that you break every yoke?
7 Is it not to share your bread with the hungry,
And that you bring to your house the poor
who are cast out;
When you see the naked, that you cover him,
And not hide yourself from your own flesh?
8 Then your light shall break forth like the
morning,
Your healing shall spring forth speedily,
And your righteousness shall go before you;
The glory of Yahweh shall be your rear guard.
9 Then you shall call, and Yahweh will answer;
You shall cry, and He will say, 'Here I am.'
"If you take away the yoke from your midst,
The pointing of the finger, and speaking
wickedness,
10 If you extend your soul to the hungry
And satisfy the afflicted soul,
Then your light shall dawn in the darkness,
And your darkness shall be as the noonday.
11 Yahweh will guide you continually,
And satisfy your soul in drought,
And strengthen your bones;
You shall be like a watered garden,
And like a spring of water, whose waters do
not fail.
12 Those from among you
Shall build the old waste places;
You shall raise up the foundations of many
generations;
And you shall be called the Repairer of the
Breach,
The Restorer of Streets to Dwell In."

Clearly, it is important to search ourselves every day, to see where we can improve before Yahweh. However, if there is any one calendar day that it is "most important" to humble ourselves before Yahweh, and see where and how we can do more righteousness, Yom Kippur would be that calendar day.

The Feast of Tabernacles (Sukkot)

In the chapter on Hanukkah we discuss why Yeshua was probably born on the first day of the Fall Feast of Tabernacles, otherwise known as the Feast of Booths, or Sukkot. But why does YHWH command us to hold the Feast of Sukkot? What is the significance? What are we to learn from it?

In Hebraic thought, a sukka is different than a tent. In ancient times, tents were typically larger structures that families could live in, which were oftentimes moved on carts with donkeys, or with camels. In contrast, the Hebrew word for a tent is an 'oh-hel' (אֹהֶל), while the word for a tabernacle or a booth is 'sukka' (סֻכָּה). The plural of sukka is sukkot (סֻכֹּת).

But what do sukkot represent? We find sukkot in Scripture whenever YHWH's people have just escaped from some grave and intense danger. For example, after Esau came out with four hundred men to kill Jacob, and YHWH delivered Jacob from the crisis, Jacob then journeyed to a place called Sukkot, where he then built sukkot for his livestock.

B'reisheet (Genesis) 33:17 17 And Jacob journeyed to Succoth, built himself a house, and made booths for his livestock. Therefore the name of the place is called Sukkot.	‏(17) וְיַעֲקֹב נָסַע סֻכֹּתָה וַיִּבֶן לוֹ בָּיִת ׀ וּלְמִקְנֵהוּ עָשָׂה סֻכֹּת עַל כֵּן קָרָא שֵׁם הַמָּקוֹם סֻכּוֹת

Sukkot are also a place of freedom. For example, when Pharaoh finally let the children of Israel go after the plague on the firstborn and they were driven out of Egypt, they went to a place called Sukkot.

> *Shemote (Exodus) 12:36-38*
> *36 And YHWH had given the people favor in the sight of the Egyptians, so that they granted them what they requested. Thus they plundered the Egyptians.*
> *37 Then the children of Israel journeyed from Rameses to Sukkot, about six hundred thousand men on foot, besides children.*
> *38 A mixed multitude went up with them also, and flocks and herds — a great deal of livestock.*

According to Jewish tradition, a sukka is a rather flimsy structure. This is meant to symbolize how, when the children of Israel had just left Egypt, they were basically unarmed, unprotected, and vulnerable to the elements. Even though the flimsy structures they built gave hardly any protection from the elements, it acknowledges that safety and security do not ultimately come from thick walls, fortifications, armies, gold, silver, or securities. Safety does not come from alliances, but only from the hand of YHWH. When YHWH is with us, even a weak shelter can give us sufficient protection from heat, cold, and enemies. However, if YHWH is against us, no shelter can protect us, no matter how sturdily it is built, or how well it is defended. This may be one reason why YHWH has us dwell in sukkot every year, so we remember that our lives depend on Him, and His will.

In rabbinic thought, Israel enters mortal danger each year during the Fall Festival Season. In rabbinical thought, Yom Teruah symbolizes divine judgment, and Yom Kippur is also a time of judgment. After these times of danger, Israel then dwells in sukkot, which are places of safety and freedom. In rabbinic thought, this is also why YHWH tells us that the Feast of Sukkot is to be a time of rejoicing at the many blessings that YHWH has given us.

> *Devarim (Deuteronomy) 16:13-17*
> *13 "You shall observe the Feast of Tabernacles seven days, when you have gathered from your threshing floor and from your winepress.*
>
> *First tithe*
>
> *14 And you shall rejoice in your feast, you and your son and your daughter, your male servant and your female servant and the Levite, the stranger and the fatherless and the widow, who are within your gates.*
>
> *Third tithe*
>
> *15 Seven days you shall keep a sacred feast to YHWH your Elohim in the place which YHWH chooses, because YHWH your Elohim will bless you in all your produce and in all the work of your hands, so that you surely rejoice.*
>
> *Second tithe*

16 "Three times a year all your males shall appear before YHWH your Elohim in the place which He chooses: at the Feast of Unleavened Bread, at the Feast of Weeks, and at the Feast of Tabernacles; and they shall not appear before YHWH empty-handed.
17 Every man shall give as he is able, according to the blessing of YHWH your Elohim which He has given you.

Great Commission. Heart condition.

The Feast of Sukkot is often thought of as being eight days long. However, in actuality it is seven days long, and is then followed immediately by a one-day festival called Shemini Atzeret, which means essentially, 'The Eighth Day Assembly', or 'The Last Great Day.'

Vayiqra (Leviticus) 23:33-44
33 Then YHWH spoke to Moshe, saying,
34 "Speak to the children of Israel, saying: 'The fifteenth day of this seventh month shall be the Feast of Tabernacles for seven days to YHWH.
35 On the first day there shall be a set-apart gathering. You shall do no customary work on it.
36 For seven days you shall offer an offering made by fire to YHWH. On the eighth day you shall have a set-apart gathering, and you shall offer an offering made by fire to YHWH. It is a set-apart assembly, and you shall do no customary work on it.

37 'These are the feasts of YHWH which you shall proclaim to be set-apart gatherings, to offer an offering made by fire to YHWH, a burnt offering and a grain offering, a sacrifice and drink offerings, everything on its day,
38 besides the Sabbaths of YHWH, besides your gifts, besides all your vows, and besides all your freewill offerings which you give to YHWH.

Then in the next five verses, YHWH again tells us how He wants His festival celebrated, using different terms.

39 'Also on the fifteenth day of the seventh month, when you have gathered in the fruit of the land, you shall keep the feast of YHWH for seven days; on the first day there shall be a sabbath-rest, and on the eighth day a sabbath-rest.

In verse 40, YHWH tells us to take four species of plants on the first day of the festival.

40 And you shall take for yourselves on the first day the fruit of beautiful trees, branches of palm trees, the boughs of leafy trees, and willows of the brook; and you shall rejoice before YHWH your Elohim for seven days.	(40) וּלְקַחְתֶּם לָכֶם בַּיּוֹם הָרִאשׁוֹן פְּרִי עֵץ הָדָר כַּפֹּת תְּמָרִים וַעֲנַף עֵץ עָבֹת וְעַרְבֵי נַחַל וּשְׂמַחְתֶּם לִפְנֵי יְהוָה אֱלֹהֵיכֶם שִׁבְעַת יָמִים

Rabbinic interpretation tells us that the fruit of beautiful trees, the branches of palm trees, the boughs of leafy trees and the willows of the brook are the etrog (citron, similar to a lemon), the lulav (palm branch), the myrtle and the aravot (willow), respectively. However, we should note that the Torah does not specify four exact species.

41 You shall keep it as a feast to YHWH for seven days in the year. It shall be a statute forever in your generations. You shall celebrate it in the seventh month.
42 You shall dwell in booths for seven days. All who are native Israelites shall dwell in booths,
43 that your generations may know that I made the children of Israel dwell in booths when I brought them out of the land of Egypt: I am YHWH your Elohim.'"
44 So Moshe declared to the children of Israel the feasts of YHWH.

When the children of Israel returned from the Exile to Babylon, they even built their sukkot out of the four species. However, this is not commanded in Torah.

Nehemiah 8:13-18
13 Now on the second day the heads of the fathers' houses of all the people, with the priests and Levites, were gathered to Ezra the scribe, in order to understand the words of the Torah.
14 And they found written in the Torah, which YHWH had commanded by Moshe, that the children of Israel

177

should dwell in sukkot during the feast of the seventh month,

15 and that they should announce and proclaim in all their cities and in Jerusalem, saying, "Go out to the mountain, and bring olive branches, branches of oil trees, myrtle branches, palm branches, and branches of leafy trees, to make booths , as it is written."

16 Then the people went out and brought them and made themselves booths, each one on the roof of his house, or in their courtyards or the courts of the house of Elohim, and in the open square of the Water Gate and in the open square of the Gate of Ephraim.

17 So the whole assembly of those who had returned from the captivity made booths and sat under the booths; for since the days of Joshua the son of Nun until that day the children of Israel had not done so. And there was very great gladness.

18 Also day by day, from the first day until the last day, he read from the Book of the Torah of Elohim. And they kept the feast seven days; and on the eighth day there was a sacred assembly, according to the prescribed manner.

Verse 18 tells us that Ezra read the entire Book of the Torah to the people during the Feast of Sukkot, in keeping with the command in Deuteronomy 31.

Devarim (Deuteronomy) 31:10-13

10 And Moshe commanded them, saying: "At the end of every seven years, at the appointed time in the year of release, at the Feast of Tabernacles,
11 when all Israel comes to appear before YHWH your Elohim in the place which He chooses, you shall read this law before all Israel in their hearing.
12 Gather the people together, men and women and little ones, and the stranger who is within your gates, that they may hear and that they may learn to fear YHWH your Elohim and carefully observe all the words of this Torah,
13 and that their children, who have not known it, may hear and learn to fear YHWH your Elohim as long as you live in the land which you cross the Jordan to possess."

That Ezra read from the Torah during the feast may indicate that it was a sabbatical year, or it may indicate that since the children of Israel had not read from the Torah for many years (and in fact may no longer have known when the sabbatical year was), they fulfilled the commandment of the sabbatical year, to be safe.

During the feast there is a traditional water drawing ceremony called Nisuch HaMayim (נסוך המים), or the 'pouring of the water.' Yeshua tells us that this festival was symbolic of Him.

Yochanan (John) 7:37-41
37 On the last day, that great day of the feast, Yeshua stood and cried out,

*saying, "If anyone thirsts, let him come
to Me and drink.*

*38 He who believes in Me, as the
Scripture has said, out of his heart will
flow rivers of living water."*

*39 But this He spoke concerning the
Spirit, whom those believing in Him
would receive; for the Set-apart Spirit
was not yet given, because Yeshua
was not yet glorified.*

*40 Therefore many from the crowd,
when they heard this saying, said,
"Truly this is the Prophet."*

41 Others said, "This is the Messiah."

Zechariah 14 tells us that in the future, the nations of
the world must come up to Jerusalem for the Feast of
Tabernacles, or else they will have no rain.

Zechariah 14:16-21
*16 And it shall come to pass that
everyone who is left of all the nations
which came against Jerusalem shall
go up from year to year to worship the
King, YHWH of hosts, and to keep the
Feast of Tabernacles.*

*17 And it shall be that whichever of the
families of the earth do not come up to
Jerusalem to worship the King, YHWH
of hosts, on them there will be no rain.*

*18 If the family of Egypt will not come
up and enter in, they shall have no
rain; they shall receive the plague with
which YHWH strikes the nations who
do not come up to keep the Feast of
Tabernacles.*

19 This shall be the punishment of Egypt and the punishment of all the nations that do not come up to keep the Feast of Tabernacles.

Ezekiel 45 further tells us that in the future, the Prince of Israel will offer burnt offerings during the feast.

Yehezqel (Ezekiel) 45:25
25 "In the seventh month, on the fifteenth day of the month, at the feast, he [the prince] shall do likewise for seven days, according to the sin offering, the burnt offering, the grain offering, and the oil."

The Book of Acts gives us an example of how YHWH protects His people with tabernacles.

Ma'aseh (Acts) 15:12-17
12 Then all the multitude kept silent and listened to Barnabas and Shaul declaring how many miracles and wonders Elohim had worked through them among the Gentiles.
13 And after they had become silent, Ya'akov answered, saying, "Men and brethren, listen to me:
14 Shimon has declared how Elohim at the first visited the Gentiles to take out of them a people for His name.
15 And with this the words of the prophets agree, just as it is written:
16 'After this I will return, and will rebuild the tabernacle of David, which has fallen down. I will rebuild its ruins, and I will set it up;

17 So that the rest of mankind may seek YHWH, even all the Gentiles who are called by My name, says YHWH who does all these things.'

Ya'akov (James) is quoting Amos 9:11, showing that YHWH's sukka is a protection for us. This same theme of YHWH protecting us in His sukka is echoed in Isaiah Chapter Four.

Yeshayahu (Isaiah) 4
1 And in that day seven women shall take hold of one man, saying, "We will eat our own food and wear our own apparel, only let us be called by your name, to take away our reproach."
2 In that day the Branch of YHWH shall be beautiful and glorious, and the fruit of the earth shall be excellent and appealing for those of Israel who have escaped.
3 And it shall come to pass that he who is left in Zion and remains in Jerusalem will be called set-apart — everyone who is recorded among the living in Jerusalem.
4 When YHWH has washed away the filth of the daughters of Zion, and purged the blood of Jerusalem from her midst, by the spirit of judgment and by the spirit of burning,
5 then YHWH will create above every dwelling place of Mount Zion, and above her assemblies, a cloud and smoke by day and the shining of a flaming fire by night. For over all the glory there will be a covering.

> *6 And there will be a tabernacle for shade in the daytime from the heat, for a place of refuge, and for a shelter from storm and rain.*

According to Talmud Tractate Succah, the priesthood lit four enormous golden candlesticks in the Court of Women within the Temple, during the Water Libation Ceremony (נסוך המים). The wicks were made from old priestly garments, and according to the Talmud, the light was so bright that there was not a courtyard in all of Jerusalem that was not illuminated by its light during the festival. If this record is true, then could it be that Yeshua said this festival rightly referred to Him?

> **Yochanan (John) 8:12**
> *12 Then Yeshua spoke to them again, saying, "I am the light of the world. He who follows Me shall not walk in darkness, but have the light of life."*

We will say more about how Yeshua was probably born on the Feast of Tabernacles in the chapter on Hanukkah, but let us take a look at the following Scripture passages, remembering that a major theme of the Feast of Sukkot is joy.

> **Luqa (Luke) 2:4-11**
> *6 So it was, that while they were there, the days were completed for her to be delivered.*
> *7 And she brought forth her firstborn Son, and wrapped Him in swaddling cloths, and laid Him in a manger, because there was no room for them in the inn.*

8 Now there were in the same country shepherds living out in the fields, keeping watch over their flock by night. 9 And behold, a messenger of YHWH stood before them, and the glory of YHWH shone around them, and they were greatly afraid.

10 Then the angel said to them, "Do not be afraid, for behold, I bring you good tidings of great joy which will be to all people.

11 For there is born to you this day in the city of David a Savior, who is Messiah YHWH.

And:

Mattai (Matthew) 2:7-12

7 Then Herod, when he had secretly called the wise men, determined from them what time the star appeared.

8 And he sent them to Bethlehem and said, "Go and search carefully for the young Child, and when you have found Him, bring back word to me, that I may come and worship Him also."

9 When they heard the king, they departed; and behold, the star which they had seen in the East went before them, till it came and stood over where the young Child was.

10 When they saw the star, they rejoiced with exceedingly great joy.

The Eighth Day Assembly

When YHWH gave us the Torah Calendar, He did not choose the days at random. Rather, He incorporated specific days into His calendar in order to give us prophetic shadow pictures of the things He has purposed to come to pass.

In the last chapter on Sukkot we spoke briefly about the Last Great Day of the feast. This Last Great Day is also called 'Shemini Atzeret,' which means, essentially, 'The Assembly of the Eighth (Day)."

While the Assembly of the Eighth is often thought of simply as the final day of the Feast of Sukkot, it is actually a separate festival. This is in much the same way as the Passover is followed by the seven Days of Unleavened Bread. However, in this case, the seven days of Sukkot are followed by the one day Assembly of the Eighth (Shemini Atzeret).

In Hebrew, the word 'Atzeret' (עֲצֶרֶת) means not just 'an assembly,' but a very special kind of assembly. It indicates that one's host is not letting one go home. Rather, one's host is 'holding one over' for an extended period of time. Strong's Concordance defines the word atzeret (עצרת) in this way:

> **OT:6116 `atsarah (ats-aw-raw'); or `atsereth (ats-eh'-reth); from OT:6113; an assembly, especially on a festival or holiday:**

When we look up the root at Strong's OT:6113, we get:

185

OT:6113 `atsar (aw-tsar'); a primitive root; to enclose; by analogy, <u>to hold back</u>; also to maintain, rule, assemble: KJV - be able, close up, <u>detain</u>, fast, <u>keep</u> (self close, still), prevail, recover, refrain, reign, restrain, <u>retain</u>, shut (up), slack, stay, stop, withhold (self).

Shemini Atzeret, then, shows us that YHWH intends to hold us back, to detain us, or to 'close us up' in some fashion for the eighth day. But in what way does YHWH intend to 'detain us', or to 'hold us over'?

The Apostle Kepha (Peter) tells us that one prophetic day can symbolize a thousand earth years.

> **Kepha Bet (2nd Peter) 3:8**
> **8 But, beloved, do not forget this one thing: that with YHWH, one day is as a thousand years, and a thousand years is as one day.**

Notice, then, that Scripture tells us that the Creation Week was seven days long.

> **B'reisheet (Genesis) 2:2**
> **2 And on the seventh day Elohim ended His work which He had done, and He rested on the seventh day from all His work which He had done.**

If the Creation Week lasted seven days, and if one prophetic day can represent a thousand earth years, then the Creation Week is symbolic of a seven thousand year plan for the earth and its inhabitants.

But if the earth is to last for seven thousand years, then why would the Feast of Sukkot last for eight days? And what is the symbolism of the eighth day?

In truth, the Feast of Sukkot lasts only seven days. We know this because it is only for seven days that the children of Israel are to dwell in booths.

> *Vayiqra (Leviticus) 23:41-43*
> *41 You shall keep it as a feast to YHWH for seven days in the year. It shall be a statute forever in your generations. You shall celebrate it in the seventh month.*
> *42 You shall dwell in booths for seven days. All who are native Israelites shall dwell in booths,*
> *43 that your generations may know that I made the children of Israel dwell in booths when I brought them out of the land of Egypt: I am YHWH your Elohim.'"*

The eighth day of Sukkot, then, is really a separate festival. Leviticus 23:36 tells us that we are to hold an assembly (עֲצֶרֶת) on this eighth day in order to bring an offering made by fire. We are also to do no ordinary or laborious work.

> *Vayiqra (Leviticus) 23:36*
> *36 For seven days you shall offer an offering made by fire to YHWH. On the eighth day you shall have a set-apart assembly, and you shall offer an offering made by fire to YHWH. It is a set-apart assembly, and you shall do no customary work on it.*

Verse 39 then tells us to keep the first and the eighth days of the festival as set-apart sabbaths of rest.

> *Vayiqra (Leviticus) 23:39*
> *39 'Also on the fifteenth day of the seventh month, when you have gathered in the fruit of the land, you shall keep the feast of YHWH for seven days; on the first day there shall be a sabbath-rest, and on the eighth day a sabbath-rest.*

It may be that the first day of the feast symbolizes the first day of the Creation Week, when YHWH Elohim created the heavens and the earth.

> *B'reisheet (Genesis) 1:1-2*
> *1 In the beginning Elohim created the heavens and the earth.*
> *2 The earth was made formless and void; and darkness was on the face of the deep.*

If the first day of the Feast of Tabernacles symbolizes the first day of Creation, could it be that Shemini Atzeret symbolizes how we will go to the New Earth, which Isaiah speaks of?

> *Yeshayahu (Isaiah) 65:17-25*
> *17 "For behold, I create new heavens and a new earth; and the former shall not be remembered or come to mind.*
> *18 But be glad and rejoice forever in what I create; for behold, I create Jerusalem as a rejoicing, and her people a joy.*

188

19 I will rejoice in Jerusalem, and joy in My people; the voice of weeping shall no longer be heard in her, nor the voice of crying.
20 "No more shall an infant from there live but a few days, nor an old man who has not fulfilled his days; for the child shall die one hundred years old, But the sinner being one hundred years old shall be accursed."

While the Feast of Tabernacles is symbolic of many things, it is also symbolic of the New Earth, for the Book of the Revelation tells us that in the New Earth, the Tabernacle of Elohim will be with men.

Gilyana (Revelation) 21:1-4
1 Now I saw a new heaven and a new earth, for the first heaven and the first earth had passed away. Also there was no more sea.
2 Then I, Yochanan, saw the set-apart city, New Jerusalem, coming down out of heaven from Elohim, prepared as a bride adorned for her husband.
3 And I heard a loud voice from heaven saying, "Behold, the Tabernacle of Elohim is with men, and He will dwell with them, and they shall be His people. Elohim Himself will be with them, and be their Elohim.
4 "And Elohim will wipe away every tear from their eyes; there shall be no more death, nor sorrow, nor crying. There shall be no more pain, for the former things have passed away."

189

If YHWH wills, we will explore this topic in much more detail in the *Joseph's Return* study, as well as explore why Yeshua returns to take us to the New Earth at the end of the earth's seven thousand years.

Once we understand the prophetic symbolism of the number eight, we can begin to see this symbolism turn up throughout the Torah.

> **Vayiqra (Leviticus) 22:26-27**
> **26 And YHWH spoke to Moshe, saying:**
> **27 "When a bull or a sheep or a goat is born, it shall be seven days with its mother; and from the eighth day and thereafter it shall be accepted as an offering made by fire to YHWH."**

Yeshua tells us that those who believe on Him are like unto sheep, or to goats.

> **Mattai (Matthew) 25:33**
> **33 "When the Son of Man comes in His glory, and all the set-apart messengers with Him, then He will sit on the throne of His glory.**
> **32 All the nations will be gathered before Him, and He will separate them one from another, as a shepherd divides his sheep from the goats.**
> **33 And He will set the sheep on His right hand, but the goats on the left."**

For seven days, our sheep and our bulls and our goats are not acceptable as sacrifice offerings unto YHWH. In much the same way, for seven thousand years, the 'sheep' and the 'goats' and the 'bulls' who believe on Yeshua are not acceptable into YHWH's kingdom.

Rather, we must wait until the start of the 'Assembly of the Eighth', after the Judgment, when YHWH will 'hold us over' in the New Earth. Then we will Tabernacle with Him.

The Jubilees and the Shemittah

The first mention of the Jubilee is in Exodus 19:13, when Moshe received the Ten Commandments from YHWH at Mount Sinai. The word 'Jubilee' is 'ha-yovel' (הַיֹּבֵל), which most English versions render simply as 'trumpet.'

Exodus 19:13b 13b "When the trumpet sounds long, they shall come near the mountain."	(13) בִּמְשֹׁךְ הַיֹּבֵל הֵמָּה יַעֲלוּ בָהָר

Strong's Concordance tells us the word 'yovel' (יֹבֵל) means 'trumpet;' particularly silver trumpets.

> *OT:3104 yowbel (yo-bale'); or yobel (yob-ale'); apparently from OT:2986; the blast of a horn (from its continuous sound); specifically, the signal of the silver trumpets; hence, the instrument itself and the festival thus introduced: -jubile [sic], ram's horn, trumpet.*

The reference at OT:2896 has to do with flowing, and bringing forth, as in sounds (especially with pomp).

> *OT:2986 yabal (yaw-bal'); a primitive root; properly, to flow; causatively, to bring (especially with pomp):*
> *KJV - bring (forth), carry, lead (forth).*

However, the 'flowing' sound of the yovel is not always associated with silver trumpets. In the conquest of the Land of Canaan, the Yovel (הַיֹּבֵל) is associated with the ram's horn (called a 'shofar'). In Joshua 6:4-6 it is called the "trumpet of ram's horns" (שׁוֹפְרוֹת הַיּוֹבְלִים).

Joshua 6:4-7	
4 "And seven priests shall bear seven trumpets of rams' horns before the ark. But the seventh day you shall march around the city seven times, and the priests shall blow the trumpets (shofarot). 5 It shall come to pass, when they make a long blast with the ram's horn, and when you hear the sound of the trumpet, that all the people shall shout with a great shout; then the wall of the city will fall down flat. And the people shall go up every man straight before him." 6 Then Joshua the son of Nun called the priests and said to them, "Take up the ark of the covenant, and let seven priests bear seven trumpets of rams' horns before the ark of YHWH."	(4) וְשִׁבְעָה כֹהֲנִים יִשְׂאוּ שִׁבְעָה שׁוֹפְרוֹת הַיּוֹבְלִים לִפְנֵי הָאָרוֹן וּבַיּוֹם הַשְּׁבִיעִי תָּסֹבּוּ אֶת הָעִיר שֶׁבַע פְּעָמִים ׀ וְהַכֹּהֲנִים יִתְקְעוּ בַּשׁוֹפָרוֹת : (5) וְהָיָה בִּמְשֹׁךְ בְּקֶרֶן הַיּוֹבֵל בשמעכם [כְּשָׁמְעֲכֶם קרי] אֶת קוֹל הַשּׁוֹפָר יָרִיעוּ כָל הָעָם תְּרוּעָה גְדוֹלָה ׀ וְנָפְלָה חוֹמַת הָעִיר תַּחְתֶּיהָ וְעָלוּ הָעָם אִישׁ נֶגְדּוֹ : (6) וַיִּקְרָא יְהוֹשֻׁעַ בֶּן נוּן אֶל הַכֹּהֲנִים וַיֹּאמֶר אֲלֵהֶם שְׂאוּ אֶת אֲרוֹן הַבְּרִית ׀ וְשִׁבְעָה כֹהֲנִים יִשְׂאוּ שִׁבְעָה שׁוֹפְרוֹת יוֹבְלִים לִפְנֵי אֲרוֹן יְהוָה

So if the Yovel (Jubilee) is not necessarily associated with silver trumpets, then what is a Yovel? To answer this question, first let us look at the seven-year land-rest cycle, in Hebrew called a 'Shemittah' (שְׁמִטָּה).

Deuteronomy 15:1-4 tells us that every seven years, we are to release all debts with our Israelite brethren. In Hebrew, this 'release' is called a 'Shemittah' (שְׁמִטָּה). This explains why the word 'Shemittah' has come to mean 'a seven-year cycle.'

Deuteronomy 15:1-4 1 "At the end of every seven years you shall grant a release. 2 And this is the form of the release: Every creditor who has lent anything to his neighbor shall release it; he shall not require it of his neighbor or his brother, because it is called YHWH's release. 3 Of a foreigner you may require it; but you shall give up your claim to what is owed by your brother, 4 except when there may be no poor among you; for YHWH will greatly bless you in the land which YHWH your Elohim is giving you to possess as an inheritance...."	(1) מִקֵּץ שֶׁבַע שָׁנִים תַּעֲשֶׂה שְׁמִטָּה : (2) וְזֶה דְּבַר הַשְּׁמִטָּה שָׁמוֹט כָּל בַּעַל מַשֵּׁה יָדוֹ אֲשֶׁר יַשֶּׁה בְּרֵעֵהוּ ׀ לֹא יִגֹּשׂ אֶת רֵעֵהוּ וְאֶת אָחִיו כִּי קָרָא שְׁמִטָּה לַיהֹוָה : (3) אֶת הַנָּכְרִי תִּגֹּשׂ ׀ וַאֲשֶׁר יִהְיֶה לְךָ אֶת אָחִיךָ תַּשְׁמֵט יָדֶךָ : (4) אֶפֶס כִּי לֹא יִהְיֶה בְּךָ אֶבְיוֹן ׀ כִּי בָרֵךְ יְבָרֶכְךָ יְהֹוָה בָּאָרֶץ אֲשֶׁר יְהֹוָה אֱלֹהֶיךָ נֹתֵן לְךָ נַחֲלָה לְרִשְׁתָּהּ :

Many scholars see a parallel between the daily 'count-seven' for the Sabbath, and the yearly 'count-seven' for the Shemittah.

Weekly Sabbath	Shemittah Cycle
Day 1 = manna	Year 1 = plant
Day 2 = manna	Year 2 = plant
Day 3 = manna	Year 3 = plant
Day 4 = manna	Year 4 = plant
Day 5 = manna	Year 5 = plant
Day 6 = prepare double	Year 6 = double harvest
Day 7 = Sabbath rest	Year 7 = Shemittah (rest)

As we saw in the chapter on the Sabbath, Exodus 16:22-30 tells us not to cook on the Sabbath. Rather, we are to prepare twice as much food on the sixth day of the week, so that we do not have to cook on the Sabbath (except perhaps to warm our food up).

> **Shemote (Exodus) 16:22-30**
> **23 Then he said to them, "This is what YHWH has said: 'Tomorrow is a Sabbath rest, a set-apart Sabbath to YHWH. Bake what you will bake today, and boil what you will boil; and lay up for yourselves all that remains, to be kept until morning.'"**
> **24 So they laid it up till morning, as Moshe commanded; and it did not stink, nor were there any worms in it.**
> **25 Then Moshe said, "Eat that today, for today is a Sabbath to YHWH; today you will not find it in the field.**
> **26 Six days you shall gather it, but on the seventh day, the Sabbath, there will be none."**

27 Now it happened that some of the people went out on the seventh day to gather, but they found none.

28 And YHWH said to Moshe, "How long do you refuse to keep My commandments and My laws?

29 See! For YHWH has given you the Sabbath; therefore He gives you on the sixth day bread for two days. Let every man remain in his place; let no man go out of his place on the seventh day."

30 So the people rested on the seventh day.

Similarly, in Leviticus 25:20, YHWH promises to provide a double-sized harvest in the sixth year, so that there is no need to plant or reap until the eighth year.

Vayiqra (Leviticus) 25:20-22
20 'And if you say, "What shall we eat in the seventh year, since we shall not sow nor gather in our produce?"

21 Then I will command My blessing on you in the sixth year, and it will bring forth produce enough for three years.

22 And you shall sow in the eighth year, and eat old produce until the ninth year; until its produce comes in, you shall eat of the old harvest.

The commandments regarding the Yovelim (Jubilees) are listed in Leviticus 25. Leviticus 25:8-10 tells us to count seven sabbaths of years, seven times seven years (i.e., forty-nine years), and then to declare a Yovel in the fiftieth year, on the Day of Atonement.

Vayiqra (Leviticus) 25:8-10
8 'And you shall count seven sabbaths of years for yourself, seven times seven years; and the time of the seven sabbaths of years shall be to you forty-nine years.
9 Then you shall cause the trumpet of the Jubilee to sound on the tenth day of the seventh month; on the Day of Atonement you shall make the trumpet to sound throughout all your land.
10 And you shall set the fiftieth year apart, and proclaim liberty throughout all the land to all its inhabitants. It shall be a Jubilee for you; and each of you shall return to his possession, and each of you shall return to his family.'

Scholars disagree as to how this passage is to be interpreted. One group believes that the Yovel is to be calculated according to a 49-year cycle, while the other group believes in a 50-year cycle. To understand how these two different groups arrive at two different conclusions, let us review the Pentecost, and the Omer Count.

In the chapter on the Pentecost we saw that while Passover can fall on any day of the week, the Omer count always begins on the first day of the week that follows the Passover. Let us emphasize that the Pentecost always falls on the first day of the week, no matter when the Passover comes. For example, the chart below shows us what happened when the children of Israel came into the land in Joshua 5:10-12: both the Wave Sheaf (the start of the Omer Count) and the Pentecost fell on the first day of the week.

						Pass.
Wave	2 Om.	3 Om.	4 Om.	5 Om.	6 Om.	Shabt
8 Om.	9 Om.	10	11	12	13	Shabt
15	16	17	18	19	20	Shabt
22	23	24	25	26	27	Shabt
29	30	31	32	33	34	Shabt
36	37	38	39	40	41	Shabt
43	44	45	46	47	48	Shabt
Pent.						

Pass. = Passover (Pesach)
Wave = The Wave Sheaf Offering
Om. = What day of the Omer Count
Shabt = Shabbat (Seventh-Day Sabbath)
Pent. = Pentecost (fiftieth day)

Those who teach a 49-year Jubilee cycle tell us that the 50th year of the Jubilee cycle is also the 1st year of the new Jubilee cycle. This, they say, is because the Yovel is built upon the Shemittot (Shemittah land sabbaths), which are based upon the concept of 'counting seven years.' They claim that the concept of recurring sevens is inviolable, and they also say that it makes sense to count this way, because it appears to follow the same pattern as the Pentecost cycle.

43	44	45	46	47	48	Shem
Yovel	2	3	4	5	6	Shem
8	9	10	11	12	13	Shem
15	16	17	18	19	20	Shem
22	23	24	25	26	27	Shem
29	30	31	32	33	34	Shem
36	37	38	39	40	41	Shem
43	44	45	46	47	48	Shem
Yovel	2	3	4	5	6	Shem

While the 49-year cycle has some attractive features, there are also some difficulties. Chief among these is that the 49-year pattern appears to violate the commandment given in Leviticus 25:3, which tells us to plant six years.

Vayiqra (Leviticus) 25:2 2 "Speak to the children of Israel, and say to them: 'When you come into the land which I give you, then the land shall keep a sabbath to YHWH. 3 Six years you shall sow your field, and six years you shall prune your vineyard, and gather its fruit; 4 but in the seventh year there shall be a sabbath of solemn rest for the land, a sabbath to YHWH. You shall neither sow your field nor prune your vineyard.	(2) דַּבֵּר אֶל בְּנֵי יִשְׂרָאֵל וְאָמַרְתָּ אֲלֵהֶם כִּי תָבֹאוּ אֶל הָאָרֶץ אֲשֶׁר אֲנִי נֹתֵן לָכֶם l וְשָׁבְתָה הָאָרֶץ שַׁבָּת לַיהוָה : (3) שֵׁשׁ שָׁנִים תִּזְרַע שָׂדֶךָ וְשֵׁשׁ שָׁנִים תִּזְמֹר כַּרְמֶךָ l וְאָסַפְתָּ אֶת תְּבוּאָתָהּ : (4) וּבַשָּׁנָה הַשְּׁבִיעִת שַׁבַּת שַׁבָּתוֹן יִהְיֶה לָאָרֶץ שַׁבָּת לַיהוָה l שָׂדְךָ לֹא תִזְרָע וְכַרְמְךָ לֹא תִזְמֹר

This commandment to plant and reap for six years before allowing the land to rest in the seventh year appears to run parallel to the Fourth Commandment, which tells us to labor six days, and then to take a rest on the seventh day.

Shemote (Exodus) 20:8-11
8 "Remember the Sabbath day, to keep it set apart.

9 Six days you shall labor and do all your work,

10 but the seventh day is the Sabbath of YHWH your Elohim. In it you shall do no work: you, nor your son, nor your daughter, nor your male servant, nor your female servant, nor your cattle, nor your stranger who is within your gates.

11 For in six days YHWH made the heavens and the earth, the sea, and all that is in them, and rested the seventh day. Therefore YHWH blessed the Sabbath day and set it apart."

Leviticus 25:3 says to sow and reap six years before giving the land a rest. This is impossible on the 49-year Jubilee model, because it is unlawful to plant or reap during a Jubilee year.

49-year model	50-year model
50 = 1 = plant ≠ Yovel	1 = plant
2 = plant	2 = plant
3 = plant	3 = plant
4 = plant	4 = plant
5 = plant	5 = plant
6 = plant	6 = plant
7 = Shemittah (rest)	7 = Shemittah (rest)

In the 49-year model, one also plants and reaps only five years before letting the land rest. This is a direct violation of Leviticus 25:3, which tells us to sow our fields and prune our vineyards for six years before allowing the land to rest. Therefore, proponents of the 50-year Jubilee model tell us that the only model that fits is the 50-year Jubilee model, shown below.

36	37	38	39	40	41	Shem
43	44	45	46	47	48	Shem
Yovel	1	2	3	4	5	6
Shem	8	9	10	11	12	13
Shem	15	16	17	18	19	20
Shem	22	23	24	25	26	27
Shem	29	30	31	32	33	34
Shem	36	37	38	39	40	41
Shem	43	44	45	46	47	48
Shem	**Yovel**	1	2	3	4	5
6	Shem	8	9	10	11	12
13	Shem	15	16	17	18	19
20	Shem	22	23	24	25	26
27	Shem	29	30	31	32	33
34	Shem	36	37	38	39	40
41	Shem	43	44	45	46	47
48	Shem	**Yovel**	1	2	3	4
5	6	Shem	8	9	10	11
12	13	Shem	15	16	17	18
19	20	Shem	22	23	24	25
26	27	Shem	29	30	31	32
33	34	Shem	36	37	38	39
40	41	Shem	43	44	45	46
47	48	Shem	**Yovel**	1	2	3
4	5	6	Shem	8	9	10
11	12	13	Shem	15	16	17
18	19	20	Shem	22	23	24....

In the chart above, the position of the Shemittah year seems to 'migrate backwards' a year for every Jubilee cycle. While this 'migration' may not seem as visually pleasing as the concept of continually 'counting seven' (as in the 49-year model), it keeps the 'work six, then rest' pattern commanded both in Exodus 20:8-11, and in Leviticus 25:2-4.

Supporters of the 50-year cycle also point out that if the earth is expected to last for some 7000 years, the number 7000 divides neatly into 140 Jubilee cycles, 140 being a multiple of 14 (and hence, also 7). They also tell us that if Yeshua came at the 4000 year mark, He would have arrived on the 80th Jubilee (8 being a number signifying new beginnings). Further, if the Millennium begins in the year 6000, then the Millennium would begin at the 120th Jubilee (which is a multiple of 12, a very common Scriptural number). This would also place Yeshua's second coming neatly at the 140th Jubilee. While all of these numbers seem to flow beautifully, in contrast, 7000 divided by 49-year cycles yields a comparatively messy 142.857+ Jubilees.

But why should it matter whether the Jubilee cycle is 49 or 50 years long? The answer is that when Ephraim returns back home to the Land of Israel, and the Torah is established as the national law, the Jubilee and the Shemittah cycles will have to be re-established. But how can that be done? When the Jews were taken into the Exile to Babylon, the Jubilee and the Shemittah cycles were lost.

Josephus and the Book of Maccabees mention the Jubilees and the Shemittot, but the dates mentioned in these sources are questionable, for the simple reason that Judah has made other corruptions to the calendar, and has not always followed YHWH's means of timing. How then, can we know for sure when YHWH wants us to observe the Shemittot and the Jubilees? In order to answer that question, we need to learn a little bit more about what we are to do in the Yovel.

Leviticus 25:11-12 tells us that in the fiftieth year, we are not to sow, and we also are not to 'reap' anything that grows of its own accord. That is, YHWH allows us to go out and pick what we need for the day (or for two days on the Sixth Day), with the manna in the wilderness. However, YHWH does not want us to 'bring in the harvest' with a sickle or a basket, in order to 'store anything up' for later.

> *Vayiqra (Leviticus) 25:11-12*
> *11 "That fiftieth year shall be a Jubilee to you; in it you shall neither sow, nor reap what grows of its own accord, nor gather the grapes of your untended vine.*
> *12 For it is the Jubilee; it shall be set apart to you; you shall eat its produce from the field."*

Thankfully, Scripture gives us a clue as to when YHWH may have last declared a Jubilee. In Second Kings 19:29-34 we read about how the King of Assyria laid siege to Jerusalem during the reign of King Hezekiah. With the Jews greatly outnumbered, King Hezekiah feared they would be overcome by the Assyrian forces. However, YHWH sent Hezekiah a message by the mouth of the Prophet Isaiah. YHWH said the people would eat that year what grew of itself (i.e., without being planted), and that in the second year they would eat that which sprang from what grew the year before (also without being planted). Then in the third year, the Jews would plant.

> *Melachim Bet (2nd Kings) 19:29-34*
> *29 'This shall be a sign to you:*
> *You shall eat this year such as grows of itself, and in the second year what springs from the same; also in the third year sow and reap, plant vineyards and eat the fruit of them.'*

As we saw earlier, this is the exact pattern YHWH commands us to keep during the Yovel: we are not to plant or reap either in the 49th or the 50th years. Rather, we are to wait for the first year, to begin planting and harvesting again.

> **Vayiqra (Leviticus) 25:20-22**
> **20 'And if you say, "What shall we eat in the seventh year, since we shall not sow nor gather in our produce?"**
> **21 Then I will command My blessing on you in the sixth year, and it will bring forth produce enough for three years.**
> **22 And you shall sow in the eighth year, and eat old produce until the ninth year; until its produce comes in, you shall eat of the old harvest.'**

Historians such as Edwin R. Thiele (The Mysterious Numbers of the Hebrew Kings) and Jack Finnegan (The Handbook of Bible Chronology) date the siege by the Assyrian forces at approximately 701 BCE. If this number is correct, then the Jubilee cycles would progress forward in the following manner:

49 Year Cycle	50 Year Cycle
701 = 49 = Shemittah	701 = 49 = Shemittah
700 = 50 = 1 = Yovel	700 = 50 = Yovel
699 = 2 = plant	699 = 1 = plant
698 = 3 = plant, etceteras	698 = 2 = plant, etceteras

Remembering that there is no 'zero year', if one does the calculations on the 49-year cycle, the last Jubilee was 1996. This date ties into numerous prophecies we earlier detailed in the Nazarene Israel study. At the time of this printing, the next Jubilee would be 2045. The Shemittot dates would then be 2003, 2010, 2017, 2024, 2031, and 2048.

Since the 50-year Jubilee cycle progresses forward by perfect fifties, the last Jubilee on the 50-year cycle was the year 2000. At the time of this printing, the last Shemitta would have been 2007, and the next Shemitta would be in 2014, followed by 2021, 2028, 2035, 2042, and then the next Jubilee will occur in 2050.

But what else happens in the Jubilee, apart from letting the land rest? Another major theme is the release of property, and the release from debt. In the Yovel, all debts between Israelites are to be canceled, and all property is to be released to its original owners. (Since land in Israel can only be sold according to the number of years until the next Jubilee, in modern-day terms, the land is only supposed to be leased.)

> *Vayiqra (Leviticus) 25:13-17*
> *13 'In this Year of Jubilee, each of you shall return to his possession.*
> *14 And if you sell anything to your neighbor or buy from your neighbor's hand, you shall not oppress one another.*
> *15 According to the number of years after the Jubilee you shall buy from your neighbor, and according to the number of years of crops he shall sell to you.*
> *16 According to the multitude of years you shall increase its price, and according to the fewer number of years you shall diminish its price; for*

he sells to you according to the
number of the years of the crops.
17 Therefore you shall not oppress
one another, but you shall fear your
Elohim; for I am YHWH your Elohim.'

Although we are only commanded to keep the Yovel and the Shemittah when we live in the Land of Israel, there are benefits and advantages to keeping the Yovel in the Dispersion. One Messianic farm family told me they made the decision not to plant in the seventh year, in obedience to the command. They reported that their harvests increased an average of 40-50%, and not just in the sixth year, but in all years. While this Messianic farm family did not know the exact earthly cause of the increase, they believed it had something to do with disruption of the natural cycles of weeds and parasites. They theorized that because the normal cycles of the weeds and parasites were disrupted, the crops were able to 'compete' much better than they would normally have been able to. However, they were also quick to point out that it was ultimately YHWH who provided the increase.

Another major theme of the Yovel is how YHWH's land and His people ultimately belong not to any earthly human being, kingship or government, but to YHWH Himself; and as such they are to be treated as His. We are to grant release of all indebtedness from our brothers (and one might also draw a 'spiritual parallel' to grudges, resentments, and lack of forgiveness).

> *Vayiqra (Leviticus) 25:23-24*
> *23 'The land shall not be sold*
> *permanently, for the land is Mine; for*
> *you are strangers and sojourners with*
> *Me.*

24 And in all the land of your possession you shall grant redemption of the land.'

While we will not delve into the specific rules for the release of land, debt and Israelite slaves here, the rules are fairly simple, and self-explanatory. No contract involving land in Israel, loans to Israelites or Israelite slaves can extend beyond the next Jubilee. At the Yovel (the 'flowing'), all land is to be released to its original owner, and all debts of every type are to be cancelled.

> **Vayiqra (Leviticus) 25:25-28**
> **25 'If one of your brethren becomes poor, and has sold some of his possession, and if his redeeming relative comes to redeem it, then he may redeem what his brother sold.**
> **26 Or if the man has no one to redeem it, but he himself becomes able to redeem it,**
> **27 then let him count the years since its sale, and restore the remainder to the man to whom he sold it, that he may return to his possession.**
> **28 But if he is not able to have it restored to himself, then what was sold shall remain in the hand of him who bought it until the Year of Jubilee; and in the Jubilee it shall be released, and he shall return to his possession.'**

Earlier we saw how YHWH's people belong to Him. In Exodus 21:1-6 and in Deuteronomy 15:12-18 we read about the Torah of the Hebrew slave who does not wish to be set free from his master.

Devarim (Deuteronomy) 15:12-18

12 "If your brother, a Hebrew man, or a Hebrew woman, is sold to you and serves you six years, then in the seventh year you shall let him go free from you.

13 And when you send him away free from you, you shall not let him go away empty-handed;

14 you shall supply him liberally from your flock, from your threshing floor, and from your winepress. From what YHWH has blessed you with, you shall give to him.

15 You shall remember that you were a slave in the land of Egypt, and YHWH your Elohim redeemed you; therefore I command you this thing today.

16 And if it happens that he says to you, 'I will not go away from you,' because he loves you and your house, since he prospers with you,

17 then you shall take an awl and thrust it through his ear to the door, and he shall be your servant forever. Also to your female servant you shall do likewise.

18 It shall not seem hard to you when you send him away free from you; for he has been worth a double hired servant in serving you six years. Then YHWH your Elohim will bless you in all that you do.

If an Israelite slave realizes that he has it better under his master than he knows how to do for himself, then he has the option of foregoing the release. Earlier we saw how the first six years of the Creation Week symbolize the first six thousand years of man's existence, as well as how the Sabbath symbolizes the Millennial Reign. Could it be that the slave desiring not to be sent away from his master's house (because he has it better than he knows how to provide for himself) is spiritually symbolic of all those Israelites who desire not to be set free from their Master YHWH, since they have it so much better with Him?

The releasing of slaves and of property takes place on Yom Kippur, at the sounding of the shofar.

> *Vayiqra (Leviticus) 25:8-10*
> *8 'And you shall count seven sabbaths of years for yourself, seven times seven years; and the time of the seven sabbaths of years shall be to you forty-nine years.*
> *9 Then you shall cause the trumpet of the Jubilee to sound on the tenth day of the seventh month; on the Day of Atonement you shall make the trumpet to sound throughout all your land.*
> *10 And you shall set the fiftieth year apart, and proclaim liberty throughout all the land to all its inhabitants. It shall be a Jubilee for you; and each of you shall return to his possession, and each of you shall return to his family.'*

Since one of Yeshua's purposes was to proclaim release to the captives, Messianic tradition informs us that Yeshua's ministry may have begun around the time of Yom Kippur, when the release of the captives was declared.

Judaism traditionally calls for an immersion (baptism) on the day before Yom Kippur, the most set-apart day of the year.

> *Luqa (Luke) 3:21-23*
> *21 When all the people were immersed, it came to pass that Yeshua also was immersed; and while He prayed, the heaven was opened.*
> *22 And the Ruach HaKodesh (Holy Spirit) descended in bodily form like a dove upon Him, and a voice came from heaven which said, "You are My beloved Son; in You I am well pleased."*
> *23 Now Yeshua Himself began His ministry at about thirty years of age....*

As we will show in the next chapter on Hanukkah, Yeshua was probably born on the first day of the Fall Feast of Sukkot (Tabernacles). Since Yom Kippur takes place five days before Sukkot, Yeshua would have been "about thirty years of age" when He began His ministry.

As another witness that Yeshua's ministry may have begun around the Sukkot timeframe, notice that after being tempted of the Devil for forty days, Yeshua returned to Natseret (Nazareth), and announced that He had been sent to proclaim release to the captives.

> *Luqa (Luke) 4:13-21*
> *13 Now when the devil had ended every temptation, he departed from Him until an opportune time.*

14 Then Yeshua returned in the power of the Spirit to Galilee, and news of Him went out through all the surrounding region.

15 And He taught in their synagogues, being glorified by all.

16 So He came to Nazareth, where He had been brought up. And as His custom was, He went into the synagogue on the Sabbath day, and stood up to read.

17 And He was handed the book of the prophet Isaiah. And when He had opened the book, He found the place where it was written:

18 "The Spirit of YHWH is upon Me, Because He has anointed Me

To preach the Good News to the poor; He has sent Me to heal the brokenhearted, <ins>to proclaim liberty to the captives</ins> and recovery of sight to the blind, <ins>to set at liberty those who are oppressed</ins>;

19 To proclaim the acceptable year of YHWH."

20 Then He closed the book, and gave it back to the attendant and sat down. And the eyes of all who were in the synagogue were fixed on Him.

21 And He began to say to them, "Today this Scripture is fulfilled in your hearing."

Finally, we should state that in all Shemittah and Yovel years, the Wave Sheaves are taken from wild barley, which may be symbolic of Ephraim.

Hanukkah Reconsidered

Why do people celebrate Hanukkah? And should we?

Around 332 BCE, Alexander the Great conquered the Land of Israel. A relatively gentle ruler, Alexander allowed the Jews to continue to practice traditional Judaism, so long as they paid him tribute (i.e. taxes).

> **Daniel 8:21-24**
> **21 And the male goat is the kingdom of Greece. The large horn that is between its eyes is the first (or chief) king (Alexander).**
> **22 As for the broken horn and the four that stood up in its place, four kingdoms shall arise out of that nation, but not with its power.**

In 323 BCE, some nine years after he had first conquered the Land of Israel, Alexander died. His empire then broke up into four kingdoms, fulfilling the prophecy in verse 22, above. One of these four successor kingdoms was the Seleucid Empire, which is located mainly in modern-day Syria. Next, verse 23 tells us that in the latter time of this (Seleucid) kingdom, a fierce, sinister king would arise, who would commit transgressions against the Hebrew people.

> **23 "And in the latter time of their kingdom, when the transgressors have reached their fullness, a king shall arise, having fierce features, who understands sinister schemes.**

24 His power shall be mighty, but not by his own power. He shall destroy fearfully, and shall prosper and thrive. He shall destroy the mighty, and also the set-apart people.

Approximately a century and a half later, in 175 BCE, this prophecy was fulfilled. Antiochus Epiphanies (also called Antiochus IV) rose to power in the Seleucid Empire. Not religiously tolerant at all, Antiochus Epiphanies began to commit great atrocities against the Jewish people.

In approximately 168 BCE, Antiochus heard reports that there was a great deal of treasure stored up in the Temple. Returning from Egypt, he looted the Temple, and also slaughtered a great many of the Jews.

1st Maccabees 1:20-24
20 And after that Antiochus had smitten Egypt, he returned again in the hundred forty and third year, and went up against Israel and Jerusalem with a great multitude.
21 And entered proudly into the sanctuary, and took away the golden altar, and the candlestick of light, and all the vessels thereof.
22 And the table of showbread, and the pouring vessels, and the vials, and the censers of gold, and the veil, and the crowns, and the golden ornaments that were before the Temple, all of which he pulled off.
23 He took also the silver and the gold, and the precious vessels: also he took the hidden treasures which he found.

24 And when he had taken all away, he went into his own land, having made a great massacre, and spoken very proudly.

Two years later, Antiochus sent tax collectors to speak peaceable words to the people, so as to plunder the city through deception. Then after collecting their taxes they massacred the Jewish people, and used the money to set up a fortress within sight of the Temple Mount, to kill anyone who brought an offering.

1 Maccabees 1:29-40
29 And after two years fully expired the king sent his chief collector of tribute unto the cities of Judah, who came unto Jerusalem with a great multitude,
30 and spake peaceable words unto them, but all was deceit: for when they had given him credence, he fell suddenly upon the city, and smote it very sore, and destroyed much people of Israel.
31 And when he had taken the spoils of the city, he set it on fire, and pulled down the houses and walls thereof on every side.
32 but the women and children they took captive, and possessed the cattle.
33 Then builded they the city of David with a great and strong wall, and mighty towers, and made it a strong hold for them.
34 And they put therein a sinful nation, wicked men, and fortified themselves therein.

35 They stored it also with armour and victuals, and when they had gathered together the spoils of Jerusalem, they laid them up there, and so they became a sore snare:

36 For it was a place to lie in wait against the sanctuary, and an evil adversary to Israel.

37 Thus they shed innocent blood on every side of the sanctuary, and defiled it:

38 insomuch that the inhabitants of Jerusalem fled because of them: whereupon the city was made an habitation of strangers, and became strange to those born in her; and her own children left her.

39 Her sanctuary was laid waste like a wilderness, her feasts turned into mourning, her Sabbaths into reproach, her honour into contempt.

40 As had been her glory, so was her dishonour increased, and her excellency was turned into mourning.

Antiochus encouraged everyone in his empire to convert to the Greek religious system, and issued orders for the destruction of all dissenters.

1 Maccabees 1:41-50
41 Moreover King Antiochus wrote to his whole kingdom, that all should be one people,
42 And every one should leave his laws: so all the heathen agreed according to the commandment of the king.

43 Yea, many also of the Israelites consented to his religion, and sacrificed unto idols, and profaned the Sabbath.
44 For the king had sent letters by messengers unto Jerusalem and the cities of Juda [Judea], that they should follow the strange laws of the land.
45 And forbid burnt offerings, and sacrifice, and drink offerings, in the temple; and that they should profane the Sabbaths and festival days:
46 And pollute the sanctuary and the holy people:
47 Set up altars, and groves, and chapels of idols, and sacrifice swine's flesh, and unclean beasts:
48 That they should also leave their children uncircumcised, and make their souls abominable with all manner of uncleanness and profanation:
49 To the end they might forget the Torah, and change all the ordinances.
50 And whosoever would not do according to the commandment of the king, he should die.

Between his incentives for Greek worship and penalties for YHWH worship, Antiochus was largely successful in getting many of the people to abandon the Torah.

1 Maccabees 1:51-53
51 In the selfsame manner wrote he to his whole kingdom, and appointed overseers over all the people, commanding the cities of Juda [Judea] to sacrifice, city by city.

52 Then many of the people were gathered unto them, to wit, every one that forsook the Torah; and so they committed evils in the land;

53 And drove the Israelites into secret places, even wheresoever they could flee for succour [relief].

Having courted those who had no zeal for the Torah, and persecuting YHWH's followers, Antiochus ordered a statue of Zeus to be erected in the Temple, and he commanded pigs to be sacrificed on the altar.

1 Maccabees 1:54-59

54 Now the fifteenth day of Kislev (the ninth month), in the hundred and forty fifth year, they set up the Abomination of Desolation upon the altar, and builded idol altars throughout the cities of Judea on every side.

55 And burnt incense at the doors of their homes, and in the streets.

56 And when they had rent in pieces the books of the law which they found, they burnt them with fire.

57 And wheresoever was found with any the book of the testament, or if any consented to the law, the king's commandment was, that they should be put to death.

58 Thus they did by their authority unto the Israelites every month, to as many as were found in the cities.

59 Now on the five and twentieth day of the month they did sacrifice upon the idol altar, which was upon the altar of [Elohim].

The situation soon became very desperate. Mothers who circumcised their children were put to death, along with their children.

> **1 Maccabees 1:60-63**
> **60 At which time according to the commandment they put to death certain women, that had caused their children to be circumcised.**
> **61 They hanged the infants about their necks, and rifled their houses, and slew them that had circumcised them.**
> **62 Howbeit many in Israel were fully resolved and confirmed in themselves not to eat any unclean thing.**
> **63 Wherefore they chose rather to die, that they might not be defiled with meats, and that they might not profane the holy covenant: so then they died.**

Mattithyahu ben Yochanan HaCohen and his five sons rebelled against Antiochus. Although Mattithyahu died a year later (from natural causes), his son Yehudah (Judah) continued to lead the Jewish rebellion with amazing bravery. Vastly outnumbered, the Jews placed their trust in YHWH, and YHWH gave them a miraculous victory against otherwise impossible odds. As a result, Yehudah and family became known as the 'Maccabees' (מכבי). This might be related to the Aramaic word for 'hammer', or it may be an acronym for the Jewish battle cry, "Mi Kamocha B'elim, YHWH" (who is like You among the elohim, YHWH?) (מכבי). Either way, after the Maccabeean victory they needed to build a new altar to replace the one that had become defiled; and they also needed to re-light the Menorah, which YHWH commands to burn continually.

Vayiqra (Leviticus) 24:1-2
24:1 Then YHWH spoke to Moshe, saying:
2 "Command the children of Israel that they bring to you pure oil of pressed olives for the light, to make the lamps burn continually.

Traditionally, it takes eight days to press and refine oil for the Menorah. While the Talmud tells us there was plenty of oil inside the Temple, it claims Antiochus' forces had defiled most of it, such that there was only enough set-apart oil to light the Menorah for one day: yet YHWH miraculously made it burn for eight.

What is [the reason of] Hanukkah? For our Rabbis taught: On the twenty-fifth of Kislew 22 [commence] the days of Hanukkah, which are eight on which a lamentation for the dead and fasting are forbidden. 23 For when the Greeks entered the Temple, they defiled all the oils therein, and when the Hasmonean [Maccabean] dynasty prevailed against and defeated them, they made search and found only one cruse of oil which lay with the seal of the High Priest, 24 but which contained sufficient for one day's lighting only; yet a miracle was wrought therein and they lit [the lamp] therewith for eight days. The following year these [days] were appointed a Festival with [the recital of] Hallel 25 and thanksgiving.26
[Babylonian Talmud, Tractate Shabbat, Chapter 21]

YHWH certainly has the power to make miracles, but the Talmud (written 400-700 years after the war) claims that this alleged miracle is the reason for Hanukkah; yet this alleged miracle is not recorded in the Book of Maccabees (which was written soon after the war). Rather, First Maccabees says only that the Jews cleaned up the Temple, built a new altar, and re-lit the menorah. No eight-day miracle of burning is recorded.

> **1 Maccabees 4:47-51**
> **47 Then they took whole stones according to the Torah, and built a new altar according to the former,**
> **48 And made up the sanctuary, and the things that were within the Temple, and set the courts apart.**
> **49 They made also new set-apart vessels, and into the temple they brought the candlestick (Menorah), and the altar of burnt offerings, and of incense, and the table.**
> **50 And upon the altar they burned incense, and the lamps that were upon the candlestick they lighted, that they might give light in the Temple.**
> **51 Furthermore they set the loaves upon the table, and spread out the veils, and finished all the works which they had begun to make.**

Had one day's worth of oil really burned for eight days, it seems likely First Maccabees would have recorded it. Instead, First Maccabees tells us only that the re-dedication ceremony (חֲנֻכָּה, Hanukkah) lasted for eight days; and that Yehudah Maccabee commanded the people to keep this festival each year.

1 Maccabees 4:56-59

56 And so they kept the dedication of the altar eight days, and offered burnt offerings with gladness, and sacrificed the sacrifice of deliverance and praise.

57 They decked also the forefront of the Temple with crowns of gold, and with shields, and the gates and the chambers they renewed, and hanged doors upon them.

58 Thus was there very great gladness among the people, for that the reproach of the heathen was put away.

59 Moreover Yehudah and his brethren and the whole congregation of Israel ordained that the days of dedication of the altar should be kept in their season from year to year by the space of eight days, from the twenty-fifth day of Kislev, with mirth and gladness.

Because the record in Talmud is not always reliable, and because the alleged miracle of the oil is not recorded in First Maccabees, some scholars believe the reason Hanukkah was established as an eight day festival was simply because the Jews had been unable to keep the Feast of Sukkot in its proper time (because of the war). Thus it may have been that when the war ended, the Jews simply celebrated a belated eight day festival to YHWH; and then they commanded that it be observed as a festival unto YHWH forever, much like the Fourth of July is celebrated in America.

What shall we say about man-made observances, such as Hanukkah and Purim? As with Christmas and Easter, the first thing we should admit is that these festival days are not commanded by YHWH: they are commanded by men. Yet YHWH warns us very clearly not to add anything to His Instructions, so that we might live, and be preserved in safety.

> *Devarim (Deuteronomy) 4:1-4*
> *1 "Now, O Israel, listen to the statutes and the judgments which I teach you to observe, that you may live, and go in and possess the land which YHWH Elohim of your fathers is giving you.*
> *2 You shall not add to the word which I command you, nor take from it, that you may keep the commandments of YHWH your Elohim which I command you.*
> *3 Your eyes have seen what YHWH did at Baal Peor; for YHWH your Elohim has destroyed from among you all the men who followed Baal of Peor.*
> *4 But you who held fast to YHWH your Elohim are alive today, every one of you."*

The second thing we should recognize is that, as we saw earlier in this study, whoever's calendar we keep, that is essentially whom we worship (worth-ship). The reason we keep anyone's calendar is because we consider that person worthy to instruct us, as to what we should do. Yet YHWH is clear that we are not to follow man's instructions, but that we must only follow His Instructions. He tells us cery plainly not to add to His Instructions: yet Hanukkah does this very thing.

222

It is clear that YHWH did not instruct us to keep either Hanukkah or Purim: men did. Yet since YHWH tells us to be careful not to add anything to His Instructions, then at least in one sense, if we keep Hanukkah or Purim, are we not being disobedient to His will? And might we not even be unwittingly guilty of esteeming these men as 'greater' than YHWH, since we are following their instructions, rather than YHWH's?

For a variety of reasons, Scripture indicates that men want to make up make their own festival days; but that this is never pleasing to YHWH, even when these festival days are purposed and intended to honor Him.

> **Shemote (Exodus) 32:5-6**
> **5 So when Aharon saw it (the golden calf), he built an altar before it. And Aharon made a proclamation and said, "Tomorrow is a feast to YHWH!"**
> **6 Then they rose early on the next day, offered burnt offerings, and brought peace offerings; and the people sat down to eat and drink, and rose up to play.**

Winter light festivals are common among the pagan nations; and many of these festivals have been brought inside the Church (complete with candles). These include Advent (four weeks before Christmas), Saint Nicholas' Day (December 6th), Saint Lucia day (December 13th), the Winter Solstice and the Yule Log lighting. Pagan light festivals also include Samhain, Imbolc, and many others. Yet while it seems natural for men to want to celebrate light in the darkness of winter, YHWH tells us not to add any of these pagan light festivals to His calendar.

Devarim (Deuteronomy) 12:29-32
29 "When YHWH your Elohim cuts off from before you the nations which you go to dispossess, and you displace them and dwell in their land,
30 take heed to yourself that you are not ensnared to follow them, after they are destroyed from before you, and that you do not inquire after their gods, saying, 'How did these nations serve their elohim (g-ds)? I also will do likewise.'
31 You shall not worship YHWH your Elohim in that way; for every abomination to YHWH which He hates they have done to their elohim (g-ds); for they burn even their sons and daughters in the fire to their elohim.
32 "Whatever I command you, be careful to observe it; you shall not add to it nor take away from it."

YHWH indeed gave a miraculous victory to the Jews in their war against Antiochus Epiphanies and the Seleucids, and nothing can ever take away from that. Yet there have been many other miraculous victories in Israel's history, such as when YHWH felled the wall at Jericho (Joshua 6), Gideon's miraculous victory over the Midianites (Judges 7), Shimshon's (Samson's) slaying of the Philistines (Judges 16), and many other miraculous victories. However, we do not add festival days to YHWH's calendar because of these other miracles; so why should we add to YHWH's calendar because He gave a victory against Antiochus Epiphanies or because of an alleged miracle with oil?

There is a counter-argument for Hanukkah. Those who advocate celebrating Hanukkah note that Yeshua was in Jerusalem at Hanukkah time, here called the Feast of Dedication.

> *Yochanan (John) 10:22-23*
> *22 Now it was the Feast of Dedication in Jerusalem, and it was winter.*
> *23 And Yeshua walked in the temple, in Solomon's porch.*

However, we should be careful to note that it does not say Yeshua was celebrating the Feast of Dedication: it simply states that He was in Jerusalem at that time, probably because He had stayed on in Jerusalem after Sukkot. This is not the same thing as celebrating it, or going up to Jerusalem for Hanukkah. He might well have been there for other reasons.

Those who advocate Hanukkah tell us that Hanukkah is traditionally celebrated by lighting candles, oil lamps, or other lights; and that it was during this same general time frame (during the Feast of Hanukkah) that Yeshua told us that He was the light of the world.

> *Yochanan (John) 8:12*
> *12 Then Yeshua spoke to them again, saying, "I am the light of the world. He who follows Me shall not walk in darkness, but have the light of life."*

Yeshua also says the same thing in John Chapter 9.

> *Yochanan (John) 9:5*
> *5 As long as I am in the world, I am the light of the world."*

Yet neither of these passages prove that Yeshua either celebrated, or approved of Hanukkah. We might easily imagine Yeshua telling those who went up for the festival to look to Him, rather than to the Hanukkiah.

> *Interpretation:*
> *Then Yeshua spoke to them again, saying, "The Hanukkiah is not the light of the world, so why do you look to it? I am the light of the world (not the Hanukkiah)! He who follows Me shall not walk in darkness, but have the light of life!"*

We might compare this with His words to the Woman at the Well, where Yeshua told her that He could give her Living Waters: yet the purpose was not to celebrate the waters or the well, but Him.

> *Yochanan (John) 4:13-14*
> *13 Yeshua answered and said to her, "Whoever drinks of this water will thirst again,*
> *14 but whoever drinks of the water that I shall give him will never thirst. But the water that I shall give him will become in him a fountain of water springing up into everlasting life."*

We might also imagine Yeshua's words this way:

> *Interpretation:*
> *"You are celebrating a Winter Light Festival: but why do you do that? For as long as I am in the world, I am the light of the world! So why do you focus on the light from a Hanukkiah?"*

226

There is an argument which suggests that Yeshua may have been conceived during Hanukkah; and yet we should note that this argument does not prove that Yeshua was conceived during Hanukkah. Further, even if it did prove it, this still does not provide us with justification for adding to YHWH's calendar. The basic rule is that we human beings are not worthy to add or subtract from the Almighty's Instructions. We are not wise enough, and we are not authorized: yet we human beings seem to want to do this, time and again.

While we will not list the whole citation here, First Chronicles 24:7-19 tells us that the Levitical priesthood was separated into twenty-four divisions, and that their schedule of service was then chosen by lot.

> *Divre HaYamim Aleph (1*st *Chronicles) 24:1a, 3, 5-19*
> *1 Now these are the divisions of the sons of Aaron....*
> *3 Then David with Zadok of the sons of Eleazar, and Ahimelech of the sons of Ithamar, divided them according to the schedule of their service....*
> *5 Thus they were divided by lot, one group as another, for there were officials of the sanctuary and officials of the house of Elohim, from the sons of Eleazar and from the sons of Ithamar.*

In Antiquities 7, Josephus tells us that each division served for a period of one week.

> *365 He divided them also into courses: and when he had separated the priests*

from them, he found of these priests twenty-four courses, sixteen of the house of Eleazar, and eight of that of Ithamar; and he ordained that one course should minister to [Elohim] eight days, from Sabbath to Sabbath.
366 And thus were the courses distributed by lot, in the presence of David, and Zadok and Abiathar the high priests, and of all the rulers: and that course which came up first was written down as the first, and accordingly the second, and so on to the twenty-fourth; and this partition has remained to this day.
[Josephus, Antiquities of the Jews 7:365-366 (Alt: VII 14:7)]

Those wishing to verify Josephus' summation from Scripture alone should reference 1st Chronicles 9:1-26, 1st Chronicles 28:11-14 and 2nd Chronicles 23:1-8. However, since Josephus' summation is so much shorter and more compact, we will not reproduce all of these passages here.

Luke tells us that Yochanan HaMatbil's (John the Baptist's) father Zechariah was of the priestly division of Aviyah (Abijah).

Luqa (Luke) 1:5
5 There was in the days of Herod, the king of Judea, a certain priest named Zacharias, of the division of Aviyah. His wife was of the daughters of Aaron, and her name was Elisheva.

We know from 1st Chronicles 24:10 that the division of Aviyah served in the eighth week.

> **Divre HaYamim (1 Chronicles) 24:7-10**
> **7 Now the first lot fell to Yehoiariv, the second to Yedaiah,**
> **8 the third to Harim, the fourth to Seorim,**
> **9 the fifth to Malchiyah, the sixth to Miyamin,**
> **10 the seventh to Hakkoz, the eighth to Aviyah....**

Since the priestly courses began at the Head of the Year, and since the priests served from Sabbath to Sabbath, and since Zechariah belonged to the eighth priestly division, Zechariah would have served in the Temple from the eighth week of the year, to the ninth. However, since all the priests served in the Temple during the three annual pilgrimage festivals, and since Shavuot (Pentecost) was in the ninth week, Zechariah would not have gone home right away, but would have stayed at the Temple, returning home after Shavuot was over. Luke 1:23-24 confirms this, and it tells us that Zechariah's wife Elisheva (Elisabeth) conceived after Zechariah had returned home.

> **Luqa (Luke) 1:8-25**
> **8 So it was, that while he was serving as priest before Elohim in the order of his division,**
> **9 according to the custom of the priesthood, his lot fell to burn incense when he went into the Temple of YHWH.**

10 And the whole multitude of the people was praying outside at the hour of incense.

11 Then a messenger of YHWH appeared to him, standing on the right side of the altar of incense.

12 And when Zechariah saw him, he was troubled, and fear fell upon him.

13 But the messenger said to him, "Do not be afraid, Zechariah, for your prayer is heard; and your wife Elisheva will bear you a son, and you shall call his name Yochanan.

14 And you will have joy and gladness, and many will rejoice at his birth.

15 For he will be great in the sight of YHWH, and shall drink neither wine nor strong drink. He will also be filled with the Set apart Spirit, even from his mother's womb. 16 And he will turn many of the children of Israel to YHWH their Elohim.

17 He will also go before Him in the spirit and power of Eliyahu, 'to turn the hearts of the fathers to the children,' and the disobedient to the wisdom of the just, to make ready a people prepared for YHWH."

18 And Zechariah said to the messenger, "How shall I know this? For I am an old man, and my wife is well advanced in years."

19 And the messenger answered and said to him, "I am Gabriel, who stands in the presence of Elohim, and was sent to speak to you and bring you these glad tidings.

20 But behold, you will be mute and not able to speak until the day these things take place, because you did not believe my words which will be fulfilled in their own time."

21 And the people waited for Zechariah, and marveled that he lingered so long in the temple.

22 But when he came out, he could not speak to them; and they perceived that he had seen a vision in the temple, for he beckoned to them and remained speechless.

23 So it was, as soon as the days of his service were completed, that he departed to his own house.

24 Now after those days his wife Elizabeth conceived; and she hid herself five months, saying,

25 "Thus YHWH has dealt with me, in the days when He looked on me, to take away my reproach among people."

It would have taken Zechariah some time to get home, so if we add nine months to the date of Yochanan's conception (perhaps in the middle of the third month), we can see that Yochanan would likely have been born in the spring, right around the Passover time frame (in the middle of the first month). [Those who obey the rabbinical rituals may find this more than a coincidence, since one of the rabbinical rituals is to set a special place setting for Eliyahu (Elijah), who Yochanan came in the power and the spirit of.]

Continuing onward, verse 36 tells us that Gabriel spoke with Miriam during the sixth month of Elisheva's term.

Luqa (Luke) 1:26-38

26 Now in the sixth month the messenger Gabriel was sent by Elohim to a city of Galilee named Nazareth,

27 to a virgin betrothed to a man whose name was Yosef, of the house of David. The virgin's name was Miriam.

28 And having come in, the messenger said to her, "Rejoice, highly favored one, YHWH is with you; blessed are you among women!"

29 But when she saw him, she was troubled at his saying, and considered what manner of greeting this was.

30 Then the messenger said to her, "Do not be afraid, Miriam, for you have found favor with Elohim.

31 And behold, you will conceive in your womb and bring forth a Son, and shall call His name Yeshua.

32 He will be great, and will be called the Son of the Highest; and YHWH Elohim will give Him the throne of His father David.

33 And He will reign over the house of Jacob forever, and of His kingdom there will be no end."

34 Then Miriam said to the messenger, "How can this be, since I do not know a man?"

35 And the messenger answered and said to her, "The Set apart Spirit will come upon you, and the power of the Highest will overshadow you; therefore, also, that Set apart One who is to be born will be called the Son of Elohim.

36 Now indeed, Elizabeth your relative has also conceived a son in her old age; and this is now the sixth month for her who was called barren.

37 For with Elohim nothing will be impossible."

38 Then Miriam said, "Behold the maidservant of YHWH! Let it be to me according to your word." And the messenger departed from her.

Continuing onward, verse 39 tells us that Miriam left Nazareth 'with haste' to go visit Elisheva. We can surmise that Miriam was already pregnant at that time because Elisheva, filled with the Set-apart Spirit, blessed the fruit of Miriam's womb (i.e., Yeshua).

Luqa (Luke) 1:39-45
39 Now Miriam arose in those days and went into the hill country with haste, to a city of Judah,

40 and entered the house of Zechariah and greeted Elisheva.

41 And it happened, when Elisheva heard the greeting of Miriam, that the babe leaped in her womb; and Elisheva was filled with the Set-apart Spirit.

42 Then she spoke out with a loud voice and said, "Blessed are you among women, and blessed is the fruit of your womb!

43 But why is this granted to me, that the mother of my Master should come to me?

44 For indeed, as soon as the voice of your greeting sounded in my ears, the babe leaped in my womb for joy.
45 Blessed is she who believed, for there will be a fulfillment of those things which were told her from YHWH."

Even though Miriam left 'with haste', back in the days of transportation on foot and by camel, it would still have taken her some time to travel from Nazareth in the north, to Judea in the south. Thus, even though Yochanan HaMatbil was probably conceived about the middle of the third month, Yeshua was likely conceived around the end of the ninth month. Some argue that this may have been about the same time as Hanukkah begins, more-or-less the 25th day of the 9th month. Thus it can be argued that YHWH used Hanukkah to give us yet one more prophetic shadow picture of the One who would become the Light of the world; yet we should be clear that this is by no means proven: and even if it were, it still does not give us justification to add to the Almighty's Instructions.

Why do we keep Hanukkah? The rabbis teach that it is because there was an eight-day miracle of oil that the Book of First Maccabees does not witness to.

What is [the reason of] Hanukkah? For our Rabbis taught: On the twenty-fifth of Kislew 22 [commence] the days of Hanukkah, which are eight on which a lamentation for the dead and fasting are forbidden. 23 For when the Greeks entered the Temple, they defiled all the oils therein, and when the Hasmonean [Maccabean] dynasty prevailed against

and defeated them, they made search and found only one cruse of oil which lay with the seal of the High Priest, 24 but which contained sufficient for one day's lighting only; yet a miracle was wrought therein and they lit [the lamp] therewith for eight days. The following year these [days] were appointed a Festival with [the recital of] Hallel 25 and thanksgiving.26
[Babylonian Talmud, Tractate Shabbat, Chapter 21]

In contrast, the Book of First Maccabees tells us that it is because Judah Maccabee and his brethren told us to do so.

1 Maccabees 4:59
59 Moreover Yehudah and his brethren and the whole congregation of Israel ordained that the days of dedication of the altar should be kept in their season from year to year by the space of eight days, from the twenty-fifth day of Kislev, with mirth and gladness.

Yet as much as we might want to respect the person of Judah Maccabee and the other war heroes to whom YHWH gave such a great victory, it would be a mistake to value and esteem their word over the Instructions of the One who gave the victory.

Purim Reconsidered

YHWH commands seven major festivals in the Torah, yet Hanukkah and Purim are not among them. We have included these festivals in this book because many of His people keep them: yet let us ask, "Why do His people keep them?" YHWH set forth His festivals in the Torah, and nowhere does He say that men would have the authority to add to His calendar (and in fact He says the exact opposite). Yet many of His people do keep man-made festivals such as Hanukkah and Purim (as well as Thanksgiving, and others); so let us discuss them here. If the Purim story is true, we might learn something important, as YHWH tends to work in patterns, and history repeats itself.

As we saw in the last chapter, Hanukkah is the story of our Jewish brothers' resistance against the Seleucid Empire, which sought first to assimilate the Jews, and then to destroy those who would not assimilate. In contrast, Purim is the story of how YHWH delivered our Jewish brothers from those who sought to exterminate them outright. YHWH's name is never mentioned in the Purim story, except in acrostics; yet if the story is true, it does seem clear that YHWH was the only one who could have saved the Jews from the destruction the Babylonians had planned against them.

In order to gain some perspective, let us roll back in history, to 586 BCE. YHWH sent Nebuchadnezzar, King of Babylon, to take the Jews into exile for their failure to follow the whole of the Torah, particularly with regards to letting the land rest on the Sabbath Years.

Divre HaYamim Bet (2 Chron) 36:17-21
17 Therefore He brought against them the king of the Chaldeans, who killed their young men with the sword in the house of their sanctuary, and had no compassion on young man or virgin, on the aged or the weak; He gave them all into his hand.
18 And all the articles from the house of Elohim, great and small, the treasures of the house of YHWH, and the treasures of the king and of his leaders, all these he took to Babylon.
19 Then they burned the house of Elohim, broke down the wall of Jerusalem, burned all its palaces with fire, and destroyed all its precious possessions.
20 And those who escaped from the sword he carried away to Babylon, where they became servants to him and his sons until the rule of the kingdom of (Media-) Persia,
21 to fulfill the word of YHWH by the mouth of Jeremiah, until the land had enjoyed her Sabbaths. As long as she lay desolate she kept Sabbath, to fulfill seventy years.

Nebuchadnezzar was succeeded by Evil-Merodach, and then by Belshazzar, who made a great festival.

Daniel 5:1-4
1 Belshazzar the king made a great feast for a thousand of his lords, and drank wine in the presence of the thousand.

237

2 While he tasted the wine, Belshazzar gave the command to bring the gold and silver vessels which his (fore) father Nebuchadnezzar had taken from the temple which had been in Jerusalem, (so) that the king and his lords, his wives, and his concubines might drink from them.

3 Then they brought the gold vessels that had been taken from the temple of the house of Elohim which had been in Jerusalem; and the king and his lords, his wives, and his concubines drank from them.

4 They drank wine, and praised the gods of gold and silver, bronze and iron, wood and stone.

Because Belshazzar's heart was lifted up, and because he purposefully denigrated the Temple vessels, YHWH gave Belshazzar a sign that he was soon to die.

Daniel 5:5-6

5 In the same hour the fingers of a man's hand appeared and wrote opposite the lampstand on the plaster of the wall of the king's palace; and the king saw the part of the hand that wrote.

6 Then the king's countenance changed, and his thoughts troubled him, so that the joints of his hips were loosened and his knees knocked against each other.

However, since no one understood the writing, they brought in the prophet Daniel to interpret the sign.

Daniel 5:18-31

18 O king, the Most High Elohim gave Nebuchadnezzar your (fore) father a kingdom and majesty, glory and honor.

19 And because of the majesty that He gave him, all peoples, nations, and languages trembled and feared before him. Whomever he wished, he executed; whomever he wished, he kept alive; whomever he wished, he set up; and whomever he wished, he put down.

20 But when his heart was lifted up, and his spirit was hardened in pride, he was deposed from his kingly throne, and they took his glory from him.

21 Then he was driven from the sons of men, his heart was made like the beasts, and his dwelling was with the wild donkeys. They fed him with grass like oxen, and his body was wet with the dew of heaven, till he knew that the Most High Elohim rules in the kingdom of men, and appoints over it whomever He chooses.

22 "But you his son, Belshazzar, have not humbled your heart, although you knew all this.

23 And you have lifted yourself up against the Master of heaven. They have brought the vessels of His house before you, and you and your lords, your wives and your concubines, have drunk wine from them. And you have

239

praised the elohim (g-ds) of silver and gold, bronze and iron, wood and stone, which do not see or hear or know; and the Elohim who holds your breath in His hand and owns all your ways, you have not glorified.

24 Then the fingers of the hand were sent from Him, and this writing was written.

25 "And this is the inscription that was written:

MENE, MENE, TEKEL, UPHARSIN.

26 This is the interpretation of each word. MENE: Elohim has numbered your kingdom, and finished it;

27 TEKEL: You have been weighed in the balances, and found wanting;

28 PERES: Your kingdom has been divided, and given to the Medes and Persians."

29 Then Belshazzar gave the command, and they clothed Daniel with purple and put a chain of gold around his neck, and made a proclamation concerning him that he should be the third ruler in the kingdom.

30 That very night Belshazzar, king of the Chaldeans, was slain.

31 And Darius the Mede received the kingdom, being about sixty-two years old.

King Darius the Mede was then succeeded by Koresh (Cyrus) of Persia. YHWH then led Koresh to proclaim a release for all of the Jews, so they could return to the Land of Israel if they so chose. However, very few did.

Ezra 1:1-4
1 Now in the first year of Koresh king of Persia, that the word of YHWH by the mouth of Jeremiah might be fulfilled, YHWH stirred up the spirit of Koresh king of Persia, so that he made a proclamation throughout all his kingdom, and also put it in writing, saying,
2 Thus says Koresh king of Persia:
All the kingdoms of the earth YHWH Elohim of heaven has given me. And He has commanded me to build Him a house at Jerusalem which is in Judah.
3 Who is among you of all His people? May his Elohim be with him, and let him go up to Jerusalem which is in Judah, and build the house of YHWH Elohim of Israel (He is Elohim), which is in Jerusalem.
4 And whoever is left in any place where he dwells, let the men of his place help him with silver and gold, with goods and livestock, besides the freewill offerings for the house of Elohim which is in Jerusalem.

The total number of Jews returning was just over forty two thousand, which was but a small percentage of the millions of Jews living in Media-Persia at that time.

Ezra 2:64
64 The whole assembly together was forty-two thousand three hundred and sixty....

241

Those who returned to the Land immediately began rebuilding the Temple, but their efforts were frustrated by the Samaritans. Though partly descended from the Ephraimites, the Samaritans were mainly descended from foreign stock that earlier Assyrian kings had brought in to resettle and repopulate the land. The Samaritans initially tried to join the Jewish efforts at building, but then sought to stymie the Jews.

Ezra 4:1-24
1 Now when the adversaries of Judah and Benjamin (i.e., the Samaritans) heard that the descendants of the captivity were building the temple of YHWH Elohim of Israel,
2 they came to Zerubbabel and the heads of the fathers' houses, and said to them, "Let us build with you, for we seek your Elohim as you do; and we have sacrificed to Him since the days of Esarhaddon king of Assyria, who brought us here."
3 But Zerubbabel and Yeshua and the rest of the heads of the fathers' houses of Israel said to them, "You may do nothing with us to build a house for our Elohim; but we alone will build to YHWH Elohim of Israel, as King Koresh the king of Persia has commanded us."
4 Then the people of the land tried to discourage the people of Judah. They troubled them in building,
5 and hired counselors against them to frustrate their purpose all the days of Koresh king of Persia, even until the reign of Darius king of Persia.

Two years later, King Koresh was succeeded by King Ahasuerus, also known as King Achashverosh, and/or Artaxerxes. The Samaritans wrote to him, saying that if he allowed the Jews to rebuild their Temple, they would soon seek to break away from his reign. Believing their allegations, Ahasuerus then gave orders that the Samaritans should halt the Temple's construction by any means necessary: even by force.

6 In the reign of Ahasuerus, in the beginning of his reign, they wrote an accusation against the inhabitants of Judah and Jerusalem.

7 And in the days of Artaxerxes Bishlam, Mithredath, Tabel, and the rest of their companions wrote to Artaxerxes (Ahasuerus) king of Persia; and the letter was written in Aramaic script, and translated into the Aramaic language.

8 Rehum the commander and Shimshai the scribe wrote a letter against Jerusalem to King Artaxerxes in this fashion:

9 From Rehum the commander, Shimshai the scribe, and the rest of their companions — representatives of the Dinaites, the Apharsathchites, the Tarpelites, the people of Persia and Erech and Babylon and Shushan, the Dehavites, the Elamites,

10 and the rest of the nations whom the great and noble Osnapper took captive and settled in the cities of Samaria and the remainder beyond the River — and so forth.

243

11 (This is a copy of the letter that they sent him): To King Artaxerxes from your servants, the men of the region beyond the River, and so forth:

12 Let it be known to the king that the Jews who came up from you have come to us at Jerusalem, and are building the rebellious and evil city, and are finishing its walls and repairing the foundations.

13 Let it now be known to the king that, if this city is built and the walls completed, they will not pay tax, tribute, or custom, and the king's treasury will be diminished.

14 Now because we receive support from the palace, it was not proper for us to see the king's dishonor; therefore we have sent and informed the king,

15 that search may be made in the book of the records of your fathers. And you will find in the book of the records and know that this city is a rebellious city, harmful to kings and provinces, and that they have incited sedition within the city in former times, for which cause this city was destroyed.

16 We inform the king that if this city is rebuilt and its walls are completed, the result will be that you will have no dominion beyond the River (i.e., the Euphrates).

17 The king sent an answer:

To Rehum the commander, to Shimshai the scribe, to the rest of their *companions who dwell in Samaria (i.e., the Samaritans), and to the remainder beyond the River:*

Peace, and so forth.

18 The letter which you sent to us has been clearly read before me.

19 And I gave the command, and a search has been made, and it was found that this city in former times has revolted against kings, and rebellion and sedition have been fostered in it.

20 There have also been mighty kings over Jerusalem, who have ruled over all the region beyond the River; and tax, tribute, and custom were paid to them.

21 Now give the command to make these men cease, that this city may not be built until the command is given by me.

22 Take heed now that you do not fail to do this. Why should damage increase to the hurt of the kings?

23 Now when the copy of King Artaxerxes' letter was read before Rehum, Shimshai the scribe, and their companions, they went up in haste to Jerusalem against the Jews, and by force of arms made them cease.

24 Thus the work of the house of Elohim which is at Jerusalem ceased, and it was discontinued until the second year of the reign of Darius king of Persia.

Now that we understand the history that took place before it, the stage is set for the Book of Ester to begin.

The Book of Ester opens with King Koresh's successor, King Ahasuerus, throwing a great festival that lasted for one hundred and eighty days (six months), to which he invited dignitaries from all throughout his empire.

> **Esther 1:1-4**
> **1 Now it came to pass in the days of Ahasuerus (this was the Ahasuerus who reigned over one hundred and twenty-seven provinces, from India to Ethiopia),**
> **2 in those days when King Ahasuerus sat on the throne of his kingdom, which was in Shushan the citadel,**
> **3 that in the third year of his reign he made a feast for all his officials and servants — the powers of Persia and Media, the nobles, and the princes of the provinces being before him —**
> **4 when he showed the riches of his glorious kingdom and the splendor of his excellent majesty for many days, one hundred and eighty days in all.**

Babylon's king was exceedingly wealthy. He could sure throw a big party without having to worry about the cost. However, even rich kings usually throw a party only to commemorate something specific. What was so important to the king that he would celebrate it for a full six months? Let us remember that he had just halted the rebuilding effort that his predecessor Koresh had begun, fulfilling Jeremiah's prophecy about the restoration of Jerusalem. Is it possible the reason King Ahasuerus was throwing such a great festival was that he believed Jeremiah's prophecy about the return of the Jews from Exile had now been proven to be false?

Yirmeyahu (Jeremiah) 29:10-14
10 For thus says YHWH: After seventy years are completed at Babylon, I will visit you and perform My good word toward you, and cause you to return to this place (Jerusalem).
11 For I know the thoughts that I think toward you, says YHWH, thoughts of peace and not of evil, to give you a future and a hope.
12 Then you will call upon Me and go and pray to Me, and I will listen to you.
13 And you will seek Me and find Me, when you search for Me with all your heart.
14 I will be found by you, says YHWH, and I will bring you back from your captivity; I will gather you from all the nations and from all the places where I have driven you, says YHWH, and I will bring you to the place from which I cause you to be carried away captive.

Jeremiah had prophesied that the Jews would be in exile for seventy years following the destruction of the first temple. However, is it possible King Ahasuerus had mistakenly believed that the seventy years had begun earlier, when King Nebuchadnezzar ascended his throne? If so, and King Ahasuerus mistakenly believed that the seventy years of Jeremiah's prophecy were already complete, then he would have seen that he had just put a stop to the restoration of the Temple, and most of the Jews remained out in the Exile. Could this have led King Ahasuerus to believe that Jeremiah's prophecy was false, and that therefore YHWH Elohim was dead? Could this be the reason for his party?

After the six months celebration, King Ahasuerus held another festival which lasted seven days. During this festival, the king served drinks in golden vessels that were different from each other.

> **Esther 1:5-7**
> **5 And when these days were completed, the king made a feast lasting seven days for all the people who were present in Shushan the citadel, from great to small, in the court of the garden of the king's palace.**
> **6 There were white and blue linen curtains fastened with cords of fine linen and purple on silver rods and marble pillars; and the couches were of gold and silver on a mosaic pavement of alabaster, turquoise, and white and black marble.**
> **7 And they served drinks in golden vessels, each vessel being different from the other, with royal wine in abundance, according to the generosity of the king.**

If these were the same Temple vessels that King Belshazzar had celebrated with earlier (above), then King Ahasuerus' purpose was probably to celebrate the end of the Jews as a people set apart unto YHWH, and to denigrate the Temple vessels. If so, YHWH did not terminate King Ahasuerus' life as He had done with King Belshazzar's. Rather, YHWH had an ironic bit of poetic justice in mind, for although he was an anti-Semite, King Ahasuerus was soon to marry the Jewess Ester, and sire Darius the Persian through her.

Becoming drunk with wine, King Ahasuerus called for his beautiful wife Vashti (whose name means, "And drink"), to show off her figure to the other leaders of his realm. Vashti refused to be humiliated like that; but this only enraged King Ahasuerus, who began to seek a replacement for his queen.

Esther 2:1-4
1 After these things, when the wrath of King Ahasuerus subsided, he remembered Vashti, what she had done, and what had been decreed against her.
2 Then the king's servants who attended him said: "Let beautiful young virgins be sought for the king;
3 and let the king appoint officers in all the provinces of his kingdom, that they may gather all the beautiful young virgins to Shushan the citadel, into the women's quarters, under the custody of Hegai the king's eunuch, custodian of the women. And let beauty preparations be given them.
4 Then let the young woman who pleases the king be queen instead of Vashti." This thing pleased the king, and he did so.

Enter Mordechai, a Jew of the tribe of Benjamin, whom some scholars believe was related to King Shaul, son of Kish; and also enter his beautiful adopted daughter Hadassah, also called Esther (i.e., Ishtar). Bringing Esther to the king's palace, Mordechai charges her not to tell anyone she is Jewish.

Esther 2:5-8

5 In Shushan the citadel there was a certain Jew whose name was Mordecai the son of Yair, the son of Shimei, the son of Kish, a Benjamite.

6 Kish had been carried away from Jerusalem with the captives who had been captured with Yeconiah king of Judah, whom Nebuchadnezzar the king of Babylon had carried away.

7 And Mordecai had brought up Hadassah, that is, Esther, his uncle's daughter, for she had neither father nor mother. The young woman was lovely and beautiful. When her father and mother died, Mordecai took her as his own daughter.

8 So it was, when the king's command and decree were heard, and when many young women were gathered at Shushan the citadel, under the custody of Hegai, that Esther also was taken to the king's palace, into the care of Hegai the custodian of the women.

9 Now the young woman pleased him, and she obtained his favor; so he readily gave beauty preparations to her, besides her allowance. Then seven choice maidservants were provided for her from the king's palace, and he moved her and her maidservants to the best place in the house of the women.

10 Esther had not revealed her people or family, for Mordecai had charged her not to reveal it.

11 And every day Mordecai paced in front of the court of the women's quarters, to learn of Esther's welfare and what was happening to her.

According to the world's standards, the Jewish people had never had it better. Mordechai was a high-ranking government official, and his daughter was about to become queen of the world's most powerful empire. As we will see below, the king was to decree a festival in Esther's name (i.e., Ishtar/Easter). Yet if Mordechai and Esther were really such good Jews, then why did neither of them return back to the Land of Israel when YHWH had given them the chance under King Koresh (Cyrus)? Why would Mordechai consider arranging a marriage between his daughter and a pagan such as King Ahasuerus? And why would she consent to it? Why indeed, especially considering that Esther still did not even feel secure divulging her nationality.

> **Esther 2:16-20**
> **16 So Esther was taken to King Ahasuerus, into his royal palace, in the tenth month, which is the month of Tebeth (Tevet), in the seventh year of his reign.**
> **17 The king loved Esther more than all the other women, and she obtained grace and favor in his sight more than all the virgins; so he set the royal crown upon her head and made her queen instead of Vashti.**
> **18 Then the king made a great feast, the Feast of Esther, for all his officials and servants; and he proclaimed a holiday in the provinces and gave gifts according to the generosity of a king.**

251

19 When virgins were gathered together a second time, Mordecai sat within the king's gate.
20 Now Esther had not revealed her family and her people, just as Mordecai had charged her, for Esther obeyed the command of Mordecai as when she was brought up by him.

Mordechai sat within the king's gate; and, one day, as he sat there he overheard two of the palace guards plotting to kill King Ahasuerus. Mordechai told Esther, and she told her husband the king, and Mordechai's loyalty was then recorded in the royal chronicles.

Esther 2:21-23
21 In those days, while Mordecai sat within the king's gate, two of the king's eunuchs, Bigthan and Teresh, doorkeepers, became furious and sought to lay hands on King Ahasuerus.
22 So the matter became known to Mordecai, who told Queen Esther, and Esther informed the king in Mordecai's name.
23 And when an inquiry was made into the matter, it was confirmed, and both were hanged on a gallows; and it was written in the book of the chronicles in the presence of the king.

Curiously, however, Mordechai was not rewarded. Kings rely on tips from their subjects to stay safe, and to retain their hold on power. Yet for some reason, the king never rewarded Mordechai for informing him.

Up to now, the storyline is not one of set-apartness, but of profane behavior. Only 42,000 of the many millions of Jews living in Babylon had chosen to return back home to YHWH's land when they had had the opportunity to do so. Instead, most Jews, including the hero and heroine of our story, had stayed on in Babylon. They were intermarrying with the local people, and were even preparing to marry into (royal) pagan lineages. Yet for all of this profane behavior, Mordechai never lost his identity as an Israelite. In Esther Chapter Three, Mordechai even refused to bow down before a high-ranking government official named Haman, perhaps because he was descended from Agag, king of Amalek.

> *Esther 3:1-7*
> *3:1 After these things King Ahasuerus promoted Haman, the son of Hammedatha the Agagite, and advanced him and set his seat above all the princes who were with him.*
> *2 And all the king's servants who were within the king's gate bowed and paid homage to Haman, for so the king had commanded concerning him. But Mordecai would not bow or pay homage.*
> *3 Then the king's servants who were within the king's gate said to Mordecai, "Why do you transgress the king's command?"*
> *4 Now it happened, when they spoke to him daily and he would not listen to them, that they told it to Haman, to see whether Mordecai's words would stand; for Mordecai had told them that he was a Jew.*

5 When Haman saw that Mordecai did not bow or pay him homage, Haman was filled with wrath.
6 But he disdained to lay hands on Mordecai alone, for they had told him of the people of Mordecai. Instead, Haman sought to destroy all the Jews who were throughout the whole kingdom of Ahasuerus — the people of Mordecai.
7 In the first month, which is the month of Nisan, in the twelfth year of King Ahasuerus, they cast Pur (that is, the lot), before Haman to determine the day and the month (of Israel's destruction), until it fell on the twelfth month, which is the month of Adar.

Even though YHWH's name is never mentioned in the Book of Esther, and even though Mordechai may not have set himself completely apart, Mordechai still considered himself Jewish. Just as King Shaul son of Kish had slain Agag, king of Amalek (First Samuel 15), Mordechai, of the house of Kish, refused to bow down before the son of an Amalekite. This filled Haman with such wrath that he decided he was not content just to destroy Mordechai, but all of the Jews in the empire.

Esther 3:8-11
8 Then Haman said to King Ahasuerus, "There is a certain people scattered and dispersed among the people in all the provinces of your kingdom. Their laws are different from all other people, and they do not keep the king's laws. Therefore it is not fitting for the king to let them remain.

9 If it pleases the king, let a decree be written that they be destroyed, and I will pay ten thousand talents of silver into the hands of those who do the work, to bring it into the king's treasuries."

10 So the king took his signet ring from his hand and gave it to Haman, the son of Hammedatha the Agagite, the enemy of the Jews.

11 And the king said to Haman, "The money and the people are given to you, to do with them as seems good to you."

Not long before this, the situation had seemed very good for the Jewish people, at least by the world's standards. However, now it seemed very bad. First King Ahasuerus had ordered the Jews in Israel to stop rebuilding the Temple, and now he consented to the extermination of all of the Jews. In fact, he completely consented, for normally when a king grants favor to a decree, he carefully reviews the legislation before placing his signet seal on it. However, in this case, simply upon hearing Haman suggest that the Jews should be killed, King Ahasuerus handed his signet ring over to him. Thus, a day before the Passover, on the thirteenth day of the first month, the king's order went forth that all of the Jews should be slaughtered eleven months later, on the thirteenth day of the twelfth month.

Esther 3:12-15

12 Then the king's scribes were called on the thirteenth day of the first month, and a decree was written according to all that Haman commanded — to the king's satraps, to the governors who were over each province, to the officials of all people, to every province according to its script, and to every people in their language. In the name of King Ahasuerus it was written, and sealed with the king's signet ring.

13 And the letters were sent by couriers into all the king's provinces, to destroy, to kill, and to annihilate all the Jews, both young and old, little children and women, in one day, on the thirteenth day of the twelfth month, which is the month of Adar, and to plunder their possessions.

14 A copy of the document was to be issued as law in every province, being published for all people, that they should be ready for that day.

15 The couriers went out, hastened by the king's command; and the decree was proclaimed in Shushan the citadel. So the king and Haman sat down to drink, but the city of Shushan was perplexed.

Upon hearing of the decree, Mordechai did something which makes no sense to the natural mind (but which only makes sense in the spiritual): he put on sackcloth, and went out into the midst of the city, to cry out.

Esther 4:1-4
4:1 When Mordecai learned all that had happened, he tore his clothes and put on sackcloth and ashes, and went out into the midst of the city. He cried out with a loud and bitter cry.

2 He went as far as the front of the king's gate, for no one might enter the king's gate clothed with sackcloth.

3 And in every province where the king's command and decree arrived, there was great mourning among the Jews, with fasting, weeping, and wailing; and many lay in sackcloth and ashes.

4 So Esther's maids and eunuchs came and told her, and the queen was deeply distressed. Then she sent garments to clothe Mordecai and take his sackcloth away from him, but he would not accept them.

The rabbis teach that the Festival of Purim is really about repentance, and trusting in YHWH rather than trusting in our own right hand. Up until this point, while Mordechai's has remained basically loyal to his people, he has also been 'in the world.' He has not treasured YHWH's land, or His temple, but has chosen instead to remain out in the Exile, in the service of an anti-Semitic government, even consenting for his daughter to marry a pagan, anti-Semitic emperor. However, now that his emperor decreed that both he and his people are to be exterminated, Mordechai changes. He realizes he cannot possibly save himself by his own right hand, and so his behavior reflects this knowledge. Instead of doing the 'sensible' thing by going and speaking with his daughter the queen, Mordechai puts on sack cloth so that he cannot enter the royal palace. Then he cries out in the streets, even refusing to put on regular clothes (which would allow him to speak with his daughter face to face). Even though YHWH's name is never mentioned, it seems clear that Mordechai knows only YHWH's hand can save them.

Mordechai's behavior makes no sense to the natural mind; but in Scriptural terms, Mordechai is starting to make perfect sense. He dresses in such a manner as to make it perfectly clear that he realizes that he cannot rescue himself or his people by his own power and strength. Instead, he demonstrates that his life and the lives of his people are completely dependent upon YHWH's unmerited favor: and that is the main point. However, we should notice that once Mordechai has done that he continues to do what little he can, sending a message to Esther through one of the eunuchs.

> **Esther 4:5-9**
> **5 Then Esther called Hathach, one of the king's eunuchs whom he had appointed to attend her, and she gave him a command concerning Mordecai, to learn what and why this was.**
> **6 So Hathach went out to Mordecai in the city square that was in front of the king's gate.**
> **7 And Mordecai told him all that had happened to him, and the sum of money that Haman had promised to pay into the king's treasuries to destroy the Jews.**
> **8 He also gave him a copy of the written decree for their destruction, which was given at Shushan, that he might show it to Esther and explain it to her, and that he might command her to go in to the king to make supplication to him and plead before him for her people.**
> **9 So Hathach returned and told Esther the words of Mordecai.**

Esther responds that she is unable to go see the king, for those coming into his presence without an invitation are to be put to death, unless the king takes action to stay the execution by holding out his royal scepter.

> *Esther 4:10-12*
> *10 Then Esther spoke to Hathach, and gave him a command for Mordecai:*
> *11 "All the king's servants and the people of the king's provinces know that any man or woman who goes into the inner court to the king, who has not been called, he has but one law: put all to death, except the one to whom the king holds out the golden scepter, that he may live. Yet I myself have not been called to go in to the king these thirty days."*
> *12 So they told Mordecai Esther's words.*

Mordechai responds that she must realize she will not survive just because she is married to the king. Then he reminds her that YHWH predestines all things, and proposes that YHWH may have made her queen just so she might play her part in YHWH's deliverance from this present crisis.

> *Esther 4:13-14*
> *13 And Mordecai told them to answer Esther: "Do not think in your heart that you will escape in the king's palace any more than all the other Jews.*
> *14 For if you remain completely silent at this time, relief and deliverance will arise for the Jews from another place,*

but you and your father's house will perish. Yet who knows whether you have come to the kingdom for such a time as this?"

Esther responds that Mordechai should command all the Jews throughout the Empire not to eat or drink for three days and three nights, which, amazingly, means they will be fasting over the Passover (even though the Torah commands Israel to partake of the Passover lamb on that day). Then she will go to King Ahasuerus; and if she perishes, then she will perish.

> **Esther 4:15-17**
> **15 Then Esther told them to reply to Mordecai:**
> **16 "Go, gather all the Jews who are present in Shushan, and fast for me; neither eat nor drink for three days, night or day. My maids and I will fast likewise. And so I will go to the king, which is against the law; and if I perish, I perish!"**
> **17 So Mordecai went his way and did according to all that Esther commanded him.**

Once again, the rabbis would argue that by calling for all Israel to fast on the Passover (and also by fasting herself), Esther also demonstrates her understanding of how utterly dependent they all are on YHWH's favor. Not only will Israel be violating the Torah, but normally a bride would also eat and drink before going in to see a king who chose her for her beauty, so as to look her best. However, by fasting three days she will not look her best; and all of their fates will be in YHWH's hands.

Having fasted and prayed, Esther enters the king's presence on the third day. The king, realizing that she would not have risked her life for an audience unless it was really important, asks her why she has come. She defers, asking the king to come to a banquet of wine instead, perhaps to put him in a better mood, and make him more agreeable. Interestingly, she also asks the king to bring Haman, which he does.

Esther 5:1-8
1 Now it happened on the third day that Esther put on her royal robes and stood in the inner court of the king's palace, across from the king's house, while the king sat on his royal throne in the royal house, facing the entrance of the house.
2 So it was, when the king saw Queen Esther standing in the court, that she found favor in his sight, and the king held out to Esther the golden scepter that was in his hand. Then Esther went near and touched the top of the scepter.
3 And the king said to her, "What do you wish, Queen Esther? What is your request? It shall be given to you — up to half the kingdom!"
4 So Esther answered, "If it pleases the king, let the king and Haman come today to the banquet that I have prepared for him."
5 Then the king said, "Bring Haman quickly, that he may do as Esther has said." So the king and Haman went to the banquet that Esther had prepared.

At the wine feast, still realizing that Ester would not have risked her life by entering his presence unless she felt it was really important, King Ahasuerus asks Esther again what it is that she wants.

> **6 At the banquet of wine the king said to Esther, "What is your petition? It shall be granted you. What is your request, up to half the kingdom? It shall be done!"**
> **7 Then Esther answered and said, "My petition and request is this:**
> **8 If I have found favor in the sight of the king, and if it pleases the king to grant my petition and fulfill my request, then let the king and Haman come to the banquet which I will prepare for them, and tomorrow I will do as the king has said."**

Still not realizing that Queen Esther is a Jewess, and still not realizing that she seeks to annul his evil plot, Haman leaves her wine party in high spirits. However, encountering Mordechai in the king's gate, Mordechai still refuses to bow to him. Venting to his wife, she suggests that Haman make a gallows some fifty cubits (approximately seventy five feet) high, upon which he should have Mordechai hanged.

> **Esther 5:9-14**
> **9 So Haman went out that day joyful and with a glad heart; but when Haman saw Mordecai in the king's gate, and that he did not stand or tremble before him, he was filled with indignation against Mordecai.**

10 Nevertheless Haman restrained himself and went home, and he sent and called for his friends and his wife Zeresh.

11 Then Haman told them of his great riches, the multitude of his children, everything in which the king had promoted him, and how he had advanced him above the officials and servants of the king.

12 Moreover Haman said, "Besides, Queen Esther invited no one but me to come in with the king to the banquet that she prepared; and tomorrow I am again invited by her, along with the king.

13 Yet all this avails me nothing, so long as I see Mordecai the Jew sitting at the king's gate."

14 Then his wife Zeresh and all his friends said to him, "Let a gallows be made, fifty cubits high, and in the morning suggest to the king that Mordecai be hanged on it; then go merrily with the king to the banquet." And the thing pleased Haman; so he had the gallows made.

Again, YHWH's name is never mentioned in the Book of Esther, and yet a miraculous series of coincidences occur which could only have been coordinated on high. The night before the banquet, King Ahasuerus cannot sleep. Curiously, he orders the royal chronicles to be read to him, whereupon he discovers that nothing was done to honor Mordechai after he had put himself at risk by warning the king of the plot to assassinate him.

Esther 6:1-12
1 That night the king could not sleep. So one was commanded to bring the book of the records of the chronicles; and they were read before the king.
2 And it was found written that Mordecai had told of Bigthana and Teresh, two of the king's eunuchs, the doorkeepers who had sought to lay hands on King Ahasuerus.
3 Then the king said, "What honor or dignity has been bestowed on Mordecai for this?"
And the king's servants who attended him said, "Nothing has been done for him."

What would cause a king to lose sleep? The Book of Ester does not tell us the reason, but rather it requires us to 'read in between the lines.' Kings depend upon 'inside information' to maintain power and control, and traditional sources tell us the king may have been worried because his subjects had stopped feeding him information. Perhaps the king had asked himself why that was, and had consulted his chronicles in an effort to discover the reason; and that upon inspecting the chronicles, the king realized that nothing had been done to honor Mordechai for his loyalty? This would have presented a serious problem, for had the people reasoned that it was not worth the effort to alert the king to plots against his life (because there was only risk, and no reward), it might lead to his downfall, and even his death. If that was the case, then the best solution would be for the king to make a soon public demonstration that it had only been an oversight; and that King Ahasuerus really did mean to reward those who took risks on his behalf.

4 So the king said, "Who is in the court?" Now Haman had just entered the outer court of the king's palace to suggest that the king hang Mordecai on the gallows that he had prepared for him.

5 The king's servants said to him, "Haman is there, standing in the court." And the king said, "Let him come in."

6 So Haman came in, and the king asked him, "What shall be done for the man whom the king delights to honor?"

Now Haman thought in his heart, "Whom would the king delight to honor more than me?"

7 And Haman answered the king, "For the man whom the king delights to honor,

8 let a royal robe be brought which the king has worn, and a horse on which the king has ridden, which has a royal crest placed on its head.

9 Then let this robe and horse be delivered to the hand of one of the king's most noble princes, that he may array the man whom the king delights to honor. Then parade him on horseback through the city square, and proclaim before him: 'Thus shall it be done to the man whom the king delights to honor!'"

10 Then the king said to Haman, "Hurry, take the robe and the horse, as you have suggested, and do so for

Mordecai the Jew who sits within the king's gate! Leave nothing undone of all that you have spoken."

11 So Haman took the robe and the horse, arrayed Mordecai and led him on horseback through the city square, and proclaimed before him, "Thus shall it be done to the man whom the king delights to honor!"

12 Afterward Mordecai went back to the king's gate. But Haman hurried to his house, mourning and with his head covered.

Now we might also surmise why Queen Esther had not asked King Ahasuerus her question straightaway, though it was important enough to warrant risking her life for. Perhaps she also needed some assurance that her petition and requests would be listened to, in light of the fact that the king had earlier been drinking with Haman. However, now that she sees Mordechai being honored publicly, it will seem safe to ask her question.

Esther 6:13-14
13 When Haman told his wife Zeresh and all his friends everything that had happened to him, his wise men and his wife Zeresh said to him, "If Mordecai, before whom you have begun to fall, is of Jewish descent, you will not prevail against him but will surely fall before him."

14 While they were still talking with him, the king's eunuchs came, and hastened to bring Haman to the banquet which Esther had prepared.

The Book of Esther gives us many clues, but still asks us to do some sleuthing work for ourselves. Could it be that the reason Esther originally invited Haman to the banquet was in order to give him a false sense of security, so that he might become overconfident, and show some area of weakness that could be exploited, in order to save the Jews? Could it be that what she really wanted was more visibility on him? Still aware that Esther would not have risked her life had it not been important, again King Ahasuerus asks his beloved queen what the matter of importance is.

> *Esther 7:1-6*
> *1 So the king and Haman went to dine with Queen Esther.*
> *2 And on the second day, at the banquet of wine, the king again said to Esther, "What is your petition, Queen Esther? It shall be granted you. And what is your request, up to half the kingdom? It shall be done!"*
> *3 Then Queen Esther answered and said, "If I have found favor in your sight, O king, and if it pleases the king, let my life be given me at my petition, and my people at my request.*
> *4 For we have been sold, my people and I, to be destroyed, to be killed, and to be annihilated. Had we been sold as male and female slaves, I would have held my tongue, although the enemy could never compensate for the king's loss."*
> *5 So King Ahasuerus answered and said to Queen Esther, "Who is he, and where is he, who would dare presume in his heart to do such a thing?"*

6 And Esther said, "The adversary and enemy is this wicked Haman!"
So Haman was terrified before the king and queen.

After the king has publicly honored Mordechai, Esther felt safe divulging her true nationality, as well as her reason for risking her life. In the private confines of the festival she had prepared, it became clear to the king that Haman was attempting to exterminate his chosen queen, as well as Mordechai, who has risked his life for him. As Haman tried to talk his way out of the situation, things only got worse for him.

Esther 7:7-10
7 Then the king arose in his wrath from the banquet of wine and went into the palace garden; but Haman stood before Queen Esther, pleading for his life, for he saw that evil was determined against him by the king.
8 When the king returned from the palace garden to the place of the banquet of wine, Haman had fallen across the couch where Esther was. Then the king said, "Will he also assault the queen while I am in the house?"
As the word left the king's mouth, they covered Haman's face.
9 Now Harbonah, one of the eunuchs, said to the king, "Look! The gallows, fifty cubits high, which Haman made for Mordecai, who spoke good on the king's behalf, is standing at the house of Haman."
Then the king said, "Hang him on it!"

10 So they hanged Haman on the gallows that he had prepared for Mordecai. Then the king's wrath subsided.

Then, after it is revealed to the king that Mordechai is the man who raised the queen, the formerly anti-Semitic King Ahasuerus gives his signet to Mordechai, making him the second in command of his realm. Then Queen Esther begs the king with tears to spare her life, and the lives of her people.

Esther 8:2-8
1 On that day King Ahasuerus gave Queen Esther the house of Haman, the enemy of the Jews. And Mordecai came before the king, for Esther had told how he was related to her.
2 So the king took off his signet ring, which he had taken from Haman, and gave it to Mordecai; and Esther appointed Mordecai over the house of Haman.
3 Now Esther spoke again to the king, fell down at his feet, and implored him with tears to counteract the evil of Haman the Agagite, and the scheme which he had devised against the Jews.
4 And the king held out the golden scepter toward Esther. So Esther arose and stood before the king,
5 and said, "If it pleases the king, and if I have found favor in his sight and the thing seems right to the king and I am pleasing in his eyes, let it be written to revoke the letters devised by

Haman, the son of Hammedatha the Agagite, which he wrote to annihilate the Jews who are in all the king's provinces.

6 For how can I endure to see the evil that will come to my people? Or how can I endure to see the destruction of my countrymen?"

7 Then King Ahasuerus said to Queen Esther and Mordecai the Jew, "Indeed, I have given Esther the house of Haman, and they have hanged him on the gallows because he tried to lay his hand on the Jews.

8 You yourselves write a decree concerning the Jews, as you please, in the king's name, and seal it with the king's signet ring; for whatever is written in the king's name and sealed with the king's signet ring no one can revoke."

Shortly after Pentecost, messengers went forth with a new decree, nullifying the earlier evil, and stating that the Jews could defend themselves against anyone who would attack them on that day.

Esther 8:10-12

10 And he wrote in the name of King Ahasuerus, sealed it with the king's signet ring, and sent letters by couriers on horseback, riding on royal horses bred from swift steeds.

11 By these letters the king permitted the Jews who were in every city to gather together and protect their lives — to destroy, kill, and annihilate all the

forces of any people or province that would assault them, both little children and women, and to plunder their possessions,
12 on one day in all the provinces of King Ahasuerus, on the thirteenth day of the twelfth month, which is the month of Adar.

When the thirteenth day of the twelfth month came, the Jews' enemies were overpowered.

Esther 9:1
1 Now in the twelfth month, that is, the month of Adar, on the thirteenth day, the time came for the king's command and his decree to be executed. On the day that the enemies of the Jews had hoped to overpower them, the opposite occurred, in that the Jews themselves overpowered those who hated them.

Haman's ten sons were also put to death.

Esther 9:6-14
6 And in Shushan the citadel the Jews killed and destroyed five hundred men.
7 Also Parshandatha, Dalphon, Aspatha,
8 Poratha, Adalia, Aridatha,
9 Parmashta, Arisai, Aridai, and Vajezatha —
10 the ten sons of Haman the son of Hammedatha, the enemy of the Jews — they killed; but they did not lay a hand on the plunder.

11 On that day the number of those who were killed in Shushan the citadel was brought to the king.

12 And the king said to Queen Esther, "The Jews have killed and destroyed five hundred men in Shushan the citadel, and the ten sons of Haman. What have they done in the rest of the king's provinces? Now what is your petition? It shall be granted to you. Or what is your further request? It shall be done."

13 Then Esther said, "If it pleases the king, let it be granted to the Jews who are in Shushan to do again tomorrow according to today's decree, and let Haman's ten sons be hanged on the gallows."

14 So the king commanded this to be done; the decree was issued in Shushan, and they hanged Haman's ten sons.

In verse thirteen, Ester asked the king to allow the Jews to defend themselves against their enemies once more (on the fourteenth day of the month). Yet, Ester also asked that Haman's ten sons be hanged, even though they were already dead (and even listed by name in verses seven through nine). Could it be that the reason Esther wanted to hang their corpses up in the sun was, in the aftermath of Haman's earlier order, to make it perfectly clear that no one could safely persecute the Jews in King Ahasuerus' empire? If this chronology is accurate, some of the Jews were finished defending themselves on the thirteenth of the month, while others needed an extra day.

Esther 9:15-17

15 And the Jews who were in Shushan gathered together again on the fourteenth day of the month of Adar and killed three hundred men at Shushan; but they did not lay a hand on the plunder.

16 The remainder of the Jews in the king's provinces gathered together and protected their lives, had rest from their enemies, and killed seventy-five thousand of their enemies; but they did not lay a hand on the plunder.

17 This was on the thirteenth day of the month of Adar. And on the fourteenth of the month they rested and made it a day of feasting and gladness.

18 But the Jews who were at Shushan assembled together on the thirteenth day, as well as on the fourteenth; and on the fifteenth of the month they rested, and made it a day of feasting and gladness.

19 Therefore the Jews of the villages who dwelt in the unwalled towns celebrated the fourteenth day of the month of Adar with gladness and feasting, as a holiday, and for sending presents to one another.

Then the Book of Esther reports that because of these things, Mordechai and Esther wrote to their people, and added to the Torah, commanding that the fourteenth and fifteenth days of the twelfth month ('Adar') be kept as a festival in perpetuity, among all the Jews forever.

Esther 9:20-26

20 And Mordecai wrote these things and sent letters to all the Jews, near and far, who were in all the provinces of King Ahasuerus,

21 to establish among them that they should celebrate yearly the fourteenth and fifteenth days of the month of Adar,

22 as the days on which the Jews had rest from their enemies, as the month which was turned from sorrow to joy for them, and from mourning to a holiday; that they should make them days of feasting and joy, of sending presents to one another and gifts to the poor.

23 So the Jews accepted the custom which they had begun, as Mordecai had written to them,

24 because Haman, the son of Hammedatha the Agagite, the enemy of all the Jews, had plotted against the Jews to annihilate them, and had cast Pur (that is, the lot), to consume them and destroy them;

25 but when Esther came before the king, he commanded by letter that this wicked plot which Haman had devised against the Jews should return on his own head, and that he and his sons should be hanged on the gallows.

26 So they called these days Purim, after the name Pur (lot).

Some scholars question the accuracy of the Book of Esther, for reasons we will discuss a little later on.

However, even if the Book of Ester is not completely accurate, we can still learn a great deal from it. For example, King Ahasuerus was only in the third year of his reign when he threw his six month long party.

> **Esther 1:3-4**
> **3 that in the third year of his reign he made a feast for all his officials and servants — the powers of Persia and Media, the nobles, and the princes of the provinces being before him —**
> **4 when he showed the riches of his glorious kingdom and the splendor of his excellent majesty for many days, one hundred and eighty days in all.**

Haman cast the lot (the pur) in the twelfth year of King Ahasuerus' reign (to see when the Jews would be most vulnerable and susceptible to attack).

> **Esther 3:7**
> **7 In the first month, which is the month of Nisan, in the twelfth year of King Ahasuerus, they cast Pur (that is, the lot), before Haman to determine the day and the month, until it fell on the twelfth month, which is the month of Adar.**

Esther and Mordechai's new decree allowed the Jews to defend themselves at the end of the twelfth year of king, which was perhaps nine or ten years after King Ahasuerus had originally thrown his party. However, Daniel tells us that it was not until the first year of Esther's son, Darius the Mede (not to be confused with Darius the Persian), that the seventy years of Exile (as foretold by Jeremiah) were supposed to end.

275

Daniel 9:1-3
9:1 In the first year of Darius the son of Ahasuerus, of the lineage of the Medes, who was made king over the realm of the Chaldeans —
2 in the first year of his reign I, Daniel, understood by the books the number of the years specified by the word of YHWH through Jeremiah the Prophet, that He would accomplish seventy years in the desolations of Jerusalem.
3 Then I set my face toward YHWH Elohim to make request by prayer and supplications, with fasting, sackcloth, and ashes.

It was the second year of King Darius the Mede (son of Ahasuerus and Esther), that those who had returned back home to the Land of Israel were allowed to resume work on the Temple.

Ezra 4:24
24 Thus the work of the house of Elohim which is at Jerusalem ceased, and it was discontinued until the second year of the reign of Darius king of Persia.

Ezra records how those who had returned to the Land wrote to the righteous King Darius, asking his pleasure with regards to the building of the Temple. King Darius, who probably knew that his mother was Jewish, gave great favor to those in the Land. He returned all of the temple vessels, and even paid for the Temple's reconstruction at royal expense.

Ezra 6:8-10
8 Moreover I issue a decree as to what you shall do for the elders of these Jews, for the building of this house of Elahah (Elohim): Let the cost be paid at the king's expense from taxes on the region beyond the River; this is to be given immediately to these men, so that they are not hindered.
9 And whatever they need — young bulls, rams, and lambs for the burnt offerings of the Elah of heaven, wheat, salt, wine, and oil, according to the request of the priests who are in Jerusalem — let it be given them day by day without fail,
10 that they may offer sacrifices of sweet aroma to the Elah of heaven, and pray for the life of the king and his sons.

Some rabbinical authorities define Amalek as anyone who has an unreasoning hatred for Israel. Further, they also remind us that YHWH works in patterns, and they draw heavy parallels to Nazi Germany. They also draw parallels between Haman's ten sons, and the New York Times headline of October, 1947:

GOERING ENDS LIFE BY POISON, 10 OTHERS HANGED IN NUREMBERG PRISON FOR NAZI WAR CRIMES; DOOMED MEN ON GALLOWS PRAY FOR GERMANY

Julius Streicher was one of the ten condemned men. He is reported to have shouted "Purimfest 1946!" as the trap door to the gallows was sprung, as if to draw a parallel to Haman's ten sons being hanged.

The ten men were hung on October 16, 1947. On the Rabbinical Calendar (which is different than the Torah Calendar) this was the seventh day of the Feast of Tabernacles, which the rabbis call Hoshana Rabbah. The rabbis claim that Hoshana Rabbah is the day that YHWH seals men's fates for the coming year.

Considering that YHWH is in charge of all things, many people see these things as support for the idea that we should keep the Feast of Purim. However, we should bear it in mind that YHWH did not command us to keep the Rabbinical Calendar (which is different than the calendar YHWH commands us to keep in Torah).

Many scholars see some suspicious parallels between the Feast of Purim and ancient Babylonian mythology. For example, the names Mordechai and Esther strongly resemble the Babylonian gods Marduk and Ishtar (Easter). Further, in Babylonian mythology, Marduk and Ishtar are cousins, as are Mordechai and Esther in the story (see verse 2:7). Marduk was the patron elohim (g-d) of the Babylonian capital, and Esther is another name for Ishtar (Easter), whom the Babylonians worshipped as a fertility goddess, and as 'the mother goddess.' Some also find it suspicious that King Ahasuerus commands a feast for Esther in Verse 2:18, and wonder if this is the same as the feast of Easter (Ishtar) that is practiced in within mainstream Christianity.

> **Esther 2:18**
> **18 Then the king made a great feast, the Feast of Esther, for all his officials and servants; and he proclaimed a holiday in the provinces and gave gifts according to the generosity of a king.**

Some scholars believe that Purim originally derived from the Babylonian New Year's rites, which existed long before the Jews were taken into exile in Babylon. Many of these suspect that the Book of Esther is a kind of a justification for practicing these Babylonian rituals, much like Christian mythology attempts to justify Easter and Christmas. These point out that the basic story components of Esther all occur in ancient Babylonian celebrations of their new year, including the selection of a queen, the parading of a common man dressed up in royal garments, and a fast and the giving of gifts.

On top of this, the chronology in Ester seems to depart from the historical records. Therefore, some scholars allege that the Book of Esther is not really a historically accurate document, and that it does not belong inside the canon of Scripture. However, that debate is a very involved one, and is outside the scope of this present study.

What is inside the scope of this present study is to state that if there really was an Esther and Mordechai, and if they really did command the Jews to keep a Feast called Purim, Esther and Mordechai do not have the authority to add festival days to YHWH's calendar, for YHWH commands us not to add to His word.

> *Devarim (Deuteronomy) 4:2*
> *2 "You shall not add to the word which I command you, nor take from it, that you may keep the commandments of YHWH your Elohim which I command you."*

Going Deeper

As one might expect, the Most High Perfect Elohim has created multiple layers of symbolism and meaning not only in His Torah, but also in His Festivals. While a complete discussion of the significance of the festivals is outside the scope of this work, let us take a look at the interrelationships between the spring and the fall festivals.

In Yoel (Joel) 2:23, YHWH tells us that the latter rains come in the first month.

Joel 2:23 23 Be glad then, you children of Zion, and rejoice in YHWH your Elohim, for He has given you the former rain faithfully, and He will cause the rain to come down for you — The former rain, and the latter rain in the first (month).	(23) וּבְנֵי צִיּוֹן גִּילוּ וְשִׂמְחוּ בַּיהוָה אֱלֹהֵיכֶם כִּי נָתַן לָכֶם אֶת הַמּוֹרֶה לִצְדָקָה וַיּוֹרֶד לָכֶם גֶּשֶׁם מוֹרֶה וּמַלְקוֹשׁ בָּרִאשׁוֹן :

The Land of Israel is semi-tropical, and has essentially two seasons: a hot dry summer, and a wet winter. In between these seasons are short temperate periods of transition, when the Spring and Fall Feasts take place. Most of the rain in the Land of Israel falls in the winter, after the Fall Festivals, but before the Passover. Later we will see symbolic aspects of this as well.

Scripture speaks of the early rains, and the latter rains. From a Western-Roman standpoint, one might think the earlier rains fall in the spring, and the latter rains fall in autumn. However, when we realize that the Hebrew year does not start until the spring, and that the Land of Israel is then normally sunny for at least six months, we see that the 'earlier' rains actually fall after the Fall Festival season, and the 'latter' rains fall just before the Passover, in the first month.

But when is rain more than just rain? In Joel 2:23, the word for the early 'rain' is מוֹרֶה (moreh), which is also the word for a teacher, or a teaching (i.e., instruction).

> ***OT:4175 mowreh (mo-reh'); from OT:3384; an archer; also teacher or teaching; also the early rain [see OT:3138]:***

The word for the latter rains is malqosh (מַלְקוֹשׁ), which translates figuratively as 'eloquence.'

> ***OT:4456 malqowsh (mal-koshe'); from OT:3953; the spring rain (compare OT:3954); figuratively, eloquence:***

YHWH says, then, that He will give His teachings and His eloquence at the times of the early and the latter rains, which come just before the Spring festivals, and after the Fall Festivals.

But if YHWH gives instruction and eloquence at His festival times, are there other relationships between His feasts? Other relationships turn up if we match up these festivals and their associated traditions side-by-side, reading from left to right.

Spring Festivals > > > > > > Fall Festivals

[Rabbinical Tu B'Shevat]
[Traditional Jewish New Year for Trees]

Yom Teruah (Trumpets)
The Bridegroom comes for His bride

Purim (before Pesach)
The bride-to-be is tested, and turns back to Him. Traditionally celebrated by eating and drinking, and then starting to cleanse one's house of leaven

Yom HaKippurim (can also be translated, "a Day like the Purim")
The bride-to-be is taken in marriage.
No eating, drinking, or any other pleasures of the flesh.

Pesach and Unleavened Bread. A one day feast followed by a seven day feast. All native Israelites must eat unleavened bread

Sukkot and Shemini Atzeret. A seven day feast followed by a one day feast. All native Israelites must dwell in sukkot.

Pentecost (Shavuot)
Traditionally, the bride was given the Torah on this day as a marital covenant (ketubah).

[Shemini Atzeret]
[Traditionally, the bride rejoices, from whence the tradition of 'Simchat Torah' comes]

Second Passover
A second opportunity to celebrate Passover, for those who were unclean at the first Passover

Chanukah
Originally established as a 'second sukkot', since the Maccabees were fighting the Greeks during Sukkot.

Physical renewal

Spiritual renewal

Additionally, there are parallels between the first and the seventh months.

First Month (Aviv) > > > > > > Seventh Month

Day 1
The Tabernacle was put into service on the first day of the first month (reference Exodus 40:2)

Day 1
Traditionally, Yeshua our Temple, will return on the first day of the first month (Yom Teruah)

Day 10
The Passover Lamb is chosen

Day 10
Two goats are chosen, one for YHWH, and one for Azazel (Satan).

Day 10
The Feast of the Passover and Unleavened Bread basically begins here, and five days later, Israel will be freed from bondage

Day 10
Jubilee ('Release') is declared, when Israelite slaves are released from bondage, and property returns to its owner

Day 10
Israel enters the Promised Land (Joshua 4:9)

Day 10
High Sabbath of rest

Day 14/15
YHWH's people enter inside their houses for protection

Day 15
YHWH's people enter into their sukkot for protection

Day 15
Israel begins dwelling in Sukkot while traveling in the Wilderness of Sinai

Day 15
Israel dwells in Sukkot for protection while living in the Promised Land

Day 14/15 Yeshua dies	Day 15 Yeshua is born
Day 14-22 Israel eats unleavened bread	Day 14-22 Israel lives in sukkot
Day 15 Pilgrimage festival	Day 15 Pilgrimage festival
Day 15 Opening harvest. Omer Count Begins	Day 15 Final harvest. The Four Species are waved before YHWH
Ripening of grains	Ripening of grapes and olives

But why does YHWH not give all of the commandments regarding the festivals in one place, so we can understand what He wants more easily? The answer is that there are hidden messages in how the commands are laid out within the Torah.

Pilgrimage Feasts	**Days of Judgment** (Traditional)
Exodus 23:14-19 Exodus 34:18-26 Deuteronomy 16:1-17	
Passover/Unleavened	Yom Teruah (Trumpets)
Pentecost/Weeks	Yom Kippur (Atonements)
Sukkot/Tabernacles	Shemini Atzeret

In Exodus and Deuteronomy, the date of the festival is not given with regards to its numerical or ordinal date, but with regards to the agricultural season and the harvests. This is why the tithe is mentioned in these places is that the tithe was historically timed to the animal and vegetable harvests of the land.

Shemote (Exodus) 23:14-19
14 "Three times you shall keep a feast to Me in the year:
15 You shall keep the Feast of Unleavened Bread (you shall eat unleavened bread seven days, as I commanded you, at the time appointed in the month of the Aviv, for in it you came out of Egypt; none shall appear before Me empty);
16 and the Feast of Harvest, the firstfruits of your labors which you have sown in the field; and the Feast of Ingathering at the end of the year, when you have gathered in the fruit of your labors from the field.
17 "Three times in the year all your males shall appear before YHWH Elohim.
18 "You shall not offer the blood of My sacrifice with leavened bread; nor shall the fat of My sacrifice remain until morning.
19 The first of the firstfruits of your land you shall bring into the house of YHWH your Elohim. You shall not boil a young goat in its mother's milk.

Exodus 34:18-24 gives us a similar set of commands, with the dates also being set with regards to the firstfruits of the land, both animal and vegetable.

Shemote (Exodus) 34:18-26
18 "The Feast of Unleavened Bread you shall keep. Seven days you shall eat unleavened bread, as I commanded you, in the appointed time of the month of the Aviv; for in the month of the Aviv you came out from Egypt.
19 "All that open the womb are Mine, and every male firstborn among your livestock, whether ox or sheep.
20 But the firstborn of a donkey you shall redeem with a lamb. And if you will not redeem him, then you shall break his neck. All the firstborn of your sons you shall redeem. And none shall appear before Me empty-handed.
21 "Six days you shall work, but on the seventh day you shall rest; in plowing time and in harvest you shall rest.
22 "And you shall observe the Feast of Weeks, of the firstfruits of wheat harvest, and the Feast of Ingathering at the year's end.
23 "Three times in the year all your men shall appear before the Adon, YHWH Elohim of Israel.
24 For I will cast out the nations before you and enlarge your borders; neither will any man covet your land when you go up to appear before YHWH your Elohim three times in the year.

25 "You shall not offer the blood of My sacrifice with leaven, nor shall the sacrifice of the Feast of the Passover be left until morning.
26 "The first of the <u>firstfruits</u> of your land you shall bring to the house of YHWH your Elohim. You shall not boil a young goat in its mother's milk."

Deuteronomy 16:1-15 follows this same pattern, by making reference to the animal and vegetable fruits of the land, and the harvest seasons.

Devarim (Deuteronomy) 16:1-15
1 "Observe the <u>month of the Aviv</u>, and keep the Passover to YHWH your Elohim, for in the <u>month of the Aviv</u> YHWH your Elohim brought you out of Egypt by night.
2 Therefore you shall sacrifice the Passover to YHWH your Elohim, from the <u>flock and the herd</u>, in the place where YHWH chooses to put His name.
3 You shall eat no leavened bread with it; seven days you shall eat unleavened bread with it, that is, the bread of affliction (for you came out of the land of Egypt in haste), that you may remember the day in which you came out of the land of Egypt all the days of your life.
4 And no leaven shall be seen among you in all your territory for seven days, nor shall any of the meat which you sacrifice the first day at twilight remain overnight until morning.

5 "You may not sacrifice the Passover within any of your gates which YHWH your Elohim gives you;

6 but at the place where YHWH your Elohim chooses to make His name abide, there you shall sacrifice the Passover at twilight, at the going down of the sun, at the time you came out of Egypt.

7 And you shall roast and eat it in the place which YHWH your Elohim chooses, and in the morning you shall turn and go to your tents.

8 Six days you shall eat unleavened bread, and on the seventh day there shall be a sacred assembly to YHWH your Elohim. You shall do no work on it.

9 "You shall count seven weeks for yourself; begin to count the seven weeks from the time you begin to put the <u>sickle to the grain</u>.

10 Then you shall keep the Feast of Weeks to YHWH your Elohim with the tribute of a freewill offering from your hand, which you shall give as YHWH your Elohim blesses you.

11 You shall rejoice before YHWH your Elohim, you and your son and your daughter, your male servant and your female servant, the Levite who is within your gates, the stranger and the fatherless and the widow who are among you, at the place where YHWH your Elohim chooses to make His name abide.

12 And you shall remember that you were a slave in Egypt, and you shall be careful to observe these statutes.

13 "You shall observe the Feast of Tabernacles seven days, when you have gathered from your <u>threshing floor</u> and from your <u>winepress</u>.

14 And you shall rejoice in your feast, you and your son and your daughter, your male servant and your female servant and the Levite, the stranger and the fatherless and the widow, who are within your gates.

15 Seven days you shall keep a sacred feast to YHWH your Elohim in the place which YHWH chooses, because YHWH your Elohim will bless you in all your produce and in all the work of your hands, so that you surely rejoice.

Notice also how the festivals line up with what most Westerners living in temperate climes would typically call spring, summer, and fall. However, since there are really only two seasons in the Land of Israel, these dates actually line up with the ripening of the crops at the start of summer, mid-summer, and then the transition at the summer's end.

Pilgrimage Festival	Season
Passover/Unleavened	Start-of-summer transition
Shavuot/Pentecost	Mid-summer
Sukkot/Tabernacles	End-of-summer transition

However, while Exodus and Deuteronomy describe the feasts in relation to the agricultural harvests, Leviticus and Numbers simply tell us what month and day they should be held in. However, Leviticus and Numbers do give us the offerings the priests are to make in the Temple. If we study these offerings side by side, in a chart, we can begin to see some interesting parallels. First we will look at Numbers 25:10 thru 30:1.

Feast	Numbers 25:10 - 30:1 (Parasha Pinchas)
Passover/Unleavened 15th day of the 1st month	2 bulls, 1 ram 7 male lambs, 1 male goat
Shavuot/Pentecost 50 days after the First Day of the Week after Pesach	2 bulls, 1 ram 7 male lambs, 1 male goat
Yom Teruah (Trumpets) 1st day of the 7th month	1 bull, 1 ram 7 male lambs, 1 male goat
Yom Kippur (Atonements) 10th day of the 7th month	1 bull, 1 ram 7 male lambs, 1 male goat (plus one for Azazel)
Sukkot (Tabernacles) 15th day of the 7th month Day 1	13 bulls, 2 rams, 14 male lambs, 1 male goat
Day 2	12 bulls, 2 rams, 14 male lambs, 1 male goat

Day 3	11 bulls, 2 rams, 14 male lambs, 1 male goat
Day 4	10 bulls, 2 rams, 14 male lambs, 1 male goat
Day 5	9 bulls, 2 rams, 14 male lambs, 1 male goat
Day 6	8 bulls, 2 rams, 14 male lambs, 1 male goat
Day 7	7 bulls, 2 rams, 14 male lambs, 1 male goat
Shemini Atzeret (Assembly of the Eighth) Day 8	1 bull, 1 ram, 7 male lambs, 1 male goat

Leviticus 23 (in Parasha Emor) is unique. It not only tells us what unique commandments are associated with each festival, but it also tells us which agricultural season each one of these special commandments falls into.

Feast	Special Command	Season
Unleavened Bread	Wave Sheaf (Omer)	*Leviticus 23:10 "When you enter the Land... and harvest the grain*

Shavuot (Pentecost) (Weeks)	Specially leavened loaves of wheat bread.	*Leviticus 23:16 "... count seven weeks, then... you shall bring a new grain offering...."*
Yom Teruah (Trumpets)	Blowing the shofar	
Yom Kippurim (Atonements)	Afflicting one's soul	
Sukkot (Tabernacles)	Waving the four species: Lulav, etrog, etc.	*Leviticus 23:39-40 "... when you gather the produce of the land... and you shall take on the first day a goodly fruit...."*

We do not really know why YHWH does not give us all the commandments regarding the festivals all neatly in one place. However, we do know that there are many layers of spiritual implications to His timing.

Israel's physical redemption from slavery in Egypt came in the spring. The springtime is also when Israel crossed the Jordan River, to enter the Land of Israel.

Spring is an interesting time. While some crops (such as barley) do grow and mature in winter, most crops lay dormant in the winter, and only begin to experience renewed growth in the spring. In much the same way, while YHWH does have some servants who may flourish and grow in the 'winter' (or in the 'Wilderness') the majority of Israelites need the warmth of spring before they can begin to grow and flourish.

However, just as spring only begins the onset of plant growth, we must also realize that our acceptance of Yeshua only begins the onset of our spiritual growth. Just as plant and animal life is also tenuous, salvation also is far from being certain. Each one of us needs to continue to work out his salvation in fear, and in trembling before the Father.

> *Kepha Aleph (1st Peter) 1:17-19*
> *17 And if you call on the Father, who without partiality judges according to each one's work, conduct yourselves throughout the time of your stay here in fear;*
> *18 knowing that you were not redeemed with corruptible things, like silver or gold, from your aimless conduct received by tradition from your fathers,*
> *19 but with the precious blood of Messiah, as of a lamb without blemish and without spot.*

Tradition holds the Messiah will return on Yom Teruah, at the end of the growing season, which is referred to as 'the day and the hour which no man knows.'

> *Mattai (Matthew) 24:36*
> *36 "But of that day and hour no one knows, not even the angels of heaven, but My Father only.*

Revelation also seems to imply that Messiah will return at the time of the Fall Harvests, which is when the grapes and the olives come ripe. Some among Israel will have reached a similar state of maturity then.

Gilyana (Revelation) 14:17-19

17 Then another angel came out of the temple which is in heaven, he also having a sharp sickle.

18 And another angel came out from the altar, who had power over fire, and he cried with a loud cry to him who had the sharp sickle, saying, "Thrust in your sharp sickle and gather the clusters of the vine of the earth, for her grapes are fully ripe."

19 So the angel thrust his sickle into the earth and gathered the vine of the earth, and threw it into the great winepress of the wrath of Elohim.

Just as grapes and olives have but one short season in which to mature and come ready for the harvest, we also have just one short lifetime in order to become fit and worthy companions and attendants for the King above all kings. Let us seize the opportunity, knowing that we must work while it is still day, for soon the night will come, when no man can work.

Let us prepare ourselves for Him, and be ready before Him when He comes.

The 'Seventy Week Ministry' Theory

Traditional theology tells us Yeshua's ministry lasted for some 3-1/2 years, from the fall festival season (e.g., Yom Kippur) to Yeshua's sacrifice at the Passover in the spring. As we saw before, Yeshua was probably killed on the 4th day of the week (i.e., a Wednesday), and was raised three days later, either on the Sabbath, or on the transition between the Sabbath and the first day of the week. This would fit Daniel 9:27, which tells us the Messiah was to be cut off in the middle of the week (וַחֲצִי הַשָּׁבוּעַ).

Daniel 9:24-27 24 "Seventy weeks (of years) are determined for your people and for your set-apart city, to finish the transgression, to make an end of sins, to make reconciliation for iniquity, to bring in everlasting righteousness, to seal up vision and prophecy, and to anoint the Most Set-apart. 25 "Know therefore and understand, that from the going forth of the command to restore and build Jerusalem until Messiah the Prince, there shall be seven weeks and	(24) שָׁבֻעִים שִׁבְעִים נֶחְתַּךְ עַל עַמְּךָ וְעַל עִיר קָדְשֶׁךָ לְכַלֵּא הַפֶּשַׁע ולחתם [וּלְהָתֵם קרי] חטאות [חַטָּאת קרי] וּלְכַפֵּר עָוֹן וּלְהָבִיא צֶדֶק עֹלָמִים ׀ וְלַחְתֹּם חָזוֹן וְנָבִיא וְלִמְשֹׁחַ קֹדֶשׁ קָדָשִׁים : (25) וְתֵדַע וְתַשְׂכֵּל מִן מֹצָא דָבָר לְהָשִׁיב וְלִבְנוֹת יְרוּשָׁלַ͏ִם עַד מָשִׁיחַ נָגִיד שָׁבֻעִים שִׁבְעָה ׀ וְשָׁבֻעִים שִׁשִּׁים וּשְׁנַיִם תָּשׁוּב וְנִבְנְתָה

sixty-two weeks. The street shall be built again, and the wall, even in troublesome times.

26 "And after the sixty-two weeks, Messiah shall be cut off, but not for Himself; and the people of the prince who is to come shall destroy the city and the sanctuary. The end of it shall be with a flood, and till the end of the war desolations are determined.

27 Then he shall confirm a covenant with many for one week; but in the middle of the week He shall bring an end to sacrifice and offering. And on the wing of abominations shall be one who makes desolate, even until the consummation, which is determined, is poured out on the desolate."

רְחוֹב וְחָרוּץ וּבְצוֹק הָעִתִּים : (26) וְאַחֲרֵי הַשָּׁבֻעִים שִׁשִּׁים וּשְׁנַיִם יִכָּרֵת מָשִׁיחַ וְאֵין לוֹ | וְהָעִיר וְהַקֹּדֶשׁ יַשְׁחִית עַם נָגִיד הַבָּא וְקִצּוֹ בַשֶּׁטֶף וְעַד קֵץ מִלְחָמָה נֶחֱרֶצֶת שֹׁמֵמוֹת : (27) וְהִגְבִּיר בְּרִית לָרַבִּים שָׁבוּעַ אֶחָד | וַחֲצִי הַשָּׁבוּעַ יַשְׁבִּית זֶבַח וּמִנְחָה וְעַל כְּנַף שִׁקּוּצִים מְשֹׁמֵם וְעַד כָּלָה וְנֶחֱרָצָה תִּתַּךְ עַל שֹׁמֵם

Verse 24 speaks of "seventy weeks" being determined for the Jews and for Jerusalem. Traditional scholarship tells us that this phrase refers to 'seventy weeks of years', or seventy times seven years (490 years). Then, as we also explain in the Nazarene Israel study, when verse 25 then speaks of "seven weeks and sixty-two weeks", it refers to sixty nine 'weeks of years', or

483 years. This was how many years there would be from the time when the Jews returned from the Exile in Babylon until "Messiah the Prince" (Yeshua) would come.

According to most historical accounts, the command for the Jews to return to Babylon was given in approximately 457 BCE. After four hundred and ninety years we reach approximately 26 CE, which is when many scholars believe Yeshua's ministry began. The question at hand, however, is whether Yeshua's ministry lasted for three-and-a-half years, or whether it lasted only for seventy weeks. Both sides make a good argument.

Proponents of a three-and-one-half year ministry tell us that when verse 27 tells us that Yeshua would make a covenant for one week, it meant seven years (seven being a number signifying perfection, and completion). However, when Yeshua was cut off in the middle of the week (bringing and end to sacrifice and offering in the Temple), it meant not only that He was killed on the 4th day of the week, but also that He was cut off at the 3-1/2 year mark of what should have been a seven-year ministry.

> *27 Then he shall confirm a covenant with many for one week; but in the middle of the week He shall bring an end to sacrifice and offering.*

However, there is also a case to be made for a seventy week ministry. The themes of 'seventy' and 'seven' run all throughout Scripture, with Yeshua even using the phrase 'seventy times seven' to illustrate the concept of perfection with (regards to forgiveness).

Mattithyahu (Matthew) 18:21-22
*21 Then Kepha (Peter) came to Him
and said, "Adon, how often shall my
brother sin against me, and I forgive
him? Up to seven times?"*
*22 Yeshua said to him, "I do not say to
you, up to seven times, but up to
seventy times seven.*

Some scholars feel it makes more sense that Yeshua's
ministry lasted seventy weeks, than three-and-one-half
years. In order to demonstrate their argument, we will
follow the chronology in the Book of Yochanan (John).

In John Chapter One we meet Yochanan HaMatbil
(John the Immerser/John the Baptist), who testifies that
Yeshua is the Son of Elohim. As we will see later, this
is probably the same general timeframe that Yeshua
was immersed, and that the Spirit descended upon
Him, and His ministry began.

Yochanan (John) 1:29-34
*29 The next day Yochanan saw Yeshua
coming toward him, and said, "Behold!
The Lamb of Elohim who takes away
the sin of the world!*
*30 This is He of whom I said, 'After me
comes a Man who is preferred before
me, for He was before me.'*
*31 I did not know Him; but that He
should be revealed to Israel, therefore
I came baptizing with water."*
*32 And John bore witness, saying, "I
saw the Spirit descending from heaven
like a dove, and He remained upon
Him.*

33 I did not know Him, but He who sent me to baptize with water said to me, 'Upon whom you see the Spirit descending, and remaining on Him, this is He who baptizes with the Ruach HaQodesh (Holy Spirit).'
34 And I have seen and testified that this is the Son of Elohim."

We know from the synoptic accounts (Matthew, Mark, and Luke) that Yeshua was then in the wilderness forty days and forty nights. However, according to the Seventy Week Ministry Theory, the sequence of events follows the festivals, and progresses quickly.

At the start of John Chapter Two, Yeshua turns water into wine and then goes to Kephar Nahum (Capernaum) for a few days.

Yochanan (John) 2:12
12 After this He went down to Capernaum, He, His mother, His brothers, and His disciples; and they did not stay there many days.

Next, Yeshua went up to Jerusalem for the Passover.

Yochanan (John) 2:13
13 Now the Passover of the Jews was at hand, and Yeshua went up to Jerusalem.

Yeshua stays in the Jerusalem area all during John Chapter Two, and is still in Jerusalem in John Chapter Three. There He meets with Nicodemus, and explains that one needs to be born again spiritually.

Yochanan (John) 3:1-3
1 There was a man of the Pharisees named Nicodemus, a ruler of the Jews.
2 This man came to Yeshua by night and said to Him, "Rabbi, we know that You are a teacher come from Elohim; for no one can do these signs that You do unless Elohim is with him."
3 Yeshua answered and said to him, "Most assuredly, I say to you, unless one is born again, he cannot see the kingdom of Elohim."

In John Chapter Four, Yeshua leaves Jerusalem and heads north for the Galilee by way of Samaria. It is at this time He meets the Woman at the Well.

Yochanan (John) 4:3-4
3 He left Judea and departed again to Galilee.
4 But He needed to go through Samaria.
5 So He came to a city of Samaria which is called Sychar, near the plot of ground that Jacob gave to his son Joseph.
6 Now Jacob's well was there. Yeshua therefore, being wearied from His journey, sat thus by the well. It was about the sixth hour.

Yeshua then witnesses to the townspeople for two more days, and then departs.

Yochanan (John) 4:43
43 Now after the two days He departed from there and went to Galilee.

Once Yeshua reaches the Galilee, He performs two miracles, including raising a certain nobleman's dead son.

> *Yochanan (John) 4:52-54*
> *52 Then he inquired of them the hour when he got better. And they said to him, "Yesterday at the seventh hour the fever left him."*
> *53 So the father knew that it was at the same hour in which Yeshua said to him, "Your son lives." And he himself believed, and his whole household.*
> *54 This again is the second sign Yeshua did when He had come out of Judea into Galilee.*

Then in Chapter Five it is time for the next feast, which according to the Seventy Week Ministry Theory would have been Shavuot (Pentecost).

> *Yochanan (John) 5:1*
> *5:1 After this there was a feast of the Jews, and Yeshua went up to Jerusalem.*

Proponents of a three-and-one-half year ministry dispute that this was Pentecost. They emphasize that Scripture does not say which feast this was. This becomes a critical point in John Chatper Six, where most Greek translations (and also the Peshitta) tell us that it was almost time for the Passover.

> *Yochanan (John) 6:4-6*
> *4 Now the Passover, a feast of the Jews, was near.*

5 Then Yeshua lifted up His eyes, and seeing a great multitude coming toward Him, He said to Philip, "Where shall we buy bread, that these may eat?"
6 But this He said to test him, for He Himself knew what He would do.

If it was feast time, ordinarily we would expect to see Yeshua heading for Jerusalem. Traditional scholarship tells us the reason Yeshua did not go up to Jerusalem was that the Pharisees were seeking to kill Him, and it was not yet His time to be sacrificed. However, this is precisely the point where proponents of a Seventy Week Ministry take issue. Those advocating a Seventy Week Ministry agree that the Pharisees were seeking Yeshua's life (see John 7:1), but they also point out that verse 4 does not exist in many of the most ancient Greek texts. Therefore they argue that it does not belong there, and it cannot be used as the foundation for doctrine. (John 6:4 does appear in the Peshitta: however, at the time of this writing, while I believe in a Semitic inspiration, I no longer believe that the Peshitta is the originally inspired text.)

It seems plausible that John 6:4 was added to the text later. There are other known and suspected alterations and emendations to Scripture, both in the Tanach (the 'Old Covenant') and the Brit Chadasha (the Renewed Covenant). Some other known or suspected passages that are absent in some of the most ancient manuscripts include Mark 16:9-20, John 7:53-8:11, 1st John 5:7-8, and others. Further, if one removes the reference to the Passover at John 6:4 the Seventy Week Ministry Theory seems to make perfect sense: John appears to be chronicling Yeshua's ministry after the timing of the Israelite festivals.

If John 6:4 originally read "Now a feast of the Jews was near", could that feast have been Yom Teruah (the Day of Trumpets)? And if so, then could it be that the Transfiguration on the Mount took place ten days later (on Yom Kippur)?

> *Marqaus (Mark) 9:1-6*
> *1 And He said to them, "Assuredly, I say to you that there are some standing here who will not taste death till they see the kingdom of Elohim present with power."*
> *2 Now after six days Yeshua took Kepha, Yaakov and Yochanan, and led them up on a high mountain apart by themselves; and He was transfigured before them.*
> *3 His clothes became shining, exceedingly white, like snow, such as no launderer on earth can whiten them.*
> *4 And Eliyahu (Elijah) appeared to them with Moshe (Moses), and they were talking with Yeshua.*
> *5 Then Kepha answered and said to Jesus, "Rabbi, it is good for us to be here; and let us make three tabernacles: one for You, one for Moshe, and one for Eliyahu" —*
> *6 because he did not know what to say, for they were greatly afraid.*

And is it possible that the reason Kepha suggested that they make three tabernacles in Galilee was because the Pharisees in Jerusalem sought to kill Him, and it was not yet His time to be sacrificed?

> *Yochanan (John) 7:1-2*
> *1 After these things Yeshua walked in Galilee; for He did not want to walk in Judea, because the Jews sought to kill Him.*
> *2 Now the Jews' Feast of Tabernacles was at hand.*

John then tells us that Yeshua went up to the feast, but in secret (John 7:10). Upon His arrival, Yeshua breaks a large number of rabbinic 'fence laws' (tachanot and ma'asim) by healing people on the Sabbath. Because Yeshua breaks these man-made fence laws (without ever breaking YHWH's Torah), the Pharisees wrongly declared that He was not of Elohim, since in the Pharisaic/Orthodox mind, breaking rabbinic tradition is the same as breaking YHWH's Torah.

> *Yochanan (John) 9:13-16*
> *13 They brought him who formerly was blind to the Pharisees.*
> *14 Now it was a Sabbath when Yeshua made the clay and opened his eyes.*
> *15 Then the Pharisees also asked him again how he had received his sight. He said to them, "He put clay on my eyes, and I washed, and I see."*
> *16 Therefore some of the Pharisees said, "This Man is not from Elohim, because He does not keep the Sabbath."*

A few months later it is time for the Feast of Dedication (Hanukkah). Yeshua goes up to Jerusalem, and shows that He is the light of the world.

Yochanan (John) 10:22
*22 Now it was the Feast of Dedication
in Jerusalem, and it was winter.*

So far the sequence has been following the festivals. Now Yeshua gets ready to go up to Jerusalem for the final Passover, at which He is offered up in sacrifice.

Yochanan (John) 11:55-57
*55 And the Passover of the Jews was
near, and many went from the country
up to Jerusalem before the Passover,
to purify themselves.*
*56 Then they sought Yeshua, and
spoke among themselves as they
stood in the temple, "What do you
think — that He will not come to the
feast?"*
*57 Now both the chief priests and the
Pharisees had given a command, that
if anyone knew where He was, he
should report it, that they might seize
Him.*

The concept that John chronicled a seventy week period of time, following the festivals as milestones seems to make a lot of sense, provided that John 6:4 is understood to be a later addition to the text.

Yochanan (John) 6:4-6
*4 Now the Passover, a feast of the
Jews, was near.*
*5 Then Yeshua lifted up His eyes, and
seeing a great multitude coming
toward Him, He said to Philip, "Where
shall we buy bread, that these may
eat?"*

6 But this He said to test him, for He Himself knew what He would do.

But why would anyone alter Scripture? What would be their motivation? Consider that if John 6:4 was added to the text, then it would not only strengthen the idea of a three-and-one-half year ministry, but it would also seem to support the idea that Yeshua did not keep the Torah. The Torah commands all males to go up to Jerusalem three times a year (e.g., Deuteronomy 16), and if Yeshua had stayed in the Galilee during the Feast of the Passover, then He would have given us all an example of knowingly violating the Torah, proving that the Torah was not really all that important (Elohim forbid).

While the 'Seventy Weeks' concept is very appealing, it is not without challenges. As we saw earlier in the chapter on the Jubilees, Luke 3:21-23 tells us that Yeshua's ministry began shortly after He was immersed, when He was about thirty years of age.

> *Luqa (Luke) 3:21-23*
> *21 When all the people were immersed, it came to pass that Yeshua also was immersed; and while He prayed, the heaven was opened.*
> *22 And the Ruach HaKodesh (Holy Spirit) descended in bodily form like a dove upon Him, and a voice came from heaven which said, "You are My beloved Son; in You I am well pleased."*
> *23 Now Yeshua Himself began His ministry at about thirty years of age....*

In Judaism, it is traditional to take a mikveh (immerse or 'baptise' oneself) just before Yom Kippur, as Yom Kippur is the most set-apart day of the year. Notice also that Yom Kippur falls only five days before the fall feast of Sukkot (Tabernacles). As we show in the chapter on Hanukkah, Yeshua was probably born on the first day of the Feast of Sukkot (Tabernacles). If Yeshua's immersion took place the day before Yom Kippur, then Yeshua would have been "about thirty years of age" when He began His ministry. However, it takes a minimum of seventy-three, and easily seventy-six weeks to go from Yom Kippur one year to Passover two years later, depending on the sighting of the Aviv barley and the new moons.

Further, Daniel 9:24 says nothing about Yeshua's ministry lasting for seventy weeks, and there are no obvious prophetic implications for a 'Seventy Week' ministry. Daniel only says there would be seventy weeks of years in between the time the command went forth to rebuild Jerusalem (circa 457 BCE), until Messiah the Prince appeared and began His ministry: it says nothing about its duration.

About Birthdays

While many believe birthday celebrations are harmless, this is the exact opposite of what Scripture teaches. In fact, with the possible exception of Yeshua's birth, Scripture never celebrates birthdays.

While the Book of Iyov (Job) tells us that Iyov was a righteous man, it also tells us that Iyov's children celebrated their birthdays.

> *Iyov (Job) 1:4-5*
> *4 And his sons went and held a feast in the house of each one upon his day; and they sent and called for their three sisters to eat and to drink with them.*
> *5 And it was so, when the days of their feasting were gone about, that Iyov sent and set them apart, and rose up early in the morning, and offered burnt-offerings according to the number of them all: for Iyov said, "It may be that my sons have sinned, and renounced Elohim in their hearts."*
> *Thus did Iyov continually.*

Notice that rather than telling us that these birthday celebrations were a good thing, we see that Iyov took pains to sacrifice on his children's behalf, since he was concerned that their decision to celebrate their own birthdays may have been a sin, and that it may also have served as an indication that Iyov's son's had renounced Elohim in their hearts.

YHWH allowed Satan to take Iyov's children's lives.

> *Iyov (Job) 1:18-19*
> *18 While he was yet speaking, there came also another, and said, "Your sons and your daughters were eating and drinking wine in their eldest brother's house;*
> *19 And, behold, there came a great wind (i.e., a great Spirit) from the wilderness, and smote the four corners of the house, and it fell upon the young men, and they are dead; and I only am escaped alone to tell you."*

Is it possible that the reason YHWH allowed Satan to take Iyov's children's lives was precisely because the desire to celebrate birthdays really does indicate a wrong spiritual condition? Is it possible that for one to celebrate one's birthday is really to exalt oneself in one's heart, and that Iyov equated exalting oneself in one's heart with having renounced Elohim?

> *Mattai (Matthew) 22:37-40*
> *37 Yeshua said to him, "'You shall love YHWH your Elohim with all your heart, with all your soul, and with all your mind.'*
> *38 This is the first and great commandment.*
> *39 And the second is like it: 'You shall love your neighbor as yourself.'*
> *40 On these two commandments hang all the Law and the Prophets."*

The first and the great commandment is to love YHWH our Elohim with all of our heart, soul, and mind; and the second is like unto it: that we love our neighbors as ourselves. However, if Iyov's sons were truly dedicated towards loving and serving YHWH, and building His kingdom with all of their hearts, souls and minds, then why would they have wanted to take the time to celebrate their birthdays in the first place? What does it do for YHWH? And how does it further His kingdom?

Pharaoh celebrated his own birthday.

> **B'reisheet (Genesis) 40:20**
> **And it came to pass the third day, which was Pharaoh's birthday, that he made a feast unto all his servants: and he lifted up the head of the chief butler and the head of the chief baker among his servants.**

Pharaoh, however, is not our example; and we are not supposed to walk like the Egyptians walk.

King Herod also celebrated his own day. However, once again, King Herod is not our example, and this birthday celebration led to the death of Yochanan haMatbil (John the Baptist).

> **Marqaus (Mark) 6:21-24**
> **21 And when a convenient day was come, that Herod on his birthday made a supper to his lords, and the high captains, and the chief men of Galilee;**
> **22 And when the daughter of Herodias herself came in and danced, she pleased Herod and them that sat at meat with him; and the king said unto the damsel, "Ask of me whatsoever you will, and I will give it to you."**

23 And he swore unto her, "Whatsoever you shall ask of me, I will give it to you, up to half of my kingdom."
24 And she went out, and said unto her mother, "What shall I ask?" And she said, "The head of Yochanan haMatbil (John the Baptist)."

While he was still alive, Yochanan haMatbil told us something very important. He told us that in order for the Father's will to be done, he had to decrease.

Yochanan (John) 3:30
30 He must increase, while I must decrease.

What does it mean that in order for the Father's will to be done, Yochanan had to decrease? And what does this mean to us? Do we have to decrease as well, in order for YHWH will to be done in our lives? And if so, what does that look like?

Human nature is very prideful. It is the nature of man to want to think more highly of himself than he ought, and this is why the Apostle Shaul warned us that we should not think highly of ourselves.

Romim (Romans) 12:3
3 For I say, through the favor given to me, to everyone who is among you, not to think of himself more highly than he ought to think, but to think soberly, as Elohim has dealt to each one a measure of faith.

Shaul instructed us to have a lowly mind.

Philipim (Philippians) 2:3
3 Let nothing be done through selfish ambition or conceit, but in lowliness of mind let each esteem others better than himself.

One reason most children like birthday celebrations so much is that most children like to be the center of attention. The flesh finds it very pleasing to be exalted. While we might think that the best course of behavior is to let children go ahead and celebrate their birthdays, in order to 'get it out of their systems', in truth, we need to raise up our children in the way they should go, so that when they are older they will not depart from the correct path.

Mishle (Proverbs) 22:6
6 Train up a child in the way he should go, and when he is old he will not depart from it.

One of the more difficult parts of parenting children correctly is to teach them, gently, lovingly and over time, to focus less and less upon what they want, and to focus more and more upon YHWH's will for them, and upon the needs of others. This learning process can take years, but it is the quintessence of helping children grow into mature, stable adults. Only adults who are able to put away pride, ego and selfishness are able to enter into the the kind of stable relationships that it takes to raise healthy children in turn.

Israel is really just one big extended family, and all of us are called first to be aware of our innate selfish tendencies, and then to die to them, so that we can better seek His will for us (rather than our own will).

Anton LaVey, the modern day founder of the Church of Satan, tells us that the highest of all holidays in the satanic religion is one's own birthday.

> **"THE highest of all holidays in the Satanic religion is the date of one's own birthday. This is in direct contradiction to the holy of holy days of other religions, which deify a particular god who has been created in an anthropomorphic form of their own image, thereby showing that the ego is not really buried."**
> **The Satanic Bible (Anton Szandor LaVey, [Air] Book of Lucifer – The Enlightenment, Avon Books, 1969, Ch XI, Religious Holidays, p. 96).**

LaVey asserts that the reason other religions' deities have a human form is that human beings like to project their traits upon their deities, which he takes as proof that no one's ego is ever really buried. According to his line of reasoning, since no one's ego is ever really buried, the logical thing is just to realize that it is the nature of all flesh to want to worship the self (i.e., to be selfish), and then just to give in to one's urges.

We might turn this thought process around, and say that while the desire to celebrate one's own birthday does serve as an indicator that one still wants to exalt one's own self, and while this desire does represent a victory for the Evil One, this does not serve as any kind of a justification for giving in to one's urges. Rather, we should pray to YHWH for help in controlling our selfish urges, and also in being set free from them (with His help).

313

Yeshua was probably born on the first day of the Feast of Tabernacles, but neither He nor any of His apostles are ever recorded as having celebrated it as His birthday. Yeshua and His apostles just continued to celebrate YHWH's festival as they always did, and thus the focus remained on keeping YHWH's festivals, and not on celebrating anyone's birthday (not even Yeshua's).

So while there is no clear-cut commandment not to celebrate our birthdays, let us remember that the righteous man Iyob (Job) feared that his sons' birthday celebrations were a sign that his sons had sinned, and despised Elohim in their hearts.

Let us also bear in mind that King Solomon, who at least at one time was the wisest man who had ever lived, tells us that not only is a good name better than precious oil, but that the day of one's death is better than the day of one's birth.

> *Qohelet (Ecclesiastes) 7:1*
> *1 A good name is better than precious oil; and the day of death (is better) than the day of one's birth.*

If this is the case, then why should we celebrate our birthdays? Or for that matter, why should we celebrate any day that our Master has not commanded us to celebrate?

If we truly love our Husband, then why not spend all of our time focusing on Him, and on His people, rather than on ourselves?

About 'Service'

YHWH tells us not to pay attention to the movements of the sun, the moon or the stars, lest we become drawn to worship them, and serve them like the gentiles do.

Deuteronomy 4:19 19 And lest you lift up your eyes unto heaven, and when you see the sun and the moon and the stars, even all the host of heaven, thou be drawn away and worship them, and serve them, which YHWH your Elohim has allotted unto all the peoples under the whole heaven.	(19) וּפֶן תִּשָּׂא עֵינֶיךָ הַשָּׁמַיְמָה וְרָאִיתָ אֶת הַשֶּׁמֶשׁ וְאֶת הַיָּרֵחַ וְאֶת הַכּוֹכָבִים כֹּל צְבָא הַשָּׁמַיִם וְנִדַּחְתָּ וְהִשְׁתַּחֲוִיתָ לָהֶם וַעֲבַדְתָּם ׀ אֲשֶׁר חָלַק יְהוָה אֱלֹהֶיךָ אֹתָם לְכֹל הָעַמִּים תַּחַת כָּל הַשָּׁמָיִם

Many believers understand how Deuteronomy 4:19 might prohibit Astrology, the Zodiac, and horoscopes. Fewer believers, however, understand how this verse might prohibit the observance of pagan festival days such as the vernal and autumnal (spring and fall) equinoxes, and the summer and winter solstices. Even fewer understand that Christmas and Easter are also prohibited by Deuteronomy 4:19, since these festival days are ultimately based on the Vernal Equinox (Easter), and on the Winter Solstice (Christmas). They often want to know, "We keep these days in honor of (Yeshua), so how can they be wrong?"

315

As we explain earlier in this study, and as we also explain in <u>Nazarene Israel</u>, Sunday, Christmas and Easter are all converted pagan sun-worship festivals. These festivals were not taught by Yeshua or practiced by His disciples, but slowly crept their way into the faith during a great 'falling away', and were only 'sanctified' by the Catholic Church hundreds of years later. Even though the Pope 'sanctified' these festivals, the Pope's authority does not exceed that of Scripture; and the simple fact is that YHWH never told us to keep these festivals. Instead, YHWH tells us to keep His festivals: so why would anyone who believes in YHWH keep Sunday, Christmas or Easter?

In different places, YHWH tells us that He wants us to keep His festival days forever, in all of our generations.

> *Shemote (Exodus) 12:14*
> *14 'Now this day will be a memorial to you, and you shall celebrate it as a feast to YHWH. Throughout your generations you are to celebrate it as a permanent ordinance.*

Because the timing of Sunday, Christmas and Easter are not established according to ÝHWH's commands, but instead are established by observing the heavenly bodies, Deuteronomy 4:19 prohibits them. This can at first seem confusing: if a believer intends to honor YHWH or Yeshua by keeping these festival days, then how is it homage to the sun, the moon and the stars to worship on these days?

Notice that when Aharon (Aaron) initiated the festival with the golden calf, he told the people that the festival was in honor of YHWH.

Shemote (Exodus) 32:4-8

4 And he received the gold from their hand, and he fashioned it with an engraving tool, and made a molded calf. Then they said, "This is your elohim, O Israel, that brought you out of the land of Egypt!"

5 So when Aharon saw it, he built an altar before it. And Aharon made a proclamation and said, "Tomorrow is a feast to YHWH!"

6 Then they rose early on the next day, offered burnt offerings, and brought peace offerings; and the people sat down to eat and drink, and rose up to play.

7 And YHWH said to Moshe, "Go, get down! For your people whom you brought out of the land of Egypt have corrupted themselves.

8 They have turned aside quickly out of the way which I commanded them. They have made themselves a molded calf, and worshiped it and sacrificed to it, and said, 'This is your elohim (g-d), O Israel, that brought you out of the land of Egypt!'"

Even though Aharon said that "Tomorrow is a feast to YHWH", and even though all the people may have thought that they would be honoring YHWH with this festival, the simple fact is that YHWH was not pleased. YHWH was so furious that the people had made their own festival days that He was prepared to wipe out the children of Israel, and start a new nation out of Moshe.

YHWH commands us to labor six days in order to do all our work, but then to rest on His Sabbaths.

> *Vayiqra (Leviticus) 23:3*
> *3 'Six days shall work be done, but the seventh day is a Sabbath of solemn rest, a set-apart gathering. You shall do no work on it; it is the Sabbath of YHWH in all your dwellings.*

If we believe we are to take YHWH's Instructions dead seriously, then it becomes a very important question as to when or why we might choose to deviate from His Instructions, for it identifies our lusts. If we choose to set alternate days apart to YHWH that are determined by observing the sun, the moon and the stars (rather than by following YHWH's words) then in YHWH's eyes we are serving the sun, the moon and the stars. This is because YHWH's words are not the reason we chose to set these alternate days apart. Therefore, by default it is only our desire to honor the sun, the moon and the stars that caused us to set those days apart.

In YHWH's mind, when our forefathers held a festival to the golden calf, they were worshipping the golden calf. This is because YHWH did not command it. Because this festival did not come from YHWH, it came only from our forefathers. YHWH calls this evil.

In another sense, our forefathers were also serving and worshipping Aharon, because he is the one who established that particular day of worship. If we follow this train of logic out, we should be able to see that those who keep the Rabbinical Calendar effectively worship and serve the rabbis who originally created the Rabbinical Calendar; and the same is true for the Roman Gregorian 'Christian' Calendar.

If we truly desire to worship and serve YHWH, then we need to keep only His festival days. If we keep other festival days that do not come from YHWH, then obviously they come only from within our own hearts.

In Hebrew, the word *'serve'* comes from the root word 'Abad' (or 'Oved') (עבד). This word means 'to work' or 'to serve' *in any sense.*

> *OT:5647 `abad (aw-bad'); a primitive root; to work (in any sense); by implication, to serve, till, (causatively) enslave, etc.:*
>
> *KJV - be, keep in bondage, be bondmen, bond-service, compel, do, dress, ear, execute, husbandman, keep, labour (-ing man), bring to pass, (cause to, make to) serve (-ing self,), (be, become) servant (-s), do (use) service, till (-er), transgress [from margin], (set a) work, be wrought, worshipper*

In Scripture, to *serve* something is to venerate or even to pay attention to anything in any reverential context. That is, if we modify our behavior based on the motions of the heavenly bodies, then at least in YHWH's eyes, we are worshipping and serving them. Now let us stop to consider the size and scope of the ramifications.

> *Qorintim Aleph (1 Cor.) 13:12*
> *12 For now we see in a mirror, dimly, but then face to face. Now I know in part, but then I shall know just as I also am known.*

The problem is that we limited humans do not always understand when we are venerating (or even paying attention to) something in a way that YHWH considers reverential. We saw in the last chapter that Satan is so pleased that we would consider ourselves worthy of being celebrated, that He makes one's own birthday the highest holy day on the Satanic Calendar.

The way YHWH looks at things, anything that occupies our mental, emotional, physical or spiritual energies is something we *serve*. That is, if we spend time talking about Astrology instead of talking about YHWH and Yeshua, then we are serving the sun, the moon and the stars. The same applies to money, gold, diamonds, football, basketball, pizza, home decorating, or even the latest Shakespeare festival. Anything that takes our focus off of YHWH, and places it onto a thing of the material realm detracts from the service of YHWH; and therefore it qualifies as *service*.

The question of what we spend our mental, emotional, spiritual and physical energies on is huge. It touches on the very heart of worship. Therefore, brothers and sisters, let us ask ourselves and be honest: are we spending our spiritual, mental, emotional and physical energies trying to become better servants of the Most High? Or are we doing something else with our time, our money and our energy?

Let us take a good, honest look at our living spaces through YHWH's eyes. What is the center of our house? Is Scripture truly the focus of our living room? Are YHWH's words really the focus of our family's daily lives? Are YHWH's festivals the time we purchase things for ourselves, and rest? If not, then why not?

If we love YHWH, and if we fear the Day of Judgment, then let us be honest with ourselves, and face into these issues, so that we can do something about them while it is still day. Because of His great love, our times of past ignorance YHWH overlooks: but now He commands all men everywhere to repent.

> **Acts 17:30-31**
> **30 Truly, these times of ignorance Elohim overlooked, but now He commands all men everywhere to repent,**
> **31 because He has appointed a day on which He will judge the world in righteousness by the Man whom He has ordained. He has given assurance of this to all by raising Him from the dead."**

Let us make no mistake: YHWH is all-powerful, and He can bestow eternal life upon those who do not know of His festival days: that is up to Him. But what can we say for those who know His Instructions, and who know that His festival days are shadows of prophetic things still to come, but who do not keep or cherish them? If we know what is right, but choose not to do it, is it still reckoned to us for righteousness?

> **Ya'akov (James) 4:17**
> **17 Therefore, to him who knows to do good and does not do it, to him it is sin.**

It is appointed for men to live and die but once, and then comes the Resurrection, and the Judgment. If YHWH is the same yesterday, today and tomorrow, and if we know the times and the seasons He has set aside to meet with us, but yet we choose not to meet with Him on those days, will He be pleased?

The Creator's Calendar is not as easy to keep as some of the other calendar systems of the world, because it asks us to wait on YHWH, like a servant has to wait upon his master. But when the Creator of the Universe bestows a gift upon his servant, does the wise servant say, "No, I don't want it"? Does the wise servant say, "It is too hard! Give me something easier"? But isn't this what we see every day: the same sin our fathers committed in the Wilderness, desiring to go back to a system which, while corrupt and evil, was easier?

> *Bemidbar (Numbers) 14:1-4*
> *1 So all the congregation lifted up their voices and cried, and the people wept that night.*
> *2 And all the children of Israel complained against Moshe and Aharon, and the whole congregation said to them, "If only we had died in the land of Egypt! Or if only we had died in this wilderness!*
> *3 Why has YHWH brought us to this land to fall by the sword, that our wives and children should become victims? Would it not be better for us to return to Egypt?"*
> *4 So they said to one another, "Let us select a leader and return to Egypt."*

When we read in Scripture about what our forefathers did in the Wilderness of Sinai, we often ask ourselves, "How could they do that? What were they thinking, with the Column of Fire and Cloud right there? Did they not recognize all of the miracles around them?"

Brothers and sisters, how many miracles are all around us every day that we fail to recognize? And when we do see them, do we remember them from day to day, and give glory to the Most High Elohim of the heavens?

> *Ivrim (Hebrews) 12:1-2*
> *1 Therefore we also, since we are surrounded by so great a cloud of witnesses, let us lay aside every weight, and the sin which so easily ensnares us, and let us run with endurance the race that is set before us,*
> *2 looking unto Yeshua, the author and perfecter of our faith, who for the joy that was set before Him endured the cross, despising the shame, and has sat down at the right hand of the throne of Elohim.*

When the Creator of the Universe gives us something, we need to seize it, prize it it, and safeguard it with our lives. We need to recognize that its worth is more than life itself, for it comes from the One who has the power to save those who value and treasure it.

We can visit with YHWH any time, as He is always there. However, seven special times a year, the King of the Universe makes an appointment for us to meet with Him, and He hopes to see us there. If we love Him, then what could be more important than going to meet with Him on those special times when He desires to meet with His bride?

Is there anything more important than going to be with our Beloved on the days that please Him most?

The Wave Sheaf in the Sabbath Year

Scripture tells us not to sow or harvest in the Shemittah (Sabbath Year) or in the Jubilee (fiftieth year). Crops are not to be sown or 'harvested' during that time.

Leviticus 25:11-12 11 "That fiftieth year shall be a Jubilee to you; in it you shall neither sow nor reap what grows of its own accord, nor gather the grapes of your untended vine. 12 For it is the Jubilee; it shall be set-apart to you; you shall eat its produce from the field."	(11) יוֹבֵל הוּא שְׁנַת הַחֲמִשִּׁים שָׁנָה תִּהְיֶה לָכֶם ׀ לֹא תִזְרָעוּ וְלֹא תִקְצְרוּ אֶת סְפִיחֶיהָ וְלֹא תִבְצְרוּ אֶת נְזִרֶיהָ : (12) כִּי יוֹבֵל הוּא קֹדֶשׁ תִּהְיֶה לָכֶם ׀ מִן הַשָּׂדֶה תֹּאכְלוּ אֶת תְּבוּאָתָהּ

Some teach we cannot offer a Wave Sheaf in these years because we cannot 'bring in the harvest' of barley then. However, Scripture does not say this. As we explain in The Torah Calendar, the command is not to abstain from partaking of the field altogether: rather, verse 12 tells us to eat that year's fruits "from the field" (as opposed to 'from the granary'). As in the Garden, we may eat from the field hand-to-mouth, and we may also take what we need for the day. What this passage prohibits is 'bringing in the harvest' (such as one might do with a combine), and then selling the crop (as one might do in other years): yet there is never a time that we should not give the Firstfruits of the land back to YHWH with thanksgiving and praise.

The spiritual lesson is clear: when YHWH provides for our bodily needs, He wants us to show Him our appreciation. He wants us to acknowledge that He is Elohim by giving the first of what He has just given us, back to Him. This is also what made Hevel's (Abel's) sacrifice so pleasing.

> **B'reisheet (Genesis) 4:3-5**
> **3 And in the process of time it came to pass that Qayin (Cain) brought an offering of the fruit of the ground to YHWH.**
> **4 Hevel (Abel) also brought of the firstborn of his flock and of their fat. And YHWH respected Hevel and his offering,**
> **5 but He did not respect Qayin (Cain) and his offering. And Qayin was very angry, and his countenance fell.**

YHWH was not pleased with Qayin's offering because Qayin did not think to honor YHWH with the Firstfruits of what he had been given. No matter the specifics, whether we have to work to obtain the increase (perhaps by raising crops), or whether YHWH just gives us the crops (such as when we eat 'volunteer crops' that grow on their own in the rest years), YHWH loves it when He can see that our hearts are filled with joy and spontaneous thanksgiving at His having given us what we need to survive.

YHWH does not need anything. He does not need barley, or the blood of bulls or lambs. He has no need of priests, or Levites, or even of you or me. What He wants to see, though, is that we acknowledge Him as the source of all good things; and that our hearts are

325

filled with so much love and joy that when He provides for our bodily needs, we eagerly want to give back the Firstfruits of whatever it is that He just gave us.

It is not the gift itself that YHWH wants. Rather, what He wants is for us to be eager to give it. And in the case of the annual crops that YHWH blesses us with each year, YHWH lets us know we can show Him our thanks by giving Him with the Firstfruits of the new barley harvest. That principle is not going to change in the Sabbatical years, or in the Jubilee: If anything, it is only going to apply all the more.

As we explain in The Torah Calendar, the symbolism between barley and Yeshua is very strong. Barley is the first of the crops to come ready in the Land of Israel, and the firstfruits of the barley is the first of the firstfruits of the land. In the same way, Yeshua became the first of the Firstfruits of redeemed Israel when YHWH raised Him from the dead.

> **Qorintim Aleph (1st Corinthians) 15:20**
> **20 But now Messiah is risen from the dead, and has become the Firstfruits of those who have fallen asleep.**

Yeshua fulfilled the first prophetic shadow of the Firstfruits of the Wave Sheaf. Yet as we explain in Nazarene Israel, all of YHWH's festivals have other fulfillments yet to come, in the future. Therefore, to suggest that we no longer need to perform the Wave Sheaf Offering would be to deny that more fulfillments are coming. [It would also essentially be to partake of Replacement Theology, which we know from the study, 'Tree of Knowledge, Tree of Life' is the fruit of the Tree of the Knowledge of Good and Evil. The fruit of the Tree of the Knowledge of Good and Evil is what we partake of when we decide to do what we want based on our own thoughts and intellect, rather than obeying YHWH's Voice, and the Torah.]

Another reason some teach we cannot offer a Wave Sheaf of thanks in the rest years is the mistaken idea that the Wave Sheaf can only be taken from cultivated barley. Scripture does not say this either. Rather, what Scripture says is just to offer the first of the fruits of the land up to Him (in thanksgiving, and in praise). While we can harvest the crops as they come ripe, verse 14 clearly tells us that we may not eat (or sell) any of the new crops until after we have brought this praise and worship offering to Him; and this commandment applies to us and our children forever, no matter where we live.

> *Vayiqra (Leviticus) 23:10-11, 14*
> *10 "Speak to the children of Israel, and say to them: 'When you come into the land which I give to you, and reap its harvest, then you shall bring a sheaf of the firstfruits of your harvest to the priest.*
> *11 He shall wave the sheaf before YHWH, to be accepted on your behalf; on the day after the Sabbath the priest shall wave it...."*
> *14 "You shall eat neither bread nor parched grain nor fresh grain until the same day that you have brought an offering to your Elohim; it shall be a statute forever throughout your generations in all your dwellings."*

Barley grows wild in all parts of Israel. It grows like the proverbial 'grass of the field' precisely because it is just such a field grass. Naturally, barley ripens sooner in the hotter areas (such as in the Jordan River Valley and in the Negev), but it also grows near the Temple Mount in Jerusalem, in the mountains of Samaria, and in the Golan. Of course it ripens fully a month or two later in the cooler mountain areas, but even in the years that we are to let the land rest, there is always plenty of barley to form a Wave Sheaf Offering. Further, 'volunteer barley' still springs up in the farmer's fields, even in the rest years.

Barley that is irrigated typically ripens 4-6 weeks earlier than barley that is not irrigated. It is a matter of debate as to whether or not we should use irrigated (cultivated) barley to time the Aviv. Some parties believe we should not use irrigated barley, since the Land of Israel did not need irrigation in ancient times.

> *Devarim (Deuteronomy) 11:10-12*
> *10 "For the land which you go to possess is not like the land of Egypt from which you have come, where you sowed your seed and watered it by foot, as a vegetable garden;*
> *11 but the land which you cross over to possess is a land of hills and valleys, which drinks water from the rain of heaven,*
> *12 a land for which YHWH your Elohim cares; the eyes of YHWH your Elohim are always on it, from the beginning of the year to the very end of the year."*

These believe that we should attempt to establish the "natural condition" in the Aviv sighting, and therefore they would reject irrigated barley for use in timing the Aviv since it "does not reflect the natural condition that YHWH brought about." However, others would accept cultivated barley for the Aviv, since they would not want to put undue burden on those farmers who chose to raise barley.

Those who believe we should use irrigated barley fields for the Wave Sheaf point out that while the farmers can harvest their barley as it comes ripe, they cannot eat or sell any of the new crop until after the Wave Sheaf is offered. This might create a condition where the farmers would have to harvest their grain a full four to six weeks before they could either eat it, or sell it. If this practice had been used in ancient times, it could have placed an unnecessary strain on the barley farmers.

No matter whether we use wild, domesticated, irrigated or non-irrigated barley for the Wave Sheaf, one reason it is so important to use the barley that ripens first is because YHWH cares for the poor, the widow, the orphan and the stranger. He loves all of us, whether rich or poor. He is not just concerned for those who have, but also for those who do not. In ancient times, having enough food to eat was never a given, and YHWH tells us to leave the corner of the field and the gleanings for the poor, the widow, the orphan and the stranger.

> *Vayiqra (Leviticus) 19:9-10*
> *9 'When you reap the harvest of your land, you shall not wholly reap the corners of your field, nor shall you gather the gleanings of your harvest.*
> *10 And you shall not glean your vineyard, nor shall you gather every grape of your vineyard; you shall leave them for the poor and the stranger: I am YHWH your Elohim."*

Yochanan HaMatbil (John the Immerser/Baptist) had to eat what he could find, living off of the land. In Matthew 3:4, we are told that his food was (only) locusts and wild honey.

Mattithyahu (Matthew) 3:4
4 Now Yochanan himself was clothed in camel's hair, with a leather belt around his waist; and his food was locusts and wild honey.

There were many righteous people in ancient Israel who were essentially without homes and farms. These often had to eat whatever they could find; yet they could not eat any part of the new crops until after the Wave Sheaf had been offered.

Vayiqra (Leviticus) 23:14
14 "You shall eat neither bread nor parched grain nor fresh grain until the same day that you have brought an offering to your Elohim; it shall be a statute forever throughout your generations in all your dwellings."

It is vital that the priesthood sets the Head of the Year according to the first of the firstfruits of the barley, so that the Wave Sheaf can be offered up, and then all the poor people can eat. Anything other than that puts a strain on the poor, and that is not pleasing to YHWH.

May He bring us all back to His calendar, soon and in our day.

Closing Prayer:

Master YHWH, King of Heaven and Earth,

We thank you for Your great kindnesses. Despite the mistakes of our fathers and ourselves, again You have chosen, and called us to serve You.

Master, please give strength to all who receive this message. Please give them endurance to withstand the trials that come from being called to a closer walk with You. Please give them shepherds who will serve them according to Your heart, as you promised by Your prophet Jeremiah. Please lead Your people back to Your land, and rejoin them to their brothers in Judah.

Master, please put it in our hearts to do all we can for you. Please lead us to make our service to You the priority in our lives. Please encourage us to do all we can with our few short days, before we stand in the Judgment.

Above all, Master, please bring Your Salvation to all of mankind, and cause all those who accept Your Son to walk even as He taught us to walk. Do it not for our sakes, Master; but for Your great Namesake.

Bring us back to You, YHWH, and we will be brought back to You. Renew our days, as of old.

In Yeshua's perfect Name,

Amein.

Book Ordering Information:

To find the best price on this book, please visit the Nazarene Israel website, www.nazareneisrael.org.

Other titles available at the time of this printing are:

Nazarene Israel: The original faith of the Apostles
The Post-Millennial Return

Other volumes available soon.

May the Name of YHWH of Hosts be glorified and magnified among His people Israel.

Shalom.

Donations to Nazarene Israel:

YHWH promises to bless those who cheerfully give to His work (Exodus 25:2, Malachi 3:10). If you would like to receive your blessing for cheerfully giving back part of what your Creator has given you, we ask only that you pray, and then do as He leads you.

If He should lead you to send a voluntary offering to His work, you can send it electronically through the website, at **www.nazareneisrael.org**, or else you can send it through the post, to:

Nazarene Israel
PO Box 787
Anderson, CA 96007
USA

Please know that your donations are not only needed, but that they will be carefully and fearfully handled for the betterment of the cause.

May the Name of YHWH be glorified: Shalom.

13770190R00190

Made in the USA
Lexington, KY
19 February 2012